JACK THE RIPPER

MANCHESTER
1824

Manchester University Press

Jack the Ripper

Media, culture, history

edited by Alexandra Warwick and Martin Willis

MANCHESTER UNIVERSITY PRESS
Manchester and New York
distributed exclusively in the USA by Palgrave

Published by Manchester University Press
Oxford Road, Manchester M13 9NR, UK
and Room 400, 175 Fifth Avenue, New York, NY 10010, USA
www.manchesteruniversitypress.co.uk

Distributed in the United States exclusively by
Palgrave Macmillan, 175 Fifth Avenue,
New York, NY 10010, USA

Distributed in Canada exclusively by
UBC Press, University of British Columbia, 2029 West Mall,
Vancouver, BC, Canada V6T 1Z2

British Library Cataloguing-in-Publication Data is available

Library of Congress Cataloging-in-Publication Data is available

ISBN 978 0 7190 7494 3 paperback

First published by Manchester University Press 2007

First reprinted 2013

Printed by Lightning Source

Contents

Figures

Contributors

Clive Bloom is Professor of English and American Studies at Middlesex University. He lives and works in East London and is the author and editor of many works on popular culture, cultural history and literary criticism. His recent books include *Violent London: 2000 Years of Riots, Rebels and Revolts* (2003), *Cult Fiction: Popular Reading and Pulp Theory* (1996), *Bestsellers: Popular Fiction Since 1900* (2002) and *Gothic Horror: A Reader's Guide from Poe to King and Beyond* (1998), all of which have enjoyed international recognition. His forthcoming book is *Terror Within* (a history of British terrorism).

Gary Coville is a writer and media historian. He is a former teacher and reference librarian. In collaboration with Patrick Lucanio, he has authored three works: *American Science Fiction Television Series of the 1950s* (1998), *Jack the Ripper: His Life and Crimes in Popular Entertainment* (1999) and *Smokin' Rockets: The Romance of Technology in American Film, Radio and Television, 1945–1962* (2002). In addition, he has written over a hundred magazine articles. At present, Coville is researching a book on Communism as Cold War entertainment. He resides in Dallas, Oregon, USA.

David Cunningham is Lecturer in English at the University of Westminster and an editor of the journal *Radical Philosophy*. He has published widely on modernism, critical theory, urbanism and aesthetics. Recent articles have appeared in *New Formations*, *Substance* and *Angelaki*, and he is the co-editor of *Photography and Literature in the Twentieth Century* (2005) and *Adorno and Literature* (2006). He grew up and still lives in East London.

L. Perry Curtis, Jr. retired from Brown University as Professor of Modern History in 2001, having also taught previously at Princeton and Berkeley. He has a distinguished record of research and publication in Anglo-Irish political and cultural relations, including *Coercion and Conciliation in Ireland* (1963), *Anglo-Saxons and Celts* (1968) and *Apes and Angels* (1971, 1997). After his foray into the Whitechapel murders, he continues to work on Irish culture, presently on landlords and depictions of eviction in nineteeth-century Ireland.

William (Bill) Fishman is the chronicler of London's East End. His books include *The Streets of East London* and *East End Jewish Radicals*. The son of an immigrant tailor, Fishman is a visiting professor at Queen Mary College, University of London and has held visiting professorships at Columbia University and the University of Wisconsin. Now retired, he regularly leads East End walks and lectures on East End subjects including Jack the Ripper.

Sir Christopher Frayling is Professor of Cultural History and Rector of the Royal College of Art in London. He has served as Chairman of the Arts Council, England, having also chaired its Visual Arts, Combined Arts, Education and Film, Video and Broadcasting panels. A historian, a critic and a broadcaster, he is well known for his work on BBC Radio 4, BBC Radio 3 and Channel 4. Sir Christopher is also a trustee of the Victoria and Albert Museum, and has been on the boards of many art, craft and design organizations. He has published numerous books on the arts, popular culture, design and the history of ideas, the most recent being his vast biography of the Italian film-maker Sergio Leone.

Sander L. Gilman is Professor of the Liberal Arts and Medicine at the University of Illinois in Chicago and Director of the Jewish Studies Programme at the University of Sussex. A cultural and literary historian, he is the author or editor of over seventy books. For twenty-five years he was a member of the Humanities and Medical faculties at Cornell University, where he held the Goldwin Smith Professorship of Humane Studies. For six years he held the Henry R. Luce Distinguished Service Professorship of the Liberal Arts in Human Biology at the University of Chicago, and he has been a visiting professor at Stanford, Princeton, UCLA and Syracuse, as well as at universities in Canada, Germany, South Africa and New Zealand.

Robert F. Haggard earned a BA (1989) in history and English from the University of North Carolina at Chapel Hill and an MA (1991) and PhD (1997) in European history from the University of Virginia. His dissertation was published by Greenwood Press under the title *The Persistence* *of Victorian Liberalism: The Politics of Social Reform in Britain, 1870–1900* (2000). An editor by profession, Dr Haggard has aided in the production of volumes of both *The Papers of George Washington* (1996–2001), which is published by the University of Virginia Press, and Princeton University Press's *Papers of Thomas Jefferson: Retirement Series* (2001-present).

Patrick Lucanio (PhD, MS University of Oregon; MAT, BS Western Oregon University) has served as an adjunct assistant professor of Humanities at Western Oregon University in Monmouth, and is currently a visiting instructor of multimedia design at Lane Community College in Eugene, Oregon. A myth/Jungian critic with interests in film and broadcasting history, Lucanio has written numerous articles on film/television history and genre studies. He served as an advisor to *The Celluloid Scientists*, a BBC Scotland radio documentary broadcast in June 2001, and he is currently the editor of *Radiogram*, the newsletter of the Society to Preserve and Encourage Radio Drama, Variety and Comedy. He is the author of *Them or Us* (1987), a critical history of 1950s monster movies, and *With Fire and Sword* (1994), a comprehensive study of the English-dubbed Italian spectacles of the 1960s often described as 'sword and sandal epics' and respectably known as *peplum*. He has co-authored with Gary Coville *American Science Fiction Television Series of the 1950s* (1998), *Jack the Ripper: His Life and Crimes in Popular Entertainment* (1999) and *Smokin' Rockets: The Romance of Technology in American Film, Radio and Television 1945–1962* (2002).

Darren Oldridge is Senior Lecturer in History at University College Worcester. He has published extensively in the areas of religious and cultural history, most recently *Strange Histories* (2005) and, as editor, *The Witchcraft Reader* (2001). In 2001 he wrote and taught (with Martin Willis) one of the first complete university courses on the Whitechapel murders in the UK.

Nicholas Rance lectured in English at Middlesex University – and its pre-1992 incarnation as Middlesex Polytechnic – from 1973 until 2001. He is author of *The Historical Novel and Popular Politics in Nineteenth-century England* (1975) and *Wilkie Collins and Other Sensation Novelists: Walking the Moral Hospital* (1991), and has introduced Everyman editions of Wilkie Collins, *The Woman in White* (1991), and Robert Louis Stevenson, *Dr Jekyll and Mr Hyde and Other Stories*(1992). He still pursues an interest in the literature of crime.

Andrew Smith is Professor of English Studies at the University of Glamorgan, where he is Head of Humanities. He is the author of *Victorian Demons: Medicine, Masculinity and the Gothic at the Fin de Siècle* (2004) and *Gothic Radicalism: Literature, Philosophy and Psychoanalysis in the Nineteenth Century* (2000). He has co-edited several collections of essays, including *Empire and the Gothic: The Politics of Genre* with William Hughes (2003) and *Gothic Modernisms* with Jeff Wallace (2001). He is currently writing a monograph on the ghost story for Manchester University Press. He edits, with Professor Ben Fisher, the series *Gothic Literary Studies*, published by the University of Wales Press.

Judith Walkowitz is Professor of History at Johns Hopkins University, where she has taught since 1989. Her fields of specialization are British cultural history and comparative women's history. She is the recipient of a number of awards and fellowships, and is the author of two books: *Prostitution and Victorian Society: Women, Class and the State* (1980) and *City of Dreadful Delight: Narratives of Sexual Danger in Late-Victorian London* (1992). Her recent articles have appeared in *American Historical Review*, *Representations* and *Victorian Studies*. She has served on the boards of *Feminist Studies*, *differences*, *Victorian Studies*, *Journal of British Studies* and *Cultural and Social History*.

Alexandra Warwick is Senior Lecturer in English at the University of Westminster, where she teaches in the areas of nineteenth-century literature and culture, Gothic and gender. She has most recently published in these fields – *Oscar Wilde* (2005) and *Repositioning Victorian Sciences* (2006) – but has previously written on clothes and the body, *Fashioning the Frame* (1995), and is currently working on a history of archaeology. She lives in the East End, where several generations of her family were born.

Martin Willis is Lecturer in English Literature at the University of Glamorgan, where he specializes in teaching nineteenth-century literature and the Gothic. Previously, he had written and taught (with Darren Oldridge) one of the first complete university courses on the Whitechapel murders in the UK. He has written widely on nineteenth-century literature and its relationship to science in *Essays in Criticism*, *Science Fiction Studies*, *Victorian Review* and the *Journal of Victorian Culture*. His book on nineteenth-century literature and scientific culture, *Mesmerists, Monsters, and Machines*, was published by Kent State University Press in 2006. He is presently writing on the relationship between science and stage magic, and on Arthur Conan Doyle and Harry Houdini.

Copyright acknowledgements

Christopher Frayling, 'The House that Jack Built' first appeared in Sylvia Tomaselli and Roy Porter (eds) *Rape* (Blackwell, 1986). Reproduced with permission of Blackwell Publishing.

L. Perry Curtis, Jr., 'The Pursuit of Angles' is taken from *Jack the Ripper and the London Press* (Yale University Press, 2001) and is reproduced with permission of Yale University.

Gary Coville and Patrick Lucanio, 'Order out of Chaos' is taken from *Jack the Ripper: His Life and Crimes in Popular Entertainment* © 1999 Gary Coville and Patrick Lucanio by permission of McFarland & Company, Inc., Box 611, Jefferson NC 28640. www.mcfarlandpub.com.

Clive Bloom, 'The Ripper Writing: A Cream of a Nightmare Dream' appeared in *Cult Fiction: Popular Reading and Pulp Theory* (Macmillan, 1998) Reproduced by permission of Palgrave Macmillan.

Andrew Smith, 'The Whitechapel Murders and the Medical Gaze' is taken from *Victorian Demons: Medicine, Masculinity and the Gothic at the Fin-de-Siècle* (Manchester University Press, 2004). Reproduced by kind permission of Manchester University Press and the author.

Nicholas Rance, '"Jonathan's Great Knife": Dracula meets Jack the Ripper' is taken from *Victorian Literature and Culture* (2002), copyright Cambridge University Press. Reproduced by permission of Cambridge University Press, *Victorian Literature and Culture* and the author.

Judith Walkowitz, 'Narratives of Sexual Danger' is taken from *City of Dreadful Delight: Narratives of Sexual Danger in Late Victorian London* (Virago, 1992), and is reproduced with permission of Time Warner Book Group UK.

Robert F. Haggard, 'Jack the Ripper as the Threat of Outcast London' originally appeared in *Essays in History*, 35 (1993), copyright Robert F. Haggard. Reproduced by kind permission of the author.

Sander L. Gilman, 'Who Kills Whores?' first appeared in Sarah Webster Goodwin and Elisabeth Bronfen (eds), *Death and Representation*, pp. 263–84. © 1993. Reprinted with permission of The Johns Hopkins University Press.

William Fishman, 'Crime and Punishment' is taken from *East End 1888* (Duckworth, 1988; Five Leaves, 2005), copyright William J. Fishman 1988, 2005. Reproduced by permission of the author and Five Leaves.

The Whitechapel murders: chronology

3 April 1888
Emma Smith was attacked, as she reported, by three men near Brick Lane
in Whitechapel at about 1.30 a.m. She made her way back to her lodgings in Spitalfields, but developed peritonitis from injuries inflicted
during the instrumental rape of her assault. She died on 4 April. No one
was apprehended, and although newspapers linked her death with the
later murders, and some later theorists have argued that she was a victim
of Jack the Ripper, it is more generally believed that she was attacked by
members of a gang who extracted protection money from prostitutes in
the area.

7 August 1888
In the early morning the body of Martha Tabram was discovered on the
first-floor landing of George Yard buildings, off Whitechapel High Street.
She had thirty-nine stab wounds. Witnesses failed to identify a soldier
with whom she had been seen earlier that night, and no arrests were
made. Public reaction to the violence of her murder led to the formation
of the first of the Vigilance Committees that patrolled Whitechapel in
1888. Although not counted among the five so-called 'canonical'
murders, many writers believe her to have been the first of Jack the
Ripper's victims.

31 August 1888
The body of the first 'canonical' victim, Mary Ann [Polly] Nichols, was
found in Buck's Row, Whitechapel, by two cart drivers on their way to
work at about 3.30 a.m. Her throat had been cut and she had serious
wounds to her abdomen. The press quickly linked her death with
those of Tabram and Smith, and Scotland Yard became involved in the
investigation. Popular feeling ran high, and anti-Semitism was manifest
in the press persecution of a local man: John Pizer, known as 'Leather
Apron'.

8 September 1888
Annie Chapman was found dead in the back yard of 29 Hanbury Street, Whitechapel by one of the house's many tenants at 6.00 a.m. Her throat had been cut, she had been partially disembowelled, and some of her abdominal organs were missing, including her uterus. At the inquest into her death, the coroner suggested, from anecdotal evidence, that the motive could have been the acquisition of the uterus for supply to medical investigation. Press and public interest turned to the possibility of a murderer with professional medical expertise.

27 September 1888
A letter postmarked London EC, written in red ink, and addressed 'Dear Boss' was received by the Central News Agency. It was signed 'Jack the Ripper'; the first time that this name was attached to the crimes. The letter was widely publicized, and hundreds of other communications were received by newspapers and other individuals connected to the inquiries.

30 September 1888
The first event of this night was the discovery of Elizabeth Stride's body in a yard on Berners Street, off Commercial Road. Her throat had been cut, but there were no other injuries. She was found at 1 a.m. in the yard that had been empty twenty minutes earlier. Three-quarters of a mile away in Mitre Square on the edge of the City a police constable found Catherine Eddowes dead at 1.45 a.m. Her throat had been cut and there were deep cuts to her face. She had extensive injuries to her abdomen, and her uterus and left kidney were missing. The constable had earlier patrolled the square where Eddowes was found, so it appeared that two murders had been carried out in about forty-five minutes. Some writers have suggested that Stride's murder was an opportunistic copy-cat killing, but it is more generally thought that this was a 'double event', as it came to be described. The speed of the murders and the narrowness of the killer's escape added to the growing mythology.

The police work was complicated by the fact that Eddowes's death took place just inside the boundary of the City Police jurisdiction, whereas all the other crimes were committed within the jurisdiction of the Metropolitan Police. There was also disagreement over the erasure of a message chalked on the wall of a tenement building in Goulston Street, close to the murder site and where a piece of Eddowes's apron was discovered. The message appeared to incriminate Jews, and was washed off to prevent further anti-Semitic feeling in the area, but its text was not accurately preserved. The Commissioner of the City Police protested at the decision of his opposite number in the Metropolitan force to destroy this piece of evidence.

16 October 1888

A package was received by George Lusk, Chairman of the Whitechapel Vigilance Committee, containing part of a kidney and the letter 'From Hell'. The kidney was identified as human, but beyond that there was no professional agreement as to whether it could have been the one taken from Catherine Eddowes's body.

9 November 1888

At about 11.45 a.m. the body of Mary Kelly was discovered in the room she rented in Miller's Court. She was the only one of the women found indoors, and her body had been subjected to the most extensive mutilation. Although she had died at some time the previous night, the police doctor and pathologist differed on a possible time, and there were several witnesses whose statements contradicted one another, including two who claimed to have seen her alive well after the time her body was found. Kelly's is widely regarded as the last of Jack the Ripper's murders.

On 10 November, Sir Charles Warren resigned. As Commissioner of the Metropolitan Police he had been ultimately responsible for the investigation, and many saw his resignation as a direct result of its failure, although the wider politics of the control of the Metropolitan Police are the more likely reason.

After 9 November there were three other murders in the district for which no perpetrator was apprehended: Rose Mylett on 20 December 1888, Alice McKenzie on 16 July 1889 and Frances Coles on 14 February 1890. The latter two particularly have been proposed as part of the Whitechapel series, and some writers have also suggested more, continuing until later and spread as widely as the United States, Germany, France and South America.

Introduction

Alexandra Warwick and Martin Willis

At 7.30 this evening, and every evening, a walking tour of Whitechapel will visit the sites where the bodies of the victims of Jack the Ripper were found. During today, and every day, several thousand people will visit the Jack the Ripper tableaux in Madame Tussaud's and the London Dungeon. Last year there were dozens of books on Jack the Ripper published. There are no signs of any diminution of interest in the subject and, in fact, in the two decades since the centenary of the murders the volume and availability of material on the Whitechapel murders has greatly increased. The obvious question is – why?

There are those for whom Jack the Ripper has become something like a profession, the so-called 'Ripperologists', and they almost always suggest a rather banal answer: that it is one of the most famous unsolved crimes, the great Victorian murder mystery. The interest here is in an absolutely straightforward question: who was the murderer? The range of suspects advanced over the years is bewildering, from otherwise unremarkable East End workmen, through Jewish hairdressers and butchers, doctors and medical students, suicidal barristers, all the way to the top of the establishment in the Freemasons and the figure of the Duke of Clarence, Queen Victoria's grandson. Suspects continue to be presented: in 1993 a diary was published, purporting to be that of James Maybrick, a Liverpool merchant who was later to appear as a victim in a notorious murder trial. In the diary, Maybrick confesses to the Whitechapel, and other, murders. In 2002 the crime novelist Patricia Cornwell, after some expensive research, confidently identified the painter Walter Sickert, who had previously been a very minor figure in suspect lists, as the murderer of a large number of women, including those in Whitechapel. In 2005 another eminent doctor, John Williams, who was instrumental in the foundation of the National Library of Wales, was proposed by one of his descendants.[1] Almost simultaneously, a former police detective published his suggestion that Jack the Ripper was a merchant seaman who continued his killings in Nicaragua and Germany.[2] Other names will be advanced, as will new interpretations of the sparse documentation on the familiar ones.

It must be stated here that none of the essays in this volume has any interest at all in the question of who Jack the Ripper might have been. Instead, they are all concerned, in different ways, with the discourses and representations of the murders and the murderer since the first press reports of the murders in August 1888. This is certainly not a denial of the reality of the grotesque deaths of five or more women in 1888 or of the appalling circumstances of their lives that rendered them vulnerable through their enforced work as prostitutes. It is rather the many 'true-crime' books on the Whitechapel murders, despite their often-declared intention to present only 'the facts', that serve to perpetuate the myth of Jack the Ripper, and as Roland Barthes says of myth, it: 'transforms the reality of the world into an image of the world, History into Nature ... myth has the task of giving an historical intention a natural justification, and making contingency appear eternal'.[3] In much of the writing on the Whitechapel murders the historical truth of the deaths of the women and the conditions in which they lived become mere background to a mytho-logical mystery. As Jane Caputi observes about sex murder: '[it] is lifted out of the historical tradition of gynocide and represented as a mysteri-ous force of nature, an expression of deeply repressed "human" urges, a fact of life, a supernatural evil, a monstrous aberration – anything but the logical and eminently functional product of the system of male dom-ination'.[4] Although there are many who would dispute Caputi's conclu-sions about the logical straight line from patriarchy to the murder of women, her assessment and the similar feminist work of Deborah Cameron and Elizabeth Fraser[5] are sobering interventions in a heavily masculine field – masculine in terms of research, readership and the sta-tistical truth that the majority of victims of what has come to be called serial murder are women, while the perpetrators are most frequently white men.

Caputi also identifies very succinctly the range of popular images of the serial killer, and all of them have their origin in the figure of Jack the Ripper. It is certainly the case that increasing interest in Jack the Ripper runs parallel to the increasing cultural prominence of the figure of the serial killer since the 1970s, when the FBI coined the term and began to produce psychological profiles of those they identified as such.[6] Documentary or 'true-crime' works on serial killers invariably identify Jack the Ripper as the original serial killer, even though he was certainly not the first person to commit repeated murders for no apparent mater-ial gain. Because he stands, as one writer comments, 'at the gateway of the modern age',[7] he is seen as the first example of a type that is the product of conditions recognizable as our own – industrialized urban modernity – and therefore somehow a monster of our own making.

The entanglement, from 1888 onwards, of Jack the Ripper with fictional figures and narratives is a phenomenon noted by many of the writers in this volume, and it is a confusion that persists in contemporary discourses on serial killers, where real cases are relatively rare, but fictional ones occupy a good deal of large and small screen time, and millions of pages of print. The confusion of fact and fiction is not limited to the popular imagination; it can also be seen to run deeply through professional law-enforcement bodies too. One of the first FBI profilers acknowledges that their 'antecedents actually do go back to crime fiction more than crime fact',[8] and Philip Jenkins notes that:

> It is difficult to know whether the bureaucratic law enforcement attitudes toward serial murder followed or preceded changes in popular culture ... the investigative priorities of bureaucratic agencies are formed by public and legislative expectations, which are derived from popular culture and the news media ... in coverage of serial murder, the boundaries between fiction and real life were often blurred to the point of non-distinction.[9]

It is clear that the Whitechapel murders are more than just a Victorian murder mystery: they have a profound legacy that has shaped the public and professional imagination in sometimes disturbing ways. It is perhaps then surprising that academic discussion of the significance of the Whitechapel murders and their representation has been relatively scant. In the introduction to the most recent academic study of the Whitechapel murders, L. Perry Curtis reflects on the areas of Jack the Ripper scholarship that he was unable to address:

> Among the many omissions in this study are the countless resurrections of the Ripper murders in our own time, whether these assume the forms of fiction, opera, film, television dramas, comic books, East End walking tours, or tacky memorabilia sold in Whitechapel pubs. Such topics could easily fill another book.[10]

And so they have here – although it is probable that even Curtis has underestimated the range of social, cultural, historical, creative and media representations for which the Whitechapel murders and the figure of Jack the Ripper are an impetus.

This book attempts to address the absence through a collection of essays that treat the subject from angles very different from that of the pursuit of suspects. One of the aims of the book is to assemble a critical canon that stands apart from the true-crime genre in which most of the work on the Whitechapel murders is found. Although it is clear that a good deal of painstaking research is present in the most rigorous of those books, it is directed at what even the most dedicated of 'Ripperologists' recognize to be an extremely unlikely outcome: the identification of the murderer. We suggest that the more interesting work lies in the investigation of the broader contexts of the murders and of the uses and significance of the figure of Jack the Ripper in wider culture. Our aim here is two fold: to collect and re-publish the important essays that have contributed to the nascent field of study, and to advance that scholarship through the addition of new commentaries and analyses. The re-published essays were until now scattered in very various locations; placing them alongside each other permits a view of their relationship with one another, as well as an indication of the movement in the analysis that they provide, in effect producing a reader of all earlier work in the field. The new essays draw on that work, while also addressing some of the absences noted by Curtis. The 'cultural turn', or the motion towards transdisciplinary study, in the humanities over recent years has allowed a rich exploration of cultural phenomena to emerge, one that is able to call on the critical and material resources of a number of different areas. The book is organized into three broad sections: Media, Culture and History. This to some extent reflects the major areas of media studies, cultural studies and historical studies from which the scholarship has emerged, although the range of the work represented here is such that it is possible to read with other organizational categories in mind, such as gender, genre and narrative, for example.

The Media section groups together the essays concerned with the representation of the figure of Jack the Ripper. The first three take the contemporary press reporting of the murders as their subject, showing how quickly the range of familiar stereotypes emerged and pointing to the very active role of the newspapers in producing and consolidating the image of the killer. Just as the late-Victorian press was a new medium, transformed as it had been by the 'New Journalism', the next new medium, film, also took up the character and the story, taking it forward through a new century. The first essay in the Media section is also one of the first significant attempts to read the Whitechapel murders as anything other than a whodunnit. Christopher Frayling considers the original press speculations on the identity of Jack the Ripper, and suggests that they all fall into three major stereotypes derived from contemporary moral panics. He also contends that, in general terms, these stereotypes were sustained in the work of 'Ripperologists' in the twentieth century.

While L. Perry Curtis's essay also focuses on the contemporary press reporting of the murders, he takes the period in the middle of the series of crimes when hard information was minimal and the kind of speculation that Frayling discusses was rife. Curtis traces a number of the 'angles' pursued by the news media to rumours or uncorroborated sources and plots their elaboration into major theories. In doing so he illuminates the inter-relationships of the publications and the beginnings of what can be recognized as the complex modern interaction between the press, police and community.

Darren Oldridge's essay takes a different approach to the contemporary press reports. Taking the very early press coverage of the murders as his subject, Oldridge reveals how the media were centrally involved in constructing the imagined figure of the serial killer some time before it was known with any authority that the murders were committed by a single perpetrator. Oldridge argues that Jack the Ripper was therefore part of the popular imaginary of the contemporary media even before the 'Dear Boss' and 'From Hell' letters gave him a specific name and apparent reality. The primary reason for this, Oldridge asserts, was the press's belief that newspaper sales were likely to be greatly increased by stories of a single killer rather than the other, equally plausible, 'explanations' of the Whitechapel murders. How the Whitechapel murders were represented, therefore, depended as much on circulation figures as on any objective calculation of cause.

The next essay in this section turns to another medium of representation. Almost since their inception Jack the Ripper has featured in films, making a first appearance in 1915. Colville and Lucanio explore the varying representations of the character, arguing that the complete absence of any real knowledge of his identity or appearance renders him a blank canvas on to which any number of changing anxieties can be projected. Focusing particularly on Alfred Hitchcock's use of the figure, they go on to argue that Jack the Ripper has also come to stand for a stock of shorthand references in cinematic vocabulary to Victorianism, nineteenth-century London and sexual pathology.

Although focused on two contemporary representations of the Whitechapel murders, Iain Sinclair's book *White Chappell, Scarlet Tracings* and Alan Moore and Eddie Campbell's graphic novel *From Hell*, Alex Warwick's essay suggests that all the different media representations are held together by the fundamental question of narrative. She argues that such questions are crucial not only to the understanding of the repeated telling of the Jack the Ripper story, but also to modern perceptions of the serial killer. The two novels are shown to be about the possibility of storytelling itself, and Jack the Ripper is used as an example of how narrative works in the creation of cultural meaning.

Warwick's essay provides a link to the second section: Culture. Here the writers are still concerned with issues of the creation of cultural meaning, but are focused more specifically on the production of 'bogeymen' – figures around whom particular currents of social anxiety are constellated, and who serve as short-hand for the articulation of those anxieties. Clive Bloom defines and investigates a number of historico-psychological symbols that are accepted as part of Ripper mythology. Bloom argues that Jack the Ripper has become a folk character, a multiple personality that serves a purpose as a monster in contemporary culture. Through reading the history of psycho-sexual murder, its investigation and attempts by scientists to make it knowable, he also shows how Jack the Ripper has come to appear as the essential case study of psychopathic behaviour.

Andrew Smith also turns his attention to the role of the medical profession and argues that medical opinion on the murders in 1888 was decidedly influenced first by the nature of the victims' supposed lifestyle and secondly by the popular belief that the murderer was a doctor or at least medically trained. This leads Smith to argue that the 'gothicization' of the crimes was influential in altering the gaze of the medical profession as they examined the already partially dissected bodies for evidence, leaving an uncertain dividing line between crime, deviance and medical practice.

Nicholas Rance and Martin Willis's essays both argue that the Whitechapel murders had a distinct influence upon the literary culture of the fin de siècle, in producing different versions of monsters. As many writers note, the late nineteenth century saw the creation of several figures who have become larger than the fictions that originally contained them: Dr Jekyll and Mr Hyde, Dracula, Dorian Gray, Sherlock Holmes. All of them are inextricably bound up with Jack the Ripper, a fact that is testified to by the number of later fictions that place them in the same narrative. All too are characteristic of the bogeyman – concentrating in one character a spectrum of social anxieties about deviance from perceived normality. Rance takes the position that Bram Stoker's *Dracula* owes more to the actions of Jack the Ripper than critics have allowed. Rance shows that Stoker was planning the novel at the same time as writing about the murders in his letters and diary, and highlights certain aspects of the Ripper mythology in the characterization of Harker, Van Helsing and Dracula. He suggests that popular notions of the murderer as a monstrous foreigner or a medical maniac contribute significantly to Stoker's doubling of the vampire and his pursuers.

Going further, Willis's essay argues that the whole genre of detective fiction was contributed to, and in fact altered by, the Jack the Ripper case. Taking Arthur Conan Doyle's Sherlock Holmes stories, Willis demonstrates the subtle shifts towards social reassurance that take place in the representation of crime and of the detective after 1888, in which the detective is dissociated from the criminal, and emphasis is placed on the powerlessness of the criminal when faced with scientific deductive reasoning. Given the influence of Doyle on the genre of British detective fiction, the Whitechapel murders are seen to have been instrumental in the creation of its forms and ideologies.

David Cunningham focuses on the recuperation of the bogeyman by consumer capitalism, the ways in which the forms of particular fears and anxieties of the past are drawn into commodification in contemporary London. Using recent discussions of economic and geographical categories, such as monopoly rent and land speculation, he looks at the heritage industry and the regeneration of East London, and argues that the long-standing notion of the 'undesirability' of the East End is now in the process of being replaced by a new idea of the area as both desirable and 'authentic' real estate. He shows how the Whitechapel murders have come to feature as part of a gothicized new mythology of place that has significant consequences for economic, cultural and social urban existence.

The final section, History, consists of essays by historians on the impact of the Whitechapel murders. This group shows in practice the importance of the transformation of disciplinary fields through the inclusion of wider cultural reference. Each of the essays represents one of the crucial lines of sight that have changed the humanities in recent decades: gender, class and race. In the context of this book, such perspectives are of particular value. It is to state the obvious that Jack the Ripper's victims were all women, and that the area in which the murders happened was one of the poorest in London, and that it contained a very high proportion of Jewish inhabitants, yet the accounts of the Whitechapel murders that concern themselves with 'the facts' can do little more than describe those facts. Analyses that start from the perspective of race or class or gender can offer a more finely textured commentary that provides more than simply an undifferentiated picture of the 'East End'. Judith Walkowitz's is one of very few feminist analyses in a field dominated by male scholarship and interest. She accounts for the enduring fascination with the murders by re-reading the press and popular material as constructing a highly unstable and contradictory story that both overlaps and conflicts with other discourses of sexuality and gender in the late-Victorian metropolis. Walkowitz locates the Ripper story as part of a formative moment in the production of feminist sexual politics and of popular narratives of sexual danger, narratives that still exert enormous influence on the public imagination today.

Robert Haggard also uses the idea of threat to read the reactions of the East and West Ends of London to the events of 1888. He suggests that the ingrained prejudices of the populace of Whitechapel quickly produced an idea of threat as located in foreigners, the police and upper-class society, while the economic uncertainty and fear of revolution affecting the West End meant that Whitechapel itself was viewed as the embodiment of the danger from 'outcast London'. Through the synthesis of the Jack the Ripper story and the larger crisis of the 1880s, Haggard argues that we can see the moment of the most acute fear of the two halves of London of each other, just before the modern labour movement began to assuage some of the distrust on both sides.

Sander Gilman's essay focuses on the historical position of the Jew in nineteenth-century British society. Rehearsing a history of anti-Semitism alongside a history of prostitution and the spread of syphilis, Gilman shows how the body of the Jew (like the body of the prostitute) is written as diseased and alien. Jack the Ripper's 'Jewishness', then, arises from contemporary ideas of what it is to be marginalized and vilified within a 'foreign' community.

The final essay analyses the effects of the murders on the district in which they took place. William Fishman discusses the rumours that arose in the local community and the steps taken by residents, such as the Vigilance Committee, to find the murderer. He also analyses the responses of the police, Jewish leaders and the radical press. Fishman goes on to detail the social implications of the crimes, demonstrating the alterations in policy that led to a number of material changes ranging from improved street lighting through public health and housing reform to the better treatment of homeless children and orphans.

As all these essays show, the phenomenon of Jack the Ripper is the touchstone for many of our analyses and critiques of late nineteenth-century Britain and of our own contemporary world. Sensational journalism can be said to have reached a new level during the Whitechapel murders, a level that was brought to a peak (or a nadir) by the popular press of the later twentieth century in a familiar series of scandals around press intrusion and sensationalism. In 1888 the fragility and anonymity of urban life were brought sharply into focus as the eyes of Britain's population were turned to London's East End. Such concerns with the shock of modernity were made postmodern pastiche in the return to Victorian values championed by late twentieth-century Conservative politicians in the wake of the inner-city crises of the 1980s. The depth of fin-de-siècle race and class divisions surfaced in the accusations of immigrants and of the professional and upper classes; similar suspicions are still disturbingly visible today in such apparently diverse contexts as the renewed debates on immigration and medical research and the presence of a newly militant rural community. The murders also played a defining role in the work of a national police force, early forensic science and the developing notions of sexual psychology and aberrant criminality. Twentieth-century Britain saw a new 'Ripper', this time from Yorkshire, but he is only one of several to whom the title has been applied. His series of murders of young women raised once again the spectre of police failure and scientific inadequacy in the face of the psycho-sexual predator, an anxiety that is still rehearsed in ambiguous ways with the repeated media criticism of police shortcomings in high-profile cases set against the complete successes of fictional forensic scientists and detectives.

In short, the murders of Jack the Ripper and the subsequent investigations by police, press, Whitechapel residents and social reform groups, as well as writers of journalism and fiction, became so dominant in late nineteenth-century culture that they can be said not only to indelibly mark the transition from a Victorian to a modern sensibility but still to have a powerful hold in the popular imaginary of the twentieth and twenty-first centuries. Jack the Ripper is a phenomenon that shows no sign of being incarcerated.

Notes

1 Tony Williams with Humphrey Price, *Uncle Jack* (London: Orion Books, 2005).

2 Trevor Marriott, *Jack the Ripper: The 21st Century Investigation* (London: Blake Publishing, 2005).

3 Roland Barthes, *Mythologies*, trans. Annette Lavers (London: Vintage, 1993), pp. 141–2.

4 Jane Caputi, *The Age of Sex Crime* (London: The Women's Press, 1988), p. 30.

5 Deborah Cameron and Elizabeth Frazer, *The Lust to Kill: A Feminist Investigation of Sexual Murder* (Cambridge: Polity Press, 1987); Deborah Cameron, 'Sti-i-i-i-ll Going ... The Quest for Jack the Ripper', *Social Text*, 40 (1994), pp. 147–54.

6 The work of Philip Jenkins in particular provides a strong critique of the construction of the category 'serial killer' and the vested interests of law-enforcement agencies. See *Using Murder: The Social Construction of Serial Homicide* (New York: Aldine de Gruyter, 1994) and 'Catch Me Before I Kill More: Seriality as Modern Monstrosity', *Cultural Analysis*, 3 (2002), pp. 1–17.

7 Oliver Cyriax, *The Penguin Encyclopaedia of Crime* (Harmondsworth: Penguin, 1996), p. 281.

8 John Douglas and Mark Olshaker, *Mindhunter: Inside the FBI's Elite Serial Crime Unit* (New York: Scribner, 1995), p. 32.

9 Jenkins, *Using Murder*, p. 223.

10 L. Perry Curtis, *Jack the Ripper and the London Press* (New Haven: Yale University Press, 2001), p. 5.

Part I

Media

1

The house that Jack built

Christopher Frayling

Since the *Pall Mall Gazette* synthesized all the 'suggestions' made by the morning newspapers, its articles on the Ripper present a broad cross-section of opinion about his possible identity. Other, less broad, cross-sections may be found in the correspondence columns of *The Times* and in the Home Office files (which contain suggestions penned by self-appointed guardians of law and order at the time).[1] *The Times* letters, in particular, were mainly sent in by retired members of the professions, elderly clerics and trigger-happy representatives of the armed forces, who were quick to express their moral outrage on behalf of 'all honest folk', and who sought a cure for all the ills besetting beleaguered Britain by the passage of laws against 'anti-socials' of all descriptions: clearly, they had not had such a good time since the riots of February 1886. Putting all these sources together, we find that the 'suggestions' fall into three main categories.

The Ripper as decadent English Milord[2]

Perhaps, like de Quincey's connoisseurs, Wilde's Dorian Gray or the Goncourts' bizarre version of Lord George Selwyn, this gentleman of leisure was seeking after luxurious cruelties which could stimulate his jaded sensibilities. Perhaps, as was suggested by an amateur sleuth who wrote to Scotland Yard, he was one of those 'upper or wealthy sort' who think that the working-class world exists purely 'for their pleasures – that of revenge being included – as a life business; without regard to any law but their own will'. E. W. Hornung's *Raffles* (1899) was also convinced that the Whitechapel murderer fitted this description:

> To follow crime with reasonable impunity you simply must have a parallel
> ostensible career – the more public the better. The principle is obvious. Mr
> Charles Peace, of pious memory, disarmed suspicion by acquiring a local
> reputation for playing the fiddle and taming animals, and its my profound
> conviction that Jack the Ripper was a really eminent public man, whose

speeches were very likely reported alongside his atrocities. Fill the bill in some prominent part, and you'll never be suspected of doubling it with another of equal prominence.

Raffles's naive assumption is, of course, that the 'eminent public man' who murdered whores was practising his art for art's sake: there is no suggestion that 'lower' motives came into it. In other words, the gentleman cracksman is relating the Ripper's motives to his own:

> *Necessity*, my dear Bunny? Does the writer only write when the wolf is at the door? Does the painter paint for bread alone? Must you and I be driven to crime like Tom of Bow or Dick of Whitechapel? You pain me, my dear chap; you needn't laugh, because you do. Art for art's sake is a vile catchword, but I confess it appeals to me. In this case my motives are absolutely pure.[3]

W. T. Stead, whose *Pall Mall Gazette* had cited de Quincey's *Essay on Murder Considered as one of the Fine Arts*, was also 'under the impression for more than a year' that 'the veritable Jack the Ripper' was a decadent occultist who called himself Roslyn D'Onston Stephenson, and that the crimes represented the application by a gentleman of leisure of some esoteric art. Stead's deduction is particularly interesting, in that his halfpenny evening newspaper had recently made its name by specializing in exposés of East End child prostitution (complete with two innovations on the newspaper scene, the interview and the cheaply printed illustration). When Stead opted for the 'decadent Milord' explanation, he was, on the face of it, destroying the very image of the East End which his paper had struggled so hard to present, since July 1885: an image of a place where people were exploited for cash rather than butchered for kicks.

But Stead had also been one of the many who campaigned 'with moral indignation' against the publication of Emile Zola's naturalistic novels in England. He had argued that Zola's frank presentation of sex, violence, cruelty and slang were liable to injure public morals, if translations were made easily available. In October 1888, much to the *Gazette*'s delight, Henry Vizatelly was summonsed for publishing three 'indecent' novels (including *Nana*) in translation, was fined £100 and placed on probation for twelve months. Stead, and his National Vigilance Association, had temporarily won the day, ensuring that 'slum novels', dealing among other 'putrid filth' with drunkenness and prostitution, would not be available to those who could not read French.[4] So, in a sense, Stead's explanation of the Ripper murders fitted neatly into the moral position on the role of the artist which his paper had promoted in the previous year, and which, to judge by sales, may well have been a popular one. It was simply a case of transposing the arguments against Vizatelly to the editorials on Whitechapel, and full mileage could still be got out of the 'modern Babylon' at the same time. The *Lancet* of 27 October finally made explicit the connection between the two campaigns: in an article on 'the exploits of Jack the Ripper, as detailed for our delectation at the breakfast table day after day', the writer noted with suitable disgust 'the same drift towards sensationalism in the popularity of the realistic novel'. The *Lancet* continued:

> The realism which M. Zola has popularised in France, and which threatens to invade us in England, does not consist in the truthful portraiture of all aspects of human life, but in the deliberate and systematic choice of what is vile and corrupt for the purposes of fiction. It is as if a painter, determined to paint nature and nature only, were to neglect the wood, the stream, the ocean and human beauty, and fill his canvas with nothing but sores and ulcers and deformities. Such art would be realistic at the expense of sacrificing its true ends – namely, the promotion of pleasure by means *that elevate and ennoble.*

'A healthy all-round genius, like SHAKSPEARE,' the *Lancet* went on, was 'sure to paint man as a rational, self-controlling being, and not as a wanton savage': this, in contrast to 'our French neighbours' who tended to worship people like the author of *The Beast in Man*.

Over the coming years, the novelist George Gissing and the poet Algernon Swinburne were actually to be named as possible Ripper 'types' – ironically, in Swinburne's case, since he also had campaigned against the Zola translations. It was almost as if the Gothick tradition of the penny-dreadfuls had joined forces with the fin-de-siècle realism of the novel: the *Newgate Calendar* had met working-class fiction and the murderer had as a result to be presented in the stock role of the 1820s Corinthian, the man of leisure who visited the Ratcliff Highway to watch the rat-fighting and the drunken fights, or to find a torture garden which catered for his particular taste in flesh. *La bête humaine* in a democratic setting ...

In Paris, where Stead's 'Maiden Tribute of Modern Babylon' had been something of a *succès de scandale*, the murders were immediately related to another literary phenomenon which was almost equally chauvinistic – the fictional celebration of 'le sadisme anglais': 'Jack' became easily absorbed into a perverted pantheon of English Milords which had recently included George Selwyn, Lord Byron, Algernon Swinburne and the 'Marquis of Mount Edgecumbe'. 'Le vice anglais', if enjoyed to excess outside the confines of public schools, could so easily get out of control. Most of the monographs published by Professor Lacassagne's Institute at Lyons had been about French 'vampires', necrophiliacs and sadistic murderers; now at last an Englishman could be added to the list.

The more prosaic I-know-what-I-like context for the *Pall Mall Gazette*'s coverage of the Whitechapel murders to some extent explains both the appeal of the 'decadent artist' or the 'decadent aristocrat' thesis, and the reasons why the paper had an interest in promoting it in 1888.

Less explicable is the recent fascination with 'solutions' that belong to the same category: in the past few years, the names Frank Miles and Walter Sickert have been linked with the Ripper crimes, as have those of the Duke of Clarence, his tutor at Cambridge (James Stephen) and Montague Druitt, an Oxford-educated barrister who was an active member of the MCC and Blackheath Cricket Club – a true heir to the *Raffles* tradition. Apart from the obvious advantage which these candidates share over the man-on-the-Whitechapel-omnibus – there is plenty of archive information about them, so it is not difficult to construct a full-scale biography as part of the 'solution' – the attraction of this category today may well have something to do with revelations about 'the other Victorians'[5] which were first published in the 1960s. Plays about real-life eminents in a fictional setting (such as Graham Greene's *Return of A. J. Raffles*[6]), films about fictional detectives in a real-life setting (such as *A Study in Terror* and *Murder by Decree*, both featuring Sherlock Holmes and both opting for the Clarence 'solution'), books about the Whitechapel murders (naming Druitt, Clarence, James Stephen and, most recently, the unlikely trio of Sir William Gull, Walter Sickert and the coachman John Netley as perpetrators of the crimes) have all proved popular in recent years, as have television series about assorted royal scandals of the nineteenth century – perhaps an indication of the power which the idea of 'the other Victorians' has over popular entertainers, and of the fact that the idea is not nearly as subversive as it looks. The only certain thing that can be said about 'the Ripper as other Victorian' is that there is not a shred of hard evidence to link the crimes with *any* of the blue-blooded suspects named. No matter: Stephen Knight's *Jack the Ripper: the Final Solution*, which named three eminent names, sold a lot of copies; Joseph Sickert's admission that the book was based on an elaborate hoax ('it was a whopping fib') was given a few lines in *The Sunday Times*. Readers of *The Final Solution* had all been gulled; perhaps they wanted to be.[7]

The Ripper as mad doctor

In this school of thought he was a crazed medical student who had caught syphilis from a prostitute (possibly even 'had his privy member destroyed'), and sought revenge on the whole pack of them. Or he was an American physician who was collecting as many specimens of the female uterus as he could find, to include as a free handout with a monograph he was writing on diseases of the womb. He was a ship's doctor, or perhaps an amateur whose only practical experience came from filleting fish. If he was not exactly a doctor, then he *might* have acquired his knowledge of anatomy from the slaughterhouse – thus he was a slaughterman, a Jewish ritual slaughterman, or even a woman disguised as a slaughterman. This category seems to have gained legitimation from at least some of the evidence given at the inquests on the Ripper's victims; speaking of the Nichols murder, Dr Rees Ralph Llewellyn suggested that the mutilations were 'fairly skilfully performed'; of the Chapman murder, Dr Phillips opined that 'the mode in which the uterus was extracted showed some anatomical knowledge'; Dr Frederick Brown thought that the murderer of Eddowes showed 'a good deal of knowledge as to the positions of organs in the body cavity and the way of removing them'. But other professional observers were by no means so convinced: Doctors Sequeira and Saunders disagreed with Brown about the Eddowes murder, others reckoned that Kelly had been so severely mutilated that it was impossible to judge the 'skill' of the murderer, while Dr Thomas Bond of the City Police was certain that in each case the mutilations were done 'by a person who has no scientific or anatomical knowledge. In my opinion he does not even possess the technical knowledge of a butcher or horse slaughterman or any person accustomed to cut up dead animals'.

Whether or not the evidence pointed in the direction of 'some anatomical knowledge', this category proved the most popular both in the press, and among commentators from the reading public at large. After all, the dramatization of *Jekyll and Hyde* was very much in the news at the time (one suggestion in the files actually names Richard Mansfield the actor as the murderer, since his 'transformation' was *so* convincing), and the idea that the Ripper might be a doctor who was leading a double life seemed to 'work' in much the same way: the London Hospital in the Whitechapel Road could provide a secure base for his operations.

Robert Louis Stevenson's *Jekyll and Hyde* metaphor for 'the beast in man' was first published two years before the murders, and had gone through several editions by autumn 1888. The Lyceum adaptation opened in August. In the book, a successful society doctor who mixes in all the right social circles (and some of the wrong ones – there is a suggestion that he knows all about Cleveland Street) unleashes his alter ego, a brutal counterpart who represents what Jekyll calls the other side of his 'dual nature'. The doctor is tall, pale and thin – of what the Victorians called 'refined features' (features with which the Ripper was associated by several eye-witnesses). The beast is sallow, small and squat, rather like the 'hard ruffian' archetype mentioned in the *Pall Mall Gazette*. Hyde is, in other words, the physical embodiment of Jekyll's great discovery, 'that man is not truly one but truly two'. The doctor's lecture on the subject has been featured in suitably abridged form at the beginning of all the major film versions of the story:

> I say two, because the state of my own knowledge does not pass beyond that point. Others will follow, others will outstrip me on the same lines; and I hazard the guess that man will be ultimately known for a mere polity of multifarious, incongruous and independent denizens. I for my part advanced infallibly in one direction and in one direction only. It was on the moral side, and in my own person, that I learned to recognise the thorough and primitive duality of man ... It was the curse of mankind that these incongruous faggots were thus bound together – that in the agonised womb of consciousness these polar twins should be continuously struggling.[8]

At a time when neither Freud nor Krafft-Ebing had filtered into popular consciousness, when forensic medicine was still in its infancy (after one of the murders the word went round that an official photograph had been taken of the victim's eyes, since it had been suggested by some European forensic experts that the retina at the moment of death would reflect the face of the murderer[9]), the Jekyll and Hyde model represented the most accessible 'explanation' for newspapers to exploit: an 'explanation' which had as its subtext something about 'the female principle' battling it out with 'the male principle'. Jekyll himself does not interpret the 'dual nature' of man in sexual terms at all: rather, he stresses that it is on the 'moral side' and has something to do with being just and unjust. Whatever the deeper meaning of the metaphor, in 1888 it seemed to newspapermen and their reading public to fit the idea that the Ripper could be an 'amiable-looking gentleman' *and* 'a hard ruffian' both at the same time. He was a bright young doctor who had gone off the rails; he was a soft-spoken gentleman who heard voices in the night; he was Mrs Belloc Lowndes's *Lodger*, Mr Sleuth (1911), Stevenson's Dr Jekyll, the *Pall Mall Gazette*'s version of the Marquis de Sade. This 'either ... or' explanation might account for the fact that the Ripper was likely to be as normal as thee or me – except when the dreaded beast in man came to the surface: for, apart from anything else, dialectical psychology was, of course, a thing of the future. It appears that Stevenson may have had in mind William Gull, MD, DCL, LLD, FRS, Queen Victoria's Physician Extraordinary, when he created the character of Henry Jekyll, MD, DCL, LLD, FRS. If so, it could explain why Gull, who by 1888 was aged and hemiplegic, has come to be associated with the Ripper murders – plus the fact that he seems to 'fit'.

The Ripper as anarchist, socialist or philanthropist[10]

If one literary correlative of our first category is Wilde's *The Picture of Dorian Gray* (decadent young thing indulging in murder as one of the fine arts), and of our second is Stevenson's *Dr Jekyll*, this third category has more to do with the image of the East End that had been constructed by the press in the few years before 1888. The 'mad doctor' thesis represented the most accessible 'explanation' at the time, but the Ripper as foreign agitator ran it a close second.

The fact that several of the eye-witness accounts stressed (for whatever reasons) the murderer's 'foreign' appearance, while some of the senior police officers associated with the case were on record as suggesting that the murderer was a 'Jewish Socialist', was used to legitimate this thesis. He was a Jewish agitator, an Irish revolutionary, a 'low class Asiatic', a Thug, a Russian Jew seeking to discredit the English police, an insane Russian doctor, 'a low class Polish Jew', a Polish Jewish shoemaker, King Leopold of the Belgians and a Portuguese sailor. Anyone who could write 'Mishter Lusk' must be Irish. Anyone who could chalk up the 'Juwes' message must really be Jacob the Ripper. Anyone who could mutilate in the Ripper's fashion must either be Portuguese (according to Napier's *History of the Peninsula War*, it was 'characteristic' of them) or a Malay running amok ('probably primed with opium'). He was certainly not one of us.

This category of explanation relates to the image of the East End in 1888, in two important ways: it fed off the 'anti-alienism' which had paralleled the economic decline of the dockland areas of East London and it mirrored more general fears about the spread of Socialism among members of the 'true working class'. That the economic depression of the East End – and the concomitant rise of overcrowding, sweat-shops and exploitation – had, by chance, occurred at much the same time as the peak years of immigration from Eastern Europe, was a fact duly noted by those commentators who were concerned about the 'dilution' of good old English stock in the 'outcast' areas of London. There may have been structural reasons for this depression – the shift in patterns of employment around the docks, the competition from regional factories, the changing face of industrial London – but the immigrants provided a ready-made, and simple, explanation of it all which could displace more searching questions about the root causes of economic decline in East London. The 'economy of makeshifts' which was so characteristic of the people of the abyss was thus presented as a *racial* characteristic, in the popular middle-class press. Moreover, the Ripper struck at much the same time as these connections were first

IS DETECTION A FAILURE?

In the interests of the Gutter Gazette and of the Criminal Classes, the Sensational Interviewer dogs the Detective's footsteps, and throws the strong light of publicity on his work. Under these circumstances, it is not surprising that Detection should prove a failure.

1 *Punch* takes a satirical swipe at sensational journalism.

being formulated. The *East London Observer* of 15 September 1888 duly noted:

> On Saturday in several quarters of East London the crowds who assembled in the streets began to assume a very threatening attitude towards the Hebrew population of the District. It was repeatedly asserted that no Englishman could have perpetrated such a horrible crime as that of Hanbury Street, and that it must have been done by a JEW – and forthwith the crowds began to threaten and abuse such of the unfortunate Hebrews as they found in the streets.

Then, on 30 September, Elizabeth Stride was discovered outside the International Working Men's Educational Club, by a Jew. The result was, in one commentator's words, 'the nearest thing to an East End anti-Jewish pogrom, prior to the advent of Mosley'.

When the *Church Times*, no less, suggested that the Ripper was a Jewish anarchist, the *Arbeter Fraint* retaliated with the words 'such homage to the Holy Spirit!' When *The Times* reported that a Jew named Ritter had been arrested near Cracow for the ritual murder of Christian women, and that 'the evidence touching the superstitions prevailing among some of the ignorant and degraded of his co-religionists remains on record and was never wholly disproved', the Chief Rabbi, Dr Herman

Adler, wrote in to 'assert without hesitation that in no Jewish book is such a barbarity even hinted at'. Adler added, 'the tragedies enacted in the East End are sufficiently distressing without the revival of moribund fables and the importation of prejudices abhorrent to the English nation'. But some members of the police force took more convincing than that. Sir Charles Warren thought the murderer might well be a 'Jewish Socialist'; Abberline thought he was George Chapman, a Pole whose real name was Severin Klosowski; Robert Anderson stated as 'a definitely ascertained fact' that the Ripper was 'a low-class Polish Jew'; and Melville Macnaghten named a certain Kosminski ('a Polish Jew resident in Whitechapel') as one of three key suspects (Kosminski had apparently 'become insane owing to many years' indulgence in solitary vices', and, perhaps as a result, he resembled Sgt Stephen White's eye-witness description).

Official visits were made to kosher abbatoirs, two ritual slaughtermen were arrested, and the special knife used by the shochet was examined by Dr Brown to see whether it could have inflicted wounds of the type found on the victims' bodies. The most highly publicized arrest in the whole case was that of John Pizer, or 'Leather Apron', a Polish Jewish shoemaker, and of the 130 arrests made in the London area alone, a significant proportion were of Jews; following Pizer's arrest, the Ripper became more and more 'foreign in appearance' by the hour. So, when Sir Charles Warren ordered the message about the 'Juwes' to be rubbed off the wall near Goulston Street, he was being far more responsible than many commentators have since suggested. It was strange, however, that he did not agree to let the words be photographed (by City Police photographers, significantly enough), and it may have been an error of judgement that prevented him from simply erasing the word 'Juwes', but the fact remains, that had he allowed the message to stay, he might well have had a riot on his hands (the message was written above a common stairway leading to a tenement block occupied mainly by Jewish immigrants). This was certainly the explanation he gave to the Home Secretary – who was furious – and it seems a reasonable one. (The police file implies that if the writing was done by the murderer, it may have had the intention of casting suspicion on three Jews who claimed to have seen him.) Dr Adler immediately wrote to congratulate Warren on his prompt action, reassuring him that the word 'Juwes' did not appear in any Yiddish dialect, and informing him of his conviction that 'the writing emanated from some illiterate Englishman who did not know how to spell the word correctly'. Warren's response was to publish this information in *The Times* of 15 October.

The recent thesis that Warren was 'covering up' for someone when he rubbed out the message, that the message referred to a different form of ritual slaughter based on Masonic mythology, seems not only to ignore the realities of East End history at the time, but also to fall prey to exactly the same mode of argument as led many to accuse the Jews in 1888. In the absence of any 'explanation' of the Ripper's actions, at the time of the murders, harassed police officers and sharp newspaper editors, as well as correspondents from the reading public, were irresistibly drawn to the 'secret ritual' argument: but there seems little excuse for doing so today.

If the murderer was not Jewish, then he must be Irish (the next worst thing) or Oriental. Failing that, he must be an English Socialist. Warren could not make up his mind whether the Ripper was Jewish, socialist or both; he was sure the Socialists had *something* to do with it – even if it meant suggesting that the murders were intended by one wing of the International to 'bring discredit' on another wing – but he could not work out exactly what. We have seen how Stead's *Pall Mall Gazette* put forward 'a scientific humanitarian' as the possible culprit. Others were more specific, implying that the Reverend Samuel Barnett, founder of Toynbee Hall, the signwriter to General Booth of the Salvation Army, and even Dr Barnardo were possible 'types'. John Burns, who was to lead the dock strike of 1889, was detained by the police as he walked home from a late-night workers' meeting.

In a sense, this line of thought represents the other side of the 'alien' thesis. For, if one feature of the East End which was constantly in the news was the peril of unrestricted immigration (and suggestions as to how immigrants might most humanely be deported), another was the danger that pernicious socialist ideas might spread from 'outcast London', the 'residuum of labour', to more respectable or 'true' members of the working class. Once the good old English aristocrat of labour, or the artisan, found socialist ideas attractive, then the Trafalgar Square incident, and its aftermath, would seem just like a sideshow. Warren, who had given the orders which resulted in 'Bloody Sunday', was more aware of this than anyone. It was bad enough to watch the emergence of the Independent Labour Party, and the dramatic increase in trade union membership: something had to be done, preferably by non-political action, to seize the initiative from the Socialists before their ideas spread *too* far.

In the popular press, the 'non-political actions' of 1884–8 were all treated with a greater or lesser measure of enthusiasm, for they seemed to provide ways of resolving the problem dramatized by Trafalgar Square without actually confronting it. The foundation of Oxford House (in 1884) and Toynbee Hall (a year later); the beginning of Charles Booth's survey of the East End, and the Inauguration of the People's Palace in the Mile End Road (both 1887); the announcement of the Salvation Army's new policy of social reform in 1887; the much-publicized increase in the number of 'settlers' (or 'slummers') from the upper rungs of society, all these were easy enough to satirize. (Henrietta Barnett's 'all class' East-West tea parties at the Vicarage were an obvious target – almost as obvious, in fact, as the social worker who smugly declared 'charity presents no difficulty to me; I took a First in Moral Philosophy at Cambridge'.) Nevertheless there were urgent reasons why they should be encouraged. When the Ripper struck, the 'slummers', Salvationists, university settlers, social analysts and 'do-gooders' of all descriptions were accused of murderous intentions with equal enthusiasm. Perhaps their work *was* actively dangerous, after all. More importantly, the Whitechapel murders gave editors the opportunity to associate socialism, or just plain philanthropy, with 'outcast' activities – the old-fashioned, sensational image of the East End as a den of vice – and thus to drive a wedge between the 'outcasts' and the 'respectables'. This distinction had been on the hidden agenda ever since Trafalgar Square, and the implied association between ripping and socialism brought it into focus.

If Jack was not a social analyst (like Booth), a settlement man (like Barnett, or, as has been suggested more recently, Druitt), a charity organizer (like Barnardo), a Salvationist (like the other Booth's signwriter) or a revolutionary (probably Jewish – enough said), then there was always the danger that the Socialists themselves would seize the initiative by using the crimes for their own propagandistic purposes. Jack, with a fiendish sense of timing, had succeeded in undoing the efforts of many well-intentioned people to publicize a less sensational image of the East End, just at a time when Beatrice Webb (among others) was beginning to realize that these efforts were merely the *first* stage: the East End, as a city within a city, was still little understood and much neglected.

Those who enthused over the 'non-political actions' of 1884–8, suggesting that they represented some kind of *solution* to the problem, were, predictably, shocked when various wings of the socialist movement *did* use the Ripper crimes as a symbol of the evils of capitalism. *Justice*, the organ of Hyndman's Social Democrats, thundered: 'the real criminal is the vicious bourgeois system which, based upon class injustice, condemns thousands to poverty, vice and crime'. Bernard Shaw presented a more whimsical Fabian view, in a letter headed 'Blood Money for Whitechapel', which he sent to the *Star* (a more radical evening paper than the *Gazette*) on 24 September 1888. To him, the identity of the murderer was quite simple: he was a social reformer 'of independent genius'. 'Less than a year ago, the West End press was literally clamouring for the blood of the people, and behaving as the propertied class always does behave when the workers throw it into a frenzy of terror by venturing to show their teeth'; but since the beginning to the Whitechapel murders, he said, the West End press had undergone a change of heart:

> Whilst we conventional social democrats were wasting our time on education, agitation and organisation, some independent genius has taken the matter in hand, and by simply murdering and disembowelling four women, converted the proprietary class to an inept sort of communism. The moral is a pretty one, and the Insurrectionists, the Dynamitards, and the Invincibles will not be slow to draw it ... Every gaol blown up, every window broken, every shop looted, every corpse found disembowelled means another ten pound note for 'ransom'.

William Morris's *Commonwealth* made a similar point, with less irony (and incidentally, with more taste): 'in our age of contradictions and absurdities, a fiend-murderer may become a more effective reformer than all the honest propagandists in the world'. Morris himself had, in fact, been involved in an evening of 'honest propaganda', sponsored by the Socialist League, at the International Club, 40 Berner Street, just eight days before Stride's corpse was discovered there. For these Socialist newspapers, nothing but good could arise from the murders, even if 'four women of the people' had been sacrificed to the cause. It never seemed to occur to them that the image of the East End, as an area where people did not go around murdering one another but where they were dead behind the eyes none the less, had suffered significant damage as a result of the Ripper's experiments in 'slaughterhouse anatomy' (or was it consciousness-raising?). Nor did it occur to them that the 'four women' might not be expendable.[11]

Arthur Morrison, writing an article on 'Whitechapel' for the *People's Palace Journal* of April 1889, was much more concerned than the Social Democrats, the Fabians and the Guild Socialists, about the effects of 'graphically-written descriptions of Whitechapel, by people who have never seen the place'. For Morrison, there were two types of description of the East End – one derived from accounts of Jack the Ripper, the other derived from the literature on 'outcast London' as an abyss into which intrepid missionaries might occasionally leap. Both failed to take note of the *variety* of life in that sector of London, of the 'ancient industries' which were in decline, of the ways in which those who did *not* live in 'foul slums' existed day-to-day, above all of the human beings who actually managed somehow to survive, and even establish communities, a network of support, in the East End of London. The first type of account went as follows:

> A horrible black labyrinth ... reeking from end to end with the vilest exhalations; its streets, mere kennels of horrid putrefaction; its every wall, its

every object, slimy with the indigenous ooze of the place; swarming with human vermin, whose trade is robbery, and whose recreation is murder; the catacombs of London – darker, more tortuous, and more dangerous than those of Rome, and supersaturated with foul life.

The second has a firmer basis in reality, but still could not claim in any way to be representative of the place:

Black and nasty still, a wilderness of crazy dens into which pallid wastrels crawl to die; where several families lie in each fetid room, and fathers, mothers and children watch each other starve; where bony, blear-eyed wretches, with everything beautiful, brave and worthy crushed out of them, and nothing of the glory and nobleness and jollity of this world within the range of their crippled senses, rasp away their puny lives in the sty of the sweater.

Both descriptions, said Morrison, were written by the kind of man who called Whitechapel 'a shocking place where he once went with a curate'. His own rejection of *both* models of the East End put over by the popular press (and popular novels) was to be reinforced by the publication shortly afterwards of the first volume of Charles Booth's *East London*. Booth, also, had had to fight against the public images of 'outcast London':

East London lay hidden from view behind a curtain on which were painted terrible pictures ... horrors of drunkenness and vice; monsters and demons of inhumanity ... Did these pictures truly represent what lay behind, or did they bear to the facts a relation similar to that which the pictures outside a booth at some country fair bear to the performance or show within? This curtain we have tried to lift.

According to Booth's figures only 1.2 per cent of the East End population were in the category of 'loafers and semi-criminals', while well over 60 per cent tried to lead 'decent, respectable lives' ('questions of employment' permitting). The rest were not so much 'debased', as living in conditions of almost perpetual poverty, and even so trying to support one another. Neither Jack, nor the 'do-gooders', had presented a true 'picture'.

These three images of the Whitechapel murderer – Dorian Gray, Dr Jekyll and a political version of the wandering Jew of the penny-dreadfuls – combined with the 'mental sets' with which they were associated by popular writers – decadence, the beast in man and socialism or racial pollution – sustained press coverage of the crimes for several months, and enabled editors to slot the Whitechapel events into previously constructed 'angles'. Whichever of the three categories was chosen, it could be linked with a well-defined moral panic, and moral panics were very good for sales. In a sense, the moral-panic strategy became a *substitute* for hard copy, since there was so little material available on the actual crimes, and since various steps seem to have been taken to prevent the more exploitable details from getting into print. It also provided three ready-made models of the-sort-of-person-who-might-do-such-things, at a time when the Ripper's motives appeared to go beyond the bounds of a recognizably human nature.

What is surprising, on the face of it, is that these explanations are *still* accepted by self-styled 'Ripperologists' and their readers, when there is so much evidence, social *and* psychological, to contradict them. The Ripper was much more likely to have been the victim himself of the syndrome that leads some deeply depressed, and highly impressionable, men to see a 'fallen woman' as the one last person they can push around than to have been one of the more famous 'other Victorians'; the frustrated victim of (apparent) powerlessness rather than the possessor of real power. We now have the language to describe what 'Jack' was up to, and perhaps why he was up to it, but the literature has continued to rely on *Gazette*-like solutions, displacing the only usable evidence there is, in favour of the criminal stereotypes of late Victorian England – one philistine, one pre-Freudian, one racialist, all of them deeply misogynistic in character. Moreover, the image of the East End as the kind of place where Nancy was regularly murdered by Bill Sikes has also survived into recent books on the Whitechapel murders, although we know better.

In 1888, reporters covering the crimes did not have much else to write about, and in any case were bound to exploit the moral panics of the moment as far as they could; this, to some extent, explains the unprecedented interest shown by newspapers catering for such widely different reading publics. True, these were serial murders, and several newspapers were quick to spot the commercial potential of the serial, often inventing fresh 'episodes' of their own to keep up the readers' interest. True, the name 'Jack the Ripper' seems to have struck a distinct chord – hardly surprising, really, since penny-bloods had for years been chronicling the exploits of Gallant Jack, Left-handed Jack, Roving Jack the Pirate Hunter, Jolly Jack Tar, Arab Jack the London Boy, Blind Jack of Knaresborough, Gentleman Jack, Jack Harkaway, Jack the Giant-Killer, Jack Spry, Jack's the Lad, Jack at Eton, Moonlight Jack King of the Road, Sixteen-String Jack the Hero Highwayman, Spring-Heeled Jack the Terror of London, Three-fingered Jack the Terror of the Antilles, Thrice-Hung Jack, Jack O'Lantern, Jack O'the Cudgel, Jack O'Legs, Jack and Joe the troublesome twins, Slippery Jack, Jack Rann, Jack Junk, Crusoe Jack, and, most famous of them all, Jack Sheppard. Meanwhile, newspaper reports of the 'High Rippers', or 'High Rips' – gangs of youths who like the Hoxton Market and old Nichol Street mobs, went around attacking unaccompanied prostitutes in the East End – filled many column inches in the early 1880s.

True, the internal squabble between various branches of the police force (and the resignations which resulted around the time of the Ripper inquiry – James Monro, head of the CID, in August, Sir Charles Warren in November) were always a stand-by, when material on the Ripper became *too* thin on the ground, or when a newspaper wanted to score points at the expense of those who were hindering inquiries (in the public interest, no doubt) about the more gory aspects of the story. Accepting all this, we are still left with the fact that the image of the East End in the mental landscape of late Victorian newspapermen, and the three moral panics with which the crimes were associated, provided the main support for the process of constructing a recognizable 'Jack the Ripper'.

Notes

1 For extracts from 'suggestions' in the Home Office files, see Donald Rumbelow, *The Complete Jack the Ripper* (London: W. H. Allen, 1975) and Stephen Knight, *Jack the Ripper: The Final Solution* (London: Harrap, 1976). One of the more bizarre suggestions in the files is that the Ripper was a renegade cowboy from Buffalo Bill's Wild West Show.

2 For a more detailed study of the tradition in popular culture from which this theme emerged, see my *Vampyre: Lord Ruthven to Count Dracula* (London: Gollanz, 1978), especially pp. 14–82.

3 E. W. Hornung, *Raffles the Amateur Cracksman* (London: Nelson Library, 1909), pp. 34–5 of 'A Costume Piece' and pp. 54–5 of 'Gentlemen and Players'.

4 On 'French Naturalism and English Working-class Fiction', see Peter Keating, *The Working Classes in Victorian Fiction* (London: Routledge & Kegan Paul, 1979), pp. 125–38.

5 The fashion, and the phrase, were launched by Steven Marcus, *The Other Victorians: A Study of Sexuality and Pornography in Mid-nineteenth Century England* (London: Weidenfeld and Nicolson, 1966), a book which has proved to be of some use in more recent studies of sexual ideology and social structure, but which has too undifferentiated an approach to 'Victorian culture' and 'sexual mores'.

6 Graham Greene, *The Return of A. J. Raffles* (London: Ultramarine, 1975).

7 On 18 June 1978, *The Sunday Times* reported Sickert's admission under the headline 'Jack the Ripper Solution was a Hoax, Man Confesses'. Joseph Sickert added, 'as an artist I found it easy to paint Jack the Ripper into the story'. Six years later, in 1984, Stephen Knight's *Jack the Ripper: The Final Solution* was reprinted by the Treasure Press, London, virtually uncorrected. Clearly, this story was so good that a little matter of factual inaccuracy could not be allowed to stand in its way.

8 Robert Louis Stevenson, *The Strange Case of Dr Jekyll and Mr Hyde* (London: Corgi, 1964), pp. 51–2 of 'Henry Jekyll's Full Statement of the Case'.

9 This myth may have started life in a citation from the *British Journal of Photography* (17 February 1888), which refers to a story about a French assassin, as recounted by an American journalist. Certainly, the *Journal* makes no mention of such folklore in its coverage of autumn 1888.

10 For some key sources, see Keating, *The Working Classes*; Kellow Chesney, *The Victorian Underworld* (London: Penguin, 1974). Also Gareth Stedman Jones, *Languages of Class: Studies in Working Class History 1832–1982* (Cambridge: Cambridge University Press, 1983), pp. 204–35, especially useful on the music halls of the period; and Judith R. Walkowitz, *Prostitution and Victorian Society* (Cambridge: Cambridge University Press, 1982), which, although it deals predominantly with the 1860s, provides an important frame of reference.

11 For a very welcome if all too brief analysis of the coverage of the Whitechapel murders from a feminist perspective, see Judith Walkowitz, 'Jack the Ripper and the Myth of Male Violence', *Feminist Studies*, 8 (1982), pp. 543–74. Although Judith Walkowitz and I have been researching independently for several years – and from somewhat different sources – our conclusions are congruent.

2

The pursuit of angles

L. Perry Curtis, Jr

The relatively long hiatus in the Ripper's activities from 1 October to 9 November meant that Fleet Street had to scratch hard for murder news, even though the Stride and Eddowes inquests dragged on for weeks. In their quest to keep the story alive by means of new angles and theories, reporters proved more than inventive, and they managed to fill some of the void with anecdotes, rumours, false reports and conjectures. During the five-week interval before the final murder many papers raised the volume of law-and-order news. Whether praising or damning Warren, they expressed concern about public safety and questioned the way Scotland Yard was deploying its resources.

Shortly after the double event Warren delivered his annual report on the state of the Metropolitan police and appealed for more money and more men. Virtually all the leading papers commented on his proposals. The *Morning Post* (8 October) supported his contention that the burdens of policing London had increased more rapidly than the number of constables and the funds available over the previous forty years. Given the ever-present danger posed by 'mischievous agitators' and 'unruly mobs', he was fully justified in asking for more policemen to cope with criminal elements. In this writer's view, the East End murders proved how easily the police could become the targets of unfair criticism by a panic-stricken public. The police could not have prevented these crimes because the murderer knew how to strike swiftly and evade capture. While approving Warren's annual report as well as his conduct, *The Times* (6 October) also praised the courage and intelligence of ordinary policemen, who afforded Londoners 'the safety and immunity which they enjoy', for which they should be more grateful. Another leader (12 October) denied that the police were guilty of 'culpable stupidity' in pursuing the culprit and blamed the victims for making such 'easy prey' because they chose to evade police surveillance in order to pursue clients. Since they spurned police protection, they were to all intents and purposes 'in league with the murderer'. Liberal and Radical papers continued to remind readers of Warren's role in the brutal repression of Bloody Sunday. Thus the *Daily Chronicle* (8 October) denounced Warren's claim to have won an important victory over the forces of disorder in 1887 because workers had every right to hold rallies in Trafalgar Square. In short, the paper argued, Warren's order to disperse the protesters had provoked the clash and aggravated the running feud between the police and the masses. The priority he placed on 'military drills and parades' had discouraged the police from thinking for themselves, while his neglect of the CID had reduced the detective branch to 'such crapulous decrepitude' that James Monro, the head of the CID, had been forced to resign. While the taxpayers of London deserved some assurance that Warren was making the best use of his forces, the 'ghastly list of undiscovered crimes' in recent months offered little hope on this score.[1]

Rushing to Warren's defence, the *Globe* (4 October) applauded his vigorous response to criticism from the Whitechapel Board of Works, and pointed out that constables could not be stationed on every street corner in London. To illuminate all the dark streets in the East End, moreover, would cost far too much money. Another leader (8 October) backed Warren's plea for more police, pointing out that only two-thirds of the force was available for street patrol at any given time. An editorial in the *East London Observer* (20 October) expressed dismay over the failure to catch the Whitechapel fiend despite the lapse of a full year since his first murder. In the past, multiple murderers like Burke and Hare had always been caught. But the Whitechapel horrors were different because the culprit was still at large and Scotland Yard's feeble response amounted to 'a series of false alarms, false arrests, fruitless theories, and ... useless house to house visitations'. The *East London Advertiser*'s editorial (13 October), entitled 'OUR DEFECTIVE DETECTIVE SYSTEM', heaped abuse on Warren's record as Chief Commissioner. Not only had he grossly mismanaged Scotland Yard, but his policies had driven Monro to resign. The time had come for a thorough reform of the CID along French lines, so that skilled detectives (including women) could be assigned to infiltrate the criminal class. Only when the police had acquired 'better brains and better organization' would London cease to be a place where 'most murderers go scot free'.

The *Pall Mall Gazette* (9 October) continued to rant against the breakdown of law and order in the metropolis, by publishing an interview with the Lord Mayor of London, Sir Polydore de Keyser, who called the murderer 'a human mad dog – a proper subject for Mr Pasteur', and a monomaniac who had evaded all the detectives looking for him. Barring suicide, the killer was bound to be caught during his next attack because 'a whole army of bloodhounds (metaphorical and literal) ... [are] on his track'. Convinced that reward money was 'meant more for show than use', de Keyser opposed increasing the number of police on the grounds of expense and traditional British prejudices against uniformed authority. On 12 October the *Gazette* again deplored Warren's order to destroy the message scrawled by 'the blood-red hand of the assassin' on Goulston Street without first obtaining a photograph. Here was proof positive of his 'utter unfitness' to lead Scotland Yard.

Stead was not content with merely taking the occasional potshot at the heads of a criminal justice system that had incarcerated him in 1886. Directing some of his animus at Scotland Yard and taking advantage of the growing dismay over the failure of the police to catch the killer, he warned readers in a trenchant leader on 8 October that a serious crime wave was sweeping through the metropolis while the police were looking the other way. In the same edition, he published the first of six long and data-laden articles under the headline 'THE POLICE AND THE CRIMINALS OF LONDON', about the ubiquity of crime and the virtual immunity from arrest enjoyed by the perpetrators.[2] Common criminals were thriving in central London because the police could not catch them. Among the most crime-ridden areas, in the *Gazette*'s opinion, were Gray's Inn Road, Hackney Road and Marylebone, where the police were undermanned, overworked, demoralized and poorly led. The author of this article insisted that professional criminals lacked any respect for Scotland Yard, and he accused Robert Anderson, the new head of the CID, of being a millenarian who wrote religious books. To make matters worse, Anderson had recently gone on holiday to Switzerland just when the police were losing the fight against crime. Because Warren knew so little about 'the science of criminal catching', Scotland Yard had become 'a laughing-stock'.

Another front-page leader in the *Gazette* (10 October), entitled 'LAW AND ORDER IN LONDON', lamented 'the present reign of plunder and anarchy' on Gray's Inn Road. Far from being the work of 'wild Irishmen in the remote morasses of Connaught, or [...] savage Asiatics in the recesses of the Himalayas', serious crimes were being committed by Englishmen in 'the heart of the greatest commercial centre of the world'. Embroidered by such subheads as 'Ruffianism and Rowdyism Rampant' (11 October), articles like these exemplified the alarmism of law-and-order news, the logical conclusion being that only more police, more surveillance of suspicious persons and harsher sentences would stop the criminal element in their tracks. In the twentieth century the tendency to criminalize whole districts or neighbourhoods has been seen as a vital part of 'social control strategies'.[3] If the Ripper murders made women even more terrified of 'sexual predators', as Judith Walkowitz maintains in *City of Dreadful Delight*, they also strengthened the lobby for radical reform of the police and detective forces. Only a few elite papers like *The Times* and *Morning Post* refused to join in the hue and cry for Warren's head. And when he did resign on the eve of Kelly's murder – ostensibly over a jurisdictional dispute with the Home Office – both these papers expressed sincere regret.

Under the heading of detection, the use of bloodhounds received a great deal of play in the press. Judging from the number of letters to the editor and allusions in feature articles, the idea of setting trained hounds onto the presumably bloodstained tracks of the killer clearly appealed to far more than fox-hunting enthusiasts. All kinds of dog fanciers, breeders and handlers joined in the debate about the pros and cons of deploying country-trained canine sleuths on city streets saturated with animal blood, offal and excrement. Although finding any particular human scent in congested Whitechapel posed a formidable challenge to even the smartest hound, some correspondents insisted that this was the only way that the murderer could be caught. An article entitled 'BLOOD-HOUNDS AS DETECTIVES' in the *Pall Mall Gazette* (3 October) cited several cases where hounds had tracked down slaves, poachers and criminals on the run. Evidently the killer of a little girl in Blackburn around 1876 had been pursued or 'convicted' by a hound. Of course, these animals had to be rushed to the crime scene while the scent was still fresh, and for this obvious reason some experts called on the police to register every bloodhound within striking distance of the East End so that they could be deployed as soon as the next murder occurred.[4]

Virtually every leading paper featured the bloodhound trials carried out under police supervision in Regent's Park and Hyde Park around 9 October. But few reporters bothered to point out how different the conditions were between the park's sylvan grounds and Whitechapel, where butchers threw the remains of knackered animals into the gutters every day and night. The *Evening News* (9 October) turned the Hyde Park trials into an enthralling, and almost amusing, story. Drawing on a long letter from an expert, the paper revealed that two seasoned hounds named Barnaby and Burgho had been brought at 7 a.m. to the Albert Gate entrance of the park, where they were greeted by several officials and a police surgeon. Having arrived on horseback, Warren volunteered to serve as the quarry. He then walked rapidly across the grass toward Bayswater while the hounds cast about for a few minutes and then picked up his scent. With only a few checks where his tracks crossed those of other people, they soon ran him to ground. Several more successful trials so impressed Warren that he ordered the police to keep some hounds in a kennel near Whitechapel.[5] Warren's role in the Hyde Park trials made the best kind of news, combining elements of both comedy and tragedy (and giving rise to the legend that one of the hounds had bitten him). Interviewed by the *People* (7 October), a leading veterinarian argued that well-trained hounds would be a useful 'auxiliary' to the police, but they would have to be 'familiarised with the odour of blood' before being put on the scent. Even so, the presence of so many other smells and shifting wind currents in any big city seriously reduced the chances of success. A reporter for the *East London Advertiser* (13 October) pointed out that the trials in Hyde Park could not be replicated in Whitechapel, where so many passers-by would 'obliterate' the killer's scent; for this reason he chose 'to back the biped against the quadruped'.[6]

Departing briefly from sensational prose, the *Pall Mall Gazette* (9 October) regaled readers with some doggerel under the title 'A BALLAD OF BLOOD-HOUNDS'. Although the CID did not unleash any hounds after Kelly's murder, despite reports that a police inspector had sent for them, the prospect of using these 'sleuths' inspired numerous articles and letters to the editor. Always keen to embarrass Warren, the *Pall Mall Gazette* (19 October) parodied the canine angle in an article entitled 'DISAPPEARANCE OF THE BLOODHOUNDS / THEIR ARREST ORDERED BY SIR C. WARREN'. Apparently the hounds had gone missing from their kennel and were being hunted by the police. '*Quis custodiet ipsos custodies?*' asked the writer gleefully after learning that Scotland Yard wanted to detain the missing dogs for questioning.[7]

Another large if sharp angle involved the serious disagreements among the police surgeons about how much or little the killer knew about surgery and female anatomy. Was he perchance a mad doctor, a failed medical student, a pathologist or simply a butcher? Refuting Coroner Baxter's far-out vivisection theory, surgeon George Sequeira stated firmly that the killer 'had no particular design on any organ' and lacked 'great anatomical skill' *(Globe*, 11 October). The *Star* (11 October) reported Dr William Saunders as making the same denial. Long before the coroners' juries in the Stride and Eddowes inquests returned their verdicts of 'wilful murder by some person unknown', Fleet Street was hunting and pecking for grains of Ripper news, sensationalizing even minor assaults on women. Even in the middle of the month, *Lloyd's* had no trouble filling four columns with the Eddowes inquest, her funeral at Ilford, bloodhounds, the replies of Warren and Matthews to their critics, anti-Semitism in the East End, the arrest of a suspect in Belfast and the stabbing of a detective dressed in female attire.[8] A front-page leader in the same paper (14 October), entitled 'GOOD OUT OF EVIL', trusted that these 'atrocious crimes' had aroused the authorities and the public to the urgent need for relief of all the suffering in the East End.

Almost as keen as the penny press to exploit the murders, *The Times* and *Morning Post* nevertheless featured other kinds of news. Not surprisingly, the results of horse racing around the country occupied almost as much space as events in Whitechapel. Moreover, at the height of the double-event crisis *The Times* (3 October) assigned more columns to the international Sugar Convention, the Church Congress at Manchester, and the speeches of prominent politicians. After the initial shock of these two murders had worn off, the paper continued to devote more space to financial affairs in the City than mutilation-murder further east.[9]

Between 8 October and 9 November, Ripper news – apart from the Stride and Eddowes inquests and the 'Lusk kidney', a piece of kidney sent to George Lusk, a prominent Whitechapel businessman and the president of the local vigilance committee – gradually tapered off. Because the killer had gone underground and the police remained tight-lipped about their investigation, reporters had to dig deep for new angles, and more often than not they failed to find a fresh lead. By the end of October news from Whitechapel had virtually dried up. Preoccupied with the special commission investigating Parnell's alleged complicity with agrarian violence in Ireland, *The Times* published no more feature articles about the Ripper until Kelly's death. The *Pall Mall Gazette* was so hard-pressed for Ripper news that it printed a short letter from 'Jack the Ripper' to George Lusk threatening to commit another 'double event' on the night of Saturday, 13 October – a report that turned out to be quite false.[10] The police actually caught one of the Ripper letter writers, who turned out to be a 'good-looking, respectably dressed', twenty-one-year-old seamstress named (appropriately) Maria Coroner, from Bradford. A search of her lodgings yielded copies of several Jack the Ripper letters in her handwriting, addressed to both the Chief Constable and a local newspaper, indicating Jack's intention to 'do a little business' in Bradford. After her arrest, Coroner confessed that she had simply wanted to create a sensation, but then tried to excuse her conduct as a 'joke'.[11]

Reluctant to let the Ripper story die during the last fortnight of October, the press highlighted suspects, who ranged from a tall gentleman with sandy or reddish hair to a short, dark and black-haired man. Evidently both Scotland Yard and Fleet Street continued to be swamped with letters from people claiming to know who the assassin was, or tendering advice about how to catch him. In the choice words of William Fishman, all the anxiety over the murders meant that 'the weirdos, the eccentrics, the perverts and inadequates had a field day'.[12]

One obvious angle favoured by the Liberal and Radical press was the issue of what the East End needed in the way of social reform. As we have seen, these papers blamed the murders on the pernicious effects of slum life and called for model housing, streetlights and night shelters for homeless women. A few idealistic leader writers even demanded an end to prostitution as well as overcrowding. But the big question remained unanswered: Who would foot the bill for all these heroic measures? On 21 October *Lloyd's* recommended public assistance for the honest poor who had to live amidst so much crime and vice. Even if the murders gave rise to a 'more humane spirit', this writer argued, that did not translate into radical reforms. To lift the poor out of their misery required both commitment and money, and these were bound to dwindle because public sympathy for the victims would not last. A second leader, bearing the ominous title 'THE FAILURE OF CIVILIZATION', cited the so-called rash of murders taking place all over London as evidence of how 'the large residuum of coarse brutality' continued to defy the forces of civilization and education. No doubt the 'thrill of horror' caused by the Ripper murders had stimulated philanthropy throughout the country, but much work remained to be done because too many people lived like the Ishmaelites, with their hands turned against their neighbours.[13] Needless to say, none of these middle-class nostrums offered the destitute residents of Spitalfields or Whitechapel much hope that their lives would improve before they died.

In addition to the left-wing press, several leading medical journals also championed slum improvement. Concerned about the misery and squalor in the East End, the *British Medical Journal* (22 September) pointed out that both heredity and environment produced hard-core criminals, and praised the Rev. Samuel Barnett's efforts to prevent 'evil individuals' from coalescing into a criminal class.[14] For its part, the *Lancet* (6 October) published three editorials in the same issue about the slayings. The first of these backed Barnett's call for more streetlights, fresh air and sanitation, to be financed by public funds and strictly enforced by the laws relating to working-class housing. According to the second leader, the murders proved the 'existence in every city of a criminal class whose capacity for evil' could only be reduced by more responsible journalism rather than better housing. To support this bold claim the writer pointed an accusing finger at Fleet Street and contended that morality could never vanquish immorality so long as an 'unscrupulous press' published 'grossly indecent' material. Not only were 'lower class newspapers' demoralizing boys and girls, but 'vice and crime rival one another as a means of stimulating a depraved appetite for the horrible and the bestial'. The sensationalism of the penny press merely stimulated the animal passions to the exclusion of lofty thoughts. While children in the slums were being corrupted, the Education Act was opening 'the door to this flood of filth', to the detriment of respectable youth. Calls for self-help were not enough – only

BLIND-MAN'S BUFF.

(*As played by the Police.*)

"TURN ROUND THREE TIMES,
AND CATCH WHOM YOU MAY!"

2 *Punch* follows public opinion in blaming police incompetence during the Whitechapel investigation.

censorship could put an end to such debased literature. The writer had no doubt that this prohibitive measure would promote 'the best interests' of all concerned.[15] The third leader argued that the Whitechapel tragedies had 'awaken[ed] the public conscience' to the lack of sanitation there, and the close connection between overcrowding, poverty, dirt and lethal violence. Proud of the *Lancet's* past efforts to expose the miseries of the slums, this writer dismissed recent improvements as 'wholly insufficient' and unworthy of England's 'boasted civilisation'. Unfortunately, the killer's knife had proved more potent than 'the pens of many earnest and ready writers' when it came to educating the public.

Several weeks later, the *Lancet* (27 October) returned to the attack, again accusing Fleet Street of sensationalism, and of exploiting the vice and violence that flourished in the East End. Arguing that prurient readers were almost inured to murders, divorces and 'fashionable scandals', this writer accused newspaper editors, as well as theatre-owners, of serving up 'a constant succession of highly spiced dishes'. Judging from the contents of almost any paper, one would think that the whole country was 'practically absorbed in the contemplation of revolting wickedness'. Granted that murder was 'the most anti-social of crimes', this did not warrant 'the prurient and demoralising amplification of its sickening details', which could so easily corrupt readers and stir dangerous passions in 'weaker and more ill-balanced minds'. Thus:

> the exploits of 'Jack the Ripper', as detailed for our delectation at the break-fast table day after day, are likely not only to hurt the consciences of innocent minds, but to fire the imagination, and perchance kindle the emulation, of those just hovering on the verge of criminal violence. It is in vain that such descriptions are accompanied by sententious and virtuous moralisings. When we have befouled ourselves with pitch, there is little advantage in calling for a looking glass and owning with compunction that pitch is very black and altogether objectionable.[16]

Having berated Fleet Street for sensationalizing murder (and having blamed France's population decline on the indulgence of readers in 'vile and corrupt' fiction), this indignant and righteous writer chose to ignore the fact that the *Lancet* published most of the intimate details of the Ripper's mutilations.

More concerned about the corrupting effects of poverty than those of journalism, the *British Medical Journal* praised Barnett's campaign against 'the public indifference' to the 'true causes' of the murders, which lay in the rookeries, where there was 'a vast population ... packed into dark places, festering in ignorance, in dirt, in moral degradation, accustomed to violence and crime, born and bred within touch of habitual immorality and coarse obscenity'. Not even the heroic efforts of Barnett and others to eliminate the filth and flood the district with Christian compassion had succeeded in penetrating the darkness, where 'the great residuum [remained] untouched and unpurified'. Philanthropists like Lord Shaftesbury, Baroness Burdett-Coutts, and the Rothschilds certainly deserved accolades for 'sweeping away ... nests of crime, filth, and degradation' and replacing them with 'light, cleanliness, [and] purity'. However, pockets of dire poverty and degradation remained. The East End stood in sore need not just of intelligence and altruism, but also of money to raze and rebuild the slums. This writer blamed the 'obscenity and brutality and violence' of the 'darkest spots' on, first, 'ourselves, the great public of London' for 'flagrant indifference' to the 'degradation of our fellow citizens'; second, the metropolitan authorities for neglecting the lighting as well as the paving and cleaning of streets; and third, the police, who lacked a 'higher sense of public morality' and could not even protect women in the East End. In the long run, he trusted that these horrifying murders would have 'a fruitful effect on the social well-being of the metropolis', and not just Whitechapel.[17]

One of the biggest angles constructed by journalists, the police and the public concerned the killer's frame of mind or emotional state. Once the police abandoned their punishment-gang theory, they came to share Fleet Street's belief that a homicidal maniac was lusting for blood, and that he might be leading the double life of Jekyll and Hyde. By mid-September the press was citing Forbes Winslow's views on criminal insanity as though he were the reigning expert in such matters. Although he changed his mind more than once, Winslow opted for a gentlemanly lunatic – a 'mad toff' – who had recently been discharged (or escaped) from an asylum. Other medical men quickly joined the debate over motive through interviews with reporters and letters to the editor. Leader writers also reflected on the killer's obsession, in light of the sadistic slashes and eviscerations. However much the pundits might disagree about his medical experience and psychopathology, they knew he had enough cunning to lure his victims into dark places, where he could kill them noiselessly and then escape unnoticed.

After the double event, a few journalists broached the sensitive issue of sexual motivation by alluding to *Psychopathia Sexualis*, the learned treatise by the Viennese psychiatrist Richard von Krafft-Ebing. Prefaced by a poignant testament to the importance of love in human affairs, the book dealt empirically and anecdotally with types of sexual and criminal abnormality, running the gamut from male impotence to sado-masochism, fetishism, homosexuality, rape, lust murder and cannibalism.[18] The *Evening News* (15 October) featured an article by 'A Medical

Man' about the kind of men who disembowelled women for 'volup-tuous' reasons. Alluding to Krafft-Ebing's discussion of 'the perversion of the sexual impulse' in mass murderers, he suggested that the killer was achieving sexual gratification by eviscerating or mutilating these poor women. Also under the influence of Lombroso, this expert noted that the 'sexu-psychopathically afflicted' male also derived great pleasure from 'wallowing in the steaming entrails of slaughtered animals', and argued that since such lust-murderers did not always rape their victims, the Whitechapel killer might be 'an anthropologically degenerate individ-ual', suffering from 'perversion of the sexual impulse'.

Other self-styled experts attributed the murders to rage arising out of venereal disease. Perhaps the culprit was a 'mad syphilitic doctor' bent on killing prostitutes to avenge his own infection or that of some close relative or friend. A third hypothesis with sexual overtones involved epilepsy. Both Lombroso and Krafft-Ebing believed that some men expe-rienced intense sexual desire while in the midst of a seizure and would attack women or children in a sexual frenzy without ever recalling the episode.[19] Needless to say, such learned discussions rarely found their way into the morning press, which preferred to focus on the violence of the knife attacks, and buried any inklings of sexual perversion deep inside the tropes of monster or fiend. On the other hand a few reporters working for the evening papers had no qualms about searching for prece-dents involving lethal forms of sexual perversion.[20] After perusing Krafft-Ebing's text, a reporter for the *Pall Mall Gazette* (7 October) came up with a labourer named Andreas Bichel, who in 1806 had lured several women to his house in Regensdorf, Bavaria, on the pretence of showing them a magic mirror that foretold the future. After killing them, he dis-membered their bodies.[21] Given the fact that the Ripper never dismem-bered his victims, this farfetched comparison illustrates the lengths to which some reporters went in their quest to explain the inexplicable.

Most Victorians regarded cannibalism, or anthropophagy, as the defining sign of savagery in the most primitive regions of the world. Conveniently forgetting that Englishmen were quite capable of eating cabin boys or shipmates when stranded in a lifeboat on the high seas, they excluded this 'custom of the sea' from their catalogue of depravity.[22] For this reason, the reading public must have found it hard to believe that 'gynophagism' (to coin a word) existed in their own capital city. More than curious about what exactly the killer had done with the 'portions' taken from Chapman and Eddowes, readers received a shocking answer on 19 October, when the press reported that someone had sent half a human kidney inside a small bloodstained box to George Lusk, co-founder of the Whitechapel Vigilance Committee. The crude note that accompanied this parcel, inscribed 'From Hell' at the top, indicated that the sender had 'prasarved' half of the 'kidne' taken from the Mitre Square victim. In his own words, 'tother piece I fried and ate it was very nise I may send you the bloody knif that took it out if you only wate a whil longer'. The note was signed, 'Catch me when you can – Mishter Lusk'.[23]

Like the Goulston Street inscription, the Lusk kidney became another turning point in the Ripper saga, and the press took full advantage of this fresh piece of sensation-horror. Scotland Yard's stony silence about the parcel seemed to lend more weight to its authenticity. Whether or not the kidney did belong to Eddowes, most papers attributed Lusk's parcel to 'Saucy Jacky', and they made good use of it to revive the flagging Ripper saga. Typical of the penny press's response was the six-tiered headline in the *Evening News* (19 October): 'MITRE SQUARE MURDER / STARTLING NEWS / HALF THE VICTIM'S MISSING / KIDNEY RESTORED / THE OTHER HALF EATEN BY THE / CANNIBAL ASSASSIN'. According to this account Lusk and several friends had taken the foul-smelling kidney to the offices of the *Evening News* on the previous day, even though they suspected that it was a bad joke in the form of a kidney taken from a domestic animal. Later, some friends urged him to show the 'ghastly relic' to Dr Thomas Openshaw, the pathological curator of the London Hospital Museum, who used his microscope to assert that it was half of the left kidney of an alcoholic woman aged around forty-five, who had died about the same time as Eddowes. Lusk then decided to convey the box and letter to Leman Street police station, where an officer promptly sent for Inspector Abberline.[24]

Although this 'ginny' kidney made the best kind of sensation-horror, several papers downplayed the incident either because they thought it was a hoax or because they were reluctant to deal with something as gross as domestic cannibalism. Both *The Times* and the *Pall Mall Gazette* (19 October) assigned the kidney one short paragraph, noting Openshaw's verdict that it came from an alcoholic woman. Unlike the *East London Observer* (20 October), which had no qualms about featuring the kidney, the *East End News* (19 October) ignored the whole episode. So, too, did the leading newspaper of the Jewish community, the *Jewish Chronicle*, which had not mentioned the Nichols and Chapman murders until Fleet Street floated the theory that a kosher butcher might be responsible for the crimes.[25]

The Lusk kidney stirred much debate among doctors and the police. Whoever sent this post-Gothic present to Lusk left the press and the public utterly baffled as to whether it was a perverse prank or a vital clue. Soon even this incident faded from the leading papers, whose only

Ripper news now consisted of filler stories about minor crimes in the East End, suspects and complaints from police constables about their heavy workload and the pressure to make an arrest.

Beside reporting the demands of reformers for slum clearance, more police patrols and better street lighting in the East End, the press also drew attention to petitions from concerned citizens addressed to the Home Secretary and the Queen. On 29 September, Lusk and several other local worthies petitioned Queen Victoria for an official reward to be paid to anyone with information leading to the arrest of the murderer.[26] Although Matthews opposed the use of state funds for this purpose, many East Enders hoped that he would change his mind and prove with deeds, not words, that the government really did care about Whitechapel's ordeal.

During the last week of October, Henrietta Barnett, wife of the godly Samuel and a dedicated moral and social activist in her own right, organized a petition to the Queen on behalf of the working women of the East End. Signed by more than four thousand women, this letter appeared in many papers, and conveyed the revulsion felt by respectable women over 'the dreadful sins' recently committed as well as their sorrow and shame over the new notoriety attached to Whitechapel. Admitting that the inquests had taught them much about the 'sad and degraded' condition of unfortunates, who had 'lost a firm hold on goodness', the petitioners promised to make men 'feel with horror the sins of impurity' that drove women to lead 'such wicked lives'. They also urged the Queen to remind her ministers to shut down all the 'bad houses' wherein 'wickedness is done and men and women [are] ruined in body and soul'. Most papers printed not only this petition, but also the bland reply of a government spokesman, who stated that the message had been 'graciously' received by Her Majesty and that the Home Secretary appreciated such efforts to promote morality. This bureaucrat also assured the petitioners that the police commissioners were considering ways to 'mitigate the evils' in question. But exactly what these steps might be he did not reveal.[27]

The fallout from the double event soon reached Whitehall and the Home Office in a most unexpected way. By 3 October, newspapers were announcing the discovery of a headless and limbless female body on the site of the new headquarters of the Metropolitan Police, between Cannon Row and the Embankment. A carpenter had come across a large bundle, wrapped in black cloth, lying in a corner of the unlit basement where holding cells were being built. Upon opening the parcel he recoiled – just as Alfred Stokes had done in 1875 – at the sight and smell of a rotting female torso. Only this time there were no arms, legs or head.[28] A short article in *The Times* (3 October) dwelled on this 'ghastly discovery'.

According to surgeons Thomas Bond and Thomas Neville, the body was that of a 'remarkably fine young woman'; they had no idea when the parcel had been placed there.[29] Most of the *Pall Mall Gazette*'s (3 October) article about the trunk came directly and without attribution from *The Times*. After seeing the human remains, the *Daily Telegraph*'s reporter (3 October) noted that the skin had a 'dark reddish hue' (characteristic of decomposition), as though it had been soaked in Condy's antiseptic fluid. Since the trunk weighed over fifty pounds, he reckoned that this was 'no light load' for even a strong man to carry. The victim seemed 'a mature, well-formed, and perhaps an unmarried woman, not over forty years of age'. Over the ensuing week some papers raised the possibility that the Ripper might have moved his operations into the West End. Once again, mystery surrounded this murder and led to more questions and speculations.

Notes

1 In defending his record at Scotland Yard, Warren condemned 'the sinister influence of a mob stirred into spasmodic action by restless demagogues', who posed a serious threat to the government. Calling the workers' protests of February 1886 'a three days' reign of terror' and alluding to the 'panic' that had swept through London in November 1887, he touched briefly on the Whitechapel murders and dismissed all the suggestions from the public about how to catch the killer. Sir Charles Warren, 'The Police of the Metropolis', *Murray's Magazine*, 4:23 (November 1888), pp. 577–94; *Times*, 27 October.

2 A prelude to these law-and-order articles appeared on 21 September in the form of an article, 'Undiscovered Criminals', that cited a Blue Book report stating that only 34.5 per cent of all indictable crimes in the metropolis during 1886–7 had ended in an arrest, compared with 77.3 per cent for the south and southwestern counties and an average of 44.9 per cent for England and Wales. Of 163 murders, moreover, 72 cases had gone to trial but only 35 ended in conviction. Published from 8 October to 13 October, and supplemented by three leaders, the six front-page articles totalled over 31 columns, or roughly 34,200 words.

3 Thus Steven Box contends that these strategies and tactics 'render underprivileged and powerless people more likely to be arrested, convicted and sentenced to prison', and also 'create the illusion that the "dangerous class" is primarily located at the bottom of various hierarchies by which we "measure" each other … in this illusion it fuses relative poverty and criminal propensities and sees them both as effects of moral inferiority, thus rendering the "dangerous" class deserving of both poverty and punishment'. Steven Box, *Power, Crime and Mystification* (London: Routledge, 1990), p. 13.

4 The *Gazette* (4 October) also printed a letter from 'An Old Sportsman' extolling the skill of beagles in hunting human beings as well as hares and rabbits. William Buchanan informed readers of *The Times* (9 October) that he had seen trained bloodhounds follow the scent of a woman who had murdered a small boy near Dieppe around 1861.

5 George Krehl, editor of the *Stock Keeper and Fancier's Chronicle* of 139 Fleet Street, believed that trained hounds would have no difficulty tracking a man carrying human organs or stained with blood. *Reynolds's* article (14 October) about the Hyde Park trials included sketches of the two hounds on the scent. See also the letter to *The Times* (11 October) from the hounds' owner, Edwin Brough.

6 Some papers reported that Warren instructed the police not to disturb the body of the next victim until bloodhounds from a kennel in southwest London had been brought to the scene. *Daily Chronicle*, 9 October, and Donald Rumbelow, *The Complete Jack the Ripper* (London: W. H. Allen, 1975), pp. 82–3.

7 For the bloodhound angle, see also Philip Sugden, *Jack the Ripper* (London: Robinson, 1994), pp. 136–7, 292–6, and Douglas G. Browne, *The Rise of Scotland Yard: A History of the Metropolitan Police* (London: George G Harrap and Co., 1956), pp. 180–1, 207.

8 Two cab drivers from Hackney Road were charged with assaulting Detective Sergeant Robinson, who was disguised as a woman while shadowing a suspect.

9 On 3 October, for example, *The Times* allocated 3.5 columns to the Stride inquest and other murder news, 2.8 columns to the Paris theatre, 9 columns to the Church Congress (in addition to a 1.25 column leader), and 4 columns to the money market and commercial and agricultural news. The 4 October edition contained 4 columns on the murders, 2.5 columns on the Central Asian Railway, 5 columns on stocks and shares, 4.5 columns on the Church Congress, 5.5 columns on Lord Hartington's speech at Inverness and 1.6 columns on sporting activities. On 5 October, the murders received 2.6 columns, compared with 3.3 columns on the Church Congress, 7 columns on the money market and business news, 5.3 columns on the London School Board, and 1.3 columns on sporting news. And on 11 October *The Times* gave a total of 15 columns to the speeches of prominent politicians, while Ripper news and letters received only 1.8 columns.

10 Supposedly addressed to Lusk and bearing a Kilburn postmark, this letter announced that the murders would take place outside Whitechapel, which had 'got rather too warm' of late. *Pall Mall Gazette*, 15 October.

11 The police charged her with disturbing the peace. *Times*, 22 October; *Weekly Times*, 21 October; Paul Begg, Martin Fido and Keith Skinner, *The Jack the Ripper A–Z* (London: Headline, 1991), p. 90.

12 William J. Fishman, *East End 1888: A Year in a London Borough Among the Labouring Poor* (London: Duckworth, 1988), p. 216.

13 Lacking any practical plan, this writer simply argued that 'the great safeguard of our people is ... increased self restraint and self respect.' *Lloyd's*, 21 October.

14 'The Whitechapel Murders', *British Medical Journal*, 22 September, pp. 673–74.

15 'Crime-Culture Through the Press', *Lancet*, 6 October, p. 682.

16 *Lancet*, 27 October, p. 827.

17 *British Medical Journal*, 6 October, pp. 768–9.

18 The first English edition of *Psychopathia Sexualis – With Especial Reference to Contrary Sexual Instinct: A Medico-Legal Study* appeared in 1886. By 1892, it had reached a seventh edition. See Charles G. Chaddock's translation, published by F. A. Davis in Philadelphia and London in 1892, especially the section on rape and lust murder, pp. 397–400. See also Deborah Cameron and Elizabeth Frazer, *The Lust to Kill: A Feminist Investigation of Sexual Murder* (Cambridge: Polity, 1987), pp. 94–6.

19 Krafft-Ebing, *Psychopathia Sexualis*, pp. 364–70.

20 The *British Medical Journal* had to go all the way back to the eighteenth century to find a possible precursor in Renwick Williams, 'The Monster' who had stabbed and maimed several women in London during 1789–90. *British Medical Journal*, 6 October, p. 772.

21 For Bichel's misdeeds, see Krafft-Ebing, *Psychopathia Sexualis*, pp. 62–7.

22 For a classic case of survival cannibalism involving English sailors, see A. W. B. Simpson, *Cannibalism and the Common Law: The Story of the Tragic Last Voyage of the 'Mignonette'* (Chicago: Chicago University Press, 1984).

23 Lusk received this package on the evening of Tuesday, 16 October. Apart from the *Pall Mall Gazette*, most papers reproduced this letter on 19 or 20 October. See Sugden, *Jack the Ripper*, pp. 263–7, 273–5; Begg *et al.*, *The Jack the Ripper A–Z*, pp. 262–4; Richard Whittington-Egan, *A Casebook on Jack the Ripper* (London: Wildy and Sons, 1975), pp. 51–65; Rumbelow, *Complete Jack the Ripper*, pp. 119–20; and Colin Wilson and Robin Odell, *Jack the Ripper: Summing Up the Verdict* (London: Bantam, 1987), pp. 69–71.

24 At first Lusk had wanted to throw away the putrid organ, assuming that it came from a dog or sheep but his friend Joseph Aarons persuaded him to consult a medical expert. However, the medical profession had no means of ascertaining the sex of a kidney, let alone the age of its owner. *Times*, 19 October, and *East London Observer*, 20 October.

25 Committed to reporting matters of religious, cultural, social and historical interest to Jewish readers, the *Chronicle*'s editor, Asher Myers, denounced the bigots who would blame these horrors on his people. Jews, he insisted, were repelled by 'any mutilation of the body after death'. Worried lest such accusations sully the good name of English Jewry and lead to anti-Semitic violence, he paid a visit to Divisional Surgeon F. Gordon Brown, bearing a set of sharp knives used by shochets in order to show him why they were not the murder weapon. *Jewish Chronicle*, 14 September, 5, 12 October. See also David Cesarani, *The Jewish Chronicle and Anglo-Jewry, 1841–1991* (Cambridge: Cambridge University Press, 1994), p. 81.

26 When Lusk first approached the Home Office for reward money, he was told that the government had stopped awarding money in such cases. In reply, he

pointed out that the murderer of at least four women was still at large and that the Home Office's refusal to act had angered many people. *Daily Telegraph*, 1 October; Begg *et al.*, *The Jack the Ripper A–Z*, p. 130; Rumbelow, *Complete Jack the Ripper*, p. 81.

27 Mrs Barnett, later Dame Henrietta Barnett, partnered her husband in running Toynbee Hall and worked hard to improve conditions in the East End. See *Dictionary of National Biography 1931–40*, pp. 44–5; Mrs H. O. R. Barnett, *Canon Barnett: His Life, Work, and Friends by His Wife*, 2 vols (London: Murray, 1918, 1921); *Times*, 25 October; *East London Observer*, 27 October.

28 Originally designated for the National Opera House, the new police head-quarters ran from the Embankment alongside Cannon Row – only a few minutes walk from Parliament Square. The building site was surrounded by an eight-foot wooden fence with one gate locked at night. *Pall Mall Gazette*, 3 October; *Times*, 3, 5 October.

29 Dr Thomas Bond was attached to the A Division of the Metropolitan Police. A lecturer in forensic medicine at Westminster Hospital, he played a prominent part in the autopsies of the Westminster body, Mary Kelly (10 November) and Alice McKenzie (18 July 1889). He denied that the Ripper had any 'scientific or anatomical knowledge', but believed that McKenzie was another of his victims. Wilson and Odell, *Jack the Ripper*, pp. 161–4; Rumbelow, *Complete Jack the Ripper*, pp. 126–7; Sugden, *Jack the Ripper*, pp. 346–9; and Begg *et al.*, *The Jack the Ripper A–Z*, pp. 44–50.

3

Casting the spell of terror: the press and the early Whitechapel murders

Darren Oldridge

The Whitechapel murders of 1888 were, above all, a media event. Sir Melville Macnaghten, one of the senior police officers involved in the case, later recalled the glut of press coverage that accompanied the killings:

> No one who was living in London that autumn will forget the terror created by these murders. I can recall the foggy evenings, and hear again the raucous cries of the newspaper boy: 'Another horrible murder, murder, mutilation, Whitechapel'. Such was the burden of their ghastly song.[1]

In Macnaghten's opinion, this press interest was both unhelpful and misleading. It encouraged an 'unreasonable' panic among the city population, so that 'no servant-maid deemed her life safe if she ventured out to post a letter after ten o'clock at night'.[2] Journalists also exaggerated the extent of the crimes, going far beyond the available evidence in pursuit of fresh 'Ripper' news:

> [The public] were quite ready to believe that any fresh murders, not at once elucidated, were by the same maniac's hand. Indeed, I remember three cases – two in 1888, and one early in 1891 – which the press ascribed to the so-called Jack the Ripper, to whom, at one time or another, some fourteen murders were attributed – some before, and some after, his veritable reign of terror.[3]

Macnaghten's memoirs point to one of the crucial effects of press coverage of the case: the creation of a narrative linking a series of crimes. There would have been no 'reign of terror' without this narrative. The Victorian police attributed the murders of five women to 'Jack the Ripper': these were [Mary Ann] Polly Nichols, Annie Chapman, Catharine Eddowes, Liz Stride and Mary Jane Kelly, though modern researchers have cast doubt on the status of Stride and Kelly as authentic Ripper victims. This indicates the sheer scale of the storytelling process: at least nine of Macnaghten's fourteen killings were completely unconnected. His account also hints at an intriguing but neglected stage in the construction of the Ripper story: press reports of a killer in

Whitechapel *before* the sequence of murders committed by a single assailant. This chapter will consider these early reports.

Why look at this material? First of all, these early stories illustrate the process of narrative construction in its purest form. In the period before 8 September 1888, when the body of Annie Chapman was discovered in a backyard in Hanbury Street, stories of a 'maniac' haunting the East End were based entirely on speculative connections between unrelated crimes. The police decided that Chapman's killer was also responsible for an earlier death – the murder of Polly Nichols on 31 August; and from this moment onwards a sequence of related killings was firmly established. But the idea of a lone killer responsible for a series of deaths was already circulating in print before Chapman's murder. Since these reports were completely detached from any 'real' story, they reveal much about the process of news construction. The idea of a 'Whitechapel murderer' emerged from a series of competing interpretations of the killings, and its establishment as the dominant narrative in the period before Chapman's death indicates the news agenda of the London press.

Secondly, the early stories about the murders established many of the conventions for reporting Jack the Ripper. The 'immoral' lives of the victims, the 'degraded' state of East London, and the ghostly figure of the killer himself were all established before the deeds of a real-life serial killer could be reported. Lastly, the prehistory of the case added immensely to the sensation caused by the murders in September 1888. When Annie Chapman was killed, she was widely viewed as the fourth victim of a lunatic who had been at large for several months. This allowed the *Star* to proclaim that 'London lies today under the spell of a great terror', as a 'nameless reprobate – half man, half beast – is ... daily gratifying his murderous instincts'.[4] It was one consequence of this perception that an enterprising hoaxer – probably a journalist himself – sent the infamous letter to the Central News Agency in London that coined the name 'Jack the Ripper'.[5] While no one could have predicted the subsequent course of events, the overblown coverage of the case was rooted in the early reports of an imaginary killer in the East End.

As several writers have noted, the Whitechapel murders coincided with the emergence of a distinctive style of news reporting. This 'New Journalism' was characterized by an emphasis on crime and 'sensation', and the willingness of newspapers to campaign on themes deemed important to their readers and the wider public. William Thomas Stead, the editor of the *Pall Mall Gazette* and one of the architects of the new style, sought to 'rouse the nation' with stirring reports of social ills.[6] Less high-minded journalists tried merely to create interest and sales through focusing on topics such as street crime, prostitution and sexual danger.

It was one consequence of this approach that instances of 'social evils' were construed into ongoing narratives. This is what happened when Polly Nichols was murdered in Buck's Row on 31 August 1888, following the earlier killings of Emma Smith on 4 April and Martha Tabram on 7 August. The circumstances of these crimes were quite different, but there were sufficient similarities between them for a 'story' to emerge. All three women were impoverished prostitutes; and their deaths occurred in the same small area of East London.

Several stories were possible. The first and most obvious was to report the 'degraded' conditions in which the crimes occurred. These could be presented as a public outrage demanding attention. The *Morning Advertiser* took this approach:

> The particulars of the latest dreadful murder in the East End of London will horrify the public. The outrage is almost unequalled in the annals of crime ... Our civilisation is a wretched mockery while crimes like this are committed in our streets; its boasted resources are miserably ineffectual while monsters like the murderer or murderers of this unhappy woman walk abroad.[7]

The *Advertiser* linked these grim revelations to modish theories of human evolution, noting Sir John Lubbock's claim that 'the lowest type of life in East End rookeries is lower, mentally and morally, than the life of the average savage'.[8] This report was part of a wider tendency to depict East London as a degenerate sink that threatened the moral and physical health of the nation. The murder of three prostitutes exemplified this theme. Even 'among the lower races', the *Advertiser* warned, it would 'be difficult to find ... instances of crime excelling in barbarity that which now makes the public imagination reel in angered disgust'.[9]

A more concrete way to connect the three crimes was to present them as the deeds of the same assailant. This was not inconsistent, of course, with more general warnings about social degradation: indeed, the *Morning Advertiser* combined its description of savagery in the East End with speculations about those responsible for the killings. Here two different narratives were available. The first attributed the murders to a gang of 'ruffians' enforcing a protection racket. On 1 September, *The Times* and the *Daily News* carried identical stories about a 'High Rip' gang demanding money from prostitutes and murdering those who refused to pay.[10] The *Advertiser* took the same line.[11] On 7 September, the *Weekly Herald* added some colour to this story by revealing that the attackers 'make their appearance during the early hours of morning' and 'put away their victims' to stop them talking to the police.[12] All four newspapers attributed the story to undisclosed police sources. The

Herald went so far as to claim that the gang 'have been under the observation of the police for some time past'.[13] Moreover, 'the prospect of a reward and a free pardon' meant that some of its members 'might be persuaded to turn Queen's evidence, when some startling revelations might be expected'.[14]

The second possible narrative assumed the existence of a single killer. It was the *Star* – founded in 1888 and at the forefront of the 'New Journalism' – that took the lead with this story. Like the papers that reported the 'High Rip' gang, the *Star* claimed that police sources supported its version of events. It also backed its account with speculations about the circumstances of the crimes. On the day of Polly Nichols's murder, readers were presented with this checklist of evidence:

> The other murder [of Martha Tabram], in which the woman received 30 stabs, must also have been the work of a maniac. This murder occurred on a Bank Holiday. On the Bank Holiday preceding another woman was murdered in equally brutal but even more barbarous fashion by being stabbed with a stick. She died without being able to tell anything of her murderer. All this leads to the conclusion, that the police have now formed, that there is a maniac haunting Whitechapel, and that the three women were all victims of his murderous frenzy.[15]

In a special edition the following day, the *Star* made an extended argument for the existence of this monster. 'In each case,' it noted, 'the victim has been a woman of abandoned character, each crime has been committed in the dark hours of the morning, and ... each murder has been accompanied by hideous mutilation.'[16] The crimes were committed, moreover, in the same small part of town: 'each of the ill-lighted thoroughfares to which the women were decoyed to be foully butchered are off turnings from Whitechapel Road, and all are within half a mile.'[17] With a breezy assurance that would characterize many subsequent conjectures about the case, the newspaper pointed to the obvious conclusion: all three murders were 'the work of some cool, cunning man with a mania for murder'.[18]

In the initial coverage of Polly Nichols's death, the press was divided on the most appropriate story to pursue. In addition to the *Star*, the *East London Advertiser* supported the view that a lone killer was at large. The existence of a 'High Rip' gang was also widely reported. On 1 September, the *Morning Advertiser* considered both possibilities before declaring the protection racket the 'more reasonable suggestion'.[19] Over the next few days, however, the idea of a single 'maniac' gained ground. On 3 September, W. T. Stead's *Pall Mall Gazette* lent its weight to the story. *The Times* and the *Daily News* also dropped their support for the 'High

3 One of the many theories to explain Jack the Ripper's apparent ease at
evading detection.

Rip' gang and reported instead that the 'three crimes are the work of one
individual'.[20] Two days later, the *Daily News* ran a piece on local fears
of this 'mysterious assassin'.[21] Within a week of Nichols's murder, the
idea of a lone killer was probably circulating more widely, and covered
in greater depth, than the alternative narrative of a criminal gang. After
the death of Annie Chapman, of course, the sensation surrounding the
Whitechapel murderer despatched the 'High Rip' gang to the footnotes
of media history.

This pattern reveals much about the impact of the 'New Journalism'.
For a start, it indicates the pressure on newspapers to create meaningful
stories from unrelated events. It is striking that even the *Daily News* –
which reported both the 'High Rip' gang and the 'Whitechapel maniac'
in the days following Polly Nichols's murder – described her death as no
more than an isolated tragedy in its earliest report on 31 August.[22]
Likewise, the *Pall Mall Gazette* did not link the case to any other crimes
in its initial coverage.[23] It is evident that stories linking the three deaths
spread quickly once they were established in sections of the media.
Beyond this, the pattern of reporting raises questions about the adoption

of particular stories after Nichols's killing. Why did the idea of a lone murderer become the main narrative? Since the press generally presented news about the murders as accounts of the latest police thinking, one explanation may lie in the official investigation of the crimes. By 3 September 1888, it appears that London news agencies were claiming that the police believed one individual to be responsible; and this certainly helped the story to spread. Nonetheless, it is unlikely that newspapers were simply following the police lead. First of all, journalists presented completely different interpretations of Polly Nichols's death as authentic reflections of police thinking: the *Star* was just as confident that the police backed its 'maniac' theory as other newspapers were that the 'High Rip' story reflected the official inquiry. Secondly, there is no evidence that the police really did connect the three killings. They assumed that Emma Smith was the victim of a gang attack and Martha Tabram – who was stabbed repeatedly with a bayonet – was murdered by a soldier. Melville Macnaghten later recalled that his colleagues never thought Polly Nichols's killer was involved in the earlier deaths.[24]

A more plausible explanation for the spread of the 'maniac' theory was its popular appeal. Measured in circulation figures, it appears that the *Star*'s version of events was more successful than its rivals'. L. Perry Curtis has shown that the paper took off commercially during the Whitechapel killings: indeed, its sales were 'a crude barometer of public interest' in the crimes.[25] This interest, in turn, was based on the core ingredient of the case that the *Star* was the first to publicize: the idea of a mysterious and bloody assassin. The story appears to have tapped into popular fears in the East End. According to the *East London Observer* on 1 September, the murder of Polly Nichols was 'the sole topic of conversation' in the area, and rumours were already circulating that the man responsible had also killed Martha Tabram.[26] The appearance of a broadside ballad after Nichols's death confirmed the popular appetite for this tale:

> Come listen to a dreadful tale I'm telling,
> In Whitechapel three murders have been done;
> With horror many hearts they now are swelling,
> Those fearful deeds that now to light have come.
>
> Twelve months ago a woman was found lying,
> In death's cold arms, how dreadful to relate,
> What agony they suffered here when dying
> They were nearly all found in the same state.
>
> The first poor creature's death they all are thinking
> The same hand took her life that fatal night,

Poor people now with fear they are shrinking
Oh! may this crime be quickly brought to light.[27]

Whatever the validity of these assertions – or the quality of the verse – it appears that the idea of a single killer commanded an audience beyond the usual readers of the daily press. The *Star*, of course, helped to sustain and amplify the idea through its extended coverage of the Nichols murder.

As well as striking a popular chord, the story of a single killer provided other advantages for the journalists who pursued it. Perhaps the most obvious of these was the opportunity to write speculative features on the identity of the nameless assassin. Unlike other murder news, such features did not depend on the disclosure of fresh information or the discovery of a new crime. Speculative stories about the killer also provided dramatic copy. The *Star* showed the potential of this approach in its edition of 5 September 1888, which carried a lengthy piece on 'the only name linked to the Whitechapel murders'.[28] This name, it turned out, was an elusive and vicious character called 'Leather Apron'. Based on late-night conversations with Whitechapel prostitutes, a reporter composed the suspect's portrait:

> His expression is sinister, and seems to be full of terror for the women who describe it. His eyes are small and glittering. His lips are usually parted in a grin which is not only not reassuring, but excessively repellent ... His name nobody knows, but all are united in the belief that he is a Jew or of Jewish parentage, his face being of a marked Hebrew type. But the most singular characteristic of the man, and one which tends to identify him closely with last Friday night's work [the murder of Polly Nichols], is the universal statement that in moving about he never makes any noise.[29]

In this small milestone of sensational journalism, the *Star* named the first suspect for the Whitechapel murders – three days before the real killer had even claimed his second victim. The story of Leather Apron had the flavour and appeal of melodrama. Indeed, the newspaper acknowledged that its suspect was 'much like the invention of a story writer'.[30] As this tale coincided with the recent fashion for detective novels – many of which were serialized in the weekly press – the potential market for such real-life horrors was clear.

The idea of a single killer also reflected anxieties about the 'degraded' state of East London. Fears that parts of the capital were descending into 'savagery' accorded with the concept of a maniac driven by bloodlust. The 'High Rip' gang was a less exotic proposition. Dreadful though it was, a protection racket was less brutish than a murderer impelled by 'a hellish mania for homicide'.[31] This thinking was explicit in the *East*

London Observer, which deduced that a 'fiend' was responsible for Nichols's killing because robbery was not a plausible motive.[32] In the same vein, the *Star* asserted that the killer was driven by an inhuman 'mania' in its editions of 31 August and 1 September. The paper back-tracked slightly by suggesting that Leather Apron tried to blackmail the women he attacked, but it also presented him as a degenerate monster – 'a ghoulish and devilish brute'.[33] The details of the Nichols murder appeared to support such bestial imagery. In the days following her inquest on 1 September 1888, several newspapers noted that the extensive injuries to her body and throat implied the 'inhuman ferocity' of a beast. This terrible evidence confirmed wider concerns about the 'primitive' nature of life in the East End, and encouraged the belief that a savage was roaming its streets.

One further factor that influenced the development of the story was the status of the murder victims. They were all impoverished women working as street prostitutes. Indeed, the extreme vulnerability of these women was the one truly plausible 'story' that linked their deaths: street prostitutes were – and remain – the social group most vulnerable to attacks by strangers, and whose murders were least likely to be solved. But they were also a group that attracted little public sympathy. Earlier press campaigns had focused on the 'innocent' victims of prostitution – most famously the children whose exploitation was exposed by the *Pall Mall Gazette* in 1885.[34] But the women killed in Whitechapel belonged to a different group: they had apparently chosen their careers. They therefore provided less promising subjects for crusading journalism. Melville Macnaghten probably spoke for many when he described the Ripper's victims as 'the lowest dregs of female humanity'.[35] This perception had two effects. First, it encouraged journalists seeking a 'social angle' to emphasize the general depravity of East London instead of the specific problems faced by prostitutes. In this view, the victims' lifestyle was part of the wider malaise that needed addressing. Secondly, it made the idea of a criminal gang preying on prostitutes a rather unattractive story. While readers could be expected to sympathize with the victims of child prostitution, they were less likely to take an interest in the criminal exploitation of women who had chosen a life as streetwalkers. The concept of a 'Whitechapel maniac', in contrast, allowed the press to cover the crimes without depending on their readers' sympathy for the murdered women.

The press coverage of the early Whitechapel murders was, of course, the beginning of a much greater sensation that immortalized 'Jack the Ripper' in the autumn of 1888. No one could have anticipated this sensation before the death of Annie Chapman on 8 September. Nonetheless, the early narrative of the murders was responsible for the extraordinary response to the discovery of the 'fourth victim'; and this response included most of the speculations, tall stories and lurid entertainments that have characterized the case ever since. Even before Chapman's death, sightseers were gathering at the location of Polly Nichols's killing; and by late September a sideshow on Whitechapel Road was displaying wax models of the murdered women. The press, in turn, reported these queasy diversions as part of the wider sensation surrounding the story. On 27 September, a *Daily News* correspondent described an evening stroll in East London:

> Here are the newspaper contents-bills spread out at large with some of the newsvendor's own additions and amplifications, telling of new murders or further details of the old ones ... A few yards further on there is a waxwork show with some horrible pictorial representations of the recent murders, and all the dreadful details are being [shouted] out into the night, and women with children in their arms are pushing their way to the front with their pennies to see the ghastly objects within.[36]

By crafting the story of the Whitechapel murderer from the deaths of Emma Smith, Martha Tabram and Polly Nichols, the press launched the 'Ripper industry' on an enthralled public. Since nothing connected these women except the overwhelming tragedy of their lives, the earliest stage of this industry illustrates the fundamental role of mythmaking in the process. It is hardly surprising, then, that myths about the Ripper have flourished and multiplied ever since.

Notes

1 Macnaghten's police career began shortly after the murders. His acquaintance with the case led him to devote a chapter to the subject in his memoirs. Sir Melville Macnaghten, *Days of My Years* (Edward Arnold: London, 1914), pp. 55–6.
2 Macnaghten, *Days of My Years*, p. 56.
3 Macnaghten, *Days of My Years*, pp. 54–5.
4 *Star*, 8 September 1888.
5 For a lucid and judicious discussion of this letter, see Philip Sugden, *The Complete History of Jack the Ripper* (Robinson: London, 1995), pp. 267–70.
6 Judith Walkowitz, *City of Dreadful Delight: Narratives of Sexual Danger in Late Victorian London* (Routledge: London, 1992), pp. 84–5.
7 *Morning Advertiser*, 1 September 1888.
8 *Morning Advertiser*, 1 September 1888.
9 *Morning Advertiser*, 1 September 1888.
10 *Times*, 1 September 1888; *Daily News*, 1 September 1888.

11 *Morning Advertiser*, 1 September 1888.
12 *Weekly Herald*, 7 September 1888.
13 *Weekly Herald*, 7 September 1888.
14 *Weekly Herald*, 7 September 1888.
15 *Star*, 4th edn, 31 August 1888.
16 *Star*, 1 September 1888.
17 *Star*, 1 September 1888.
18 *Star*, 1 September 1888.
19 *Morning Advertiser*, 1888.
20 *Daily News*, 3 September 1888.
21 *Daily News*, 5 September 1888.
22 *Daily News*, 31 August 1888.
23 *Pall Mall Gazette*, 31 August 1888.
24 Macnaghten, *Days of My Years*, pp. 57–8.
25 L. Perry Curtis, *Jack the Ripper and the London Press* (New Haven: Yale University Press, 2001), p. 59.
26 *East London Observer*, 1 September 1888.
27 'Lines on the Terrible Tragedy in Whitechapel' (1888). This is reproduced in Sugden, *The Complete History*, p. 56.
28 *Star*, 5th edn, 5 September 1888.
29 *Star*, 5th edn, 5 September 1888.
30 *Star*, 5th edn, 5 September 1888.
31 *Morning Advertiser*, 1 September 1888.
32 *East London Observer*, 1 September 1888.
33 *Star*, 5th edn, 5 September 1888.
34 For W. T. Stead's explosive campaign against child prostitution, see Walkowitz, *City of Dreadful Delight*, pp. 81–105.
35 Macnaghten, *Days of My Years*, p. 56.
36 *Daily News*, 27 September 1888.

4

Order out of chaos

Gary Coville and Patrick Lucanio

From the time of the first reports of the Ripper's active presence in the seamier environs of London, artists and writers had been fascinated with the whole aura and mystique surrounding Jack the Ripper. Rumbelow remarks, 'What is surprising is just how quickly the public seized on the dramatic possibilities,' and then cites Brewer's 'piece of nonsense' titled 'The Curse Upon Mitre Square A. D. 1530–1888', which appeared in only a matter of weeks following the murder of Catherine Eddowes, according to Begg, Fido and Skinner.[1]

One writer in particular, Mrs Marie Belloc Lowndes, made use of the Ripper persona to such an extent that her preeminent novel *The Lodger* has formed the basis of many of the speculative performances depicting the Ripper. Appearing first as a short story in the January 1911 edition of *McClure's* magazine, her story was so effective in reaching the more or less contemporary audiences of the Ripper that she expanded it into a novel, which saw publication two years later.[2] Detective fiction critics Chris Steinbrunner and Otto Penzler describe *The Lodger* as 'a psychological suspense thriller rather than a tale of detection', and they point out that its effect is 'more a "why-done-it" than a "who-done-it" '.[3] It is this approach, they argue, that forms the basis of Mrs Belloc Lowndes's best works. With respect to *The Lodger* specifically, the 'why-done-it' hinges on a theme of sexual madness, which registers throughout Ripper lore – as it must, given the nature of the crimes involved. For Mrs Belloc Lowndes, the 'why' was a religious fanaticism charged with sexual repression that fed and impelled the actions of the lodger himself. And it remained for Marie Belloc Lowndes to overtly establish this theme, thereby setting the principal concern for an entire school of writers caught up in pursuing the Ripper as *objet d'art*.

At this stage, then, the flesh-and-blood creature who plunged his knife into five or seven or ten or twenty ladies of the evening – or 'sisters of the abyss', as some Victorians modestly called them – has become irrelevant to the central point. The public has taken to its liking an embellished monster larger than life, one that is capable of transcending life itself, as we have stated. We have become fascinated by an effigy which speaks to us of blood and evil in surrealistic terms, figuratively seizing us by the throat and forcibly reminding us just how close we remain to our primordial heritage, and that it is only the thin, conspicuously woven fabric of civilization that separates each of us from Jack the Ripper.

The Lodger, then, provided one of the earliest and notably the strongest embodiments of this thematic presentation. Although for the purposes of *The Lodger*, Marie Belloc Lowndes elected to anoint her fiend 'The Avenger' rather than 'Jack the Ripper', there has never been any question as to the Avenger's true derivation. In fact, Mrs Belloc Lowndes has validated for her readers and us the duality of the Ripper and Avenger. In a diary entry dated 9 March 1923, she wrote: 'The story of *The Lodger* was written by me as a short story after I heard a man telling a woman at a dinner party that his mother had a butler and a cook who married and kept lodgers. They were convinced that Jack the Ripper had spent a night under their roof'.[4]

The Lodger proved popular with the reading public, although critics were much less quick to endorse the novel. As Mrs Lowndes recalled some ten years after publication, 'When *The Lodger* was published, I did not receive a single favorable review. When it came to sending a quotation for an advertisement for the American edition, I was not able to find even one sentence of tepid approval. Then, to my surprise, when *The Lodger* had been out two or three years reviewers began to rebuke me for not writing another *Lodger*'.[5]

Sensing that an audience was building for *The Lodger*, English playwright Horace Annesley Vachell adapted Mrs Belloc Lowndes's novel for the stage. Originally produced under the title *Who is He?* at London's Haymarket Theatre, the play starred Henry Ainley as the mysterious lodger. Vachell, however, transformed Mrs Belloc Lowndes's searching character study into an undistinguished comedy, which fared adversely with audiences. After its London closure, the play, with changes in cast and title, transferred to New York's Maxine Elliott Theatre, where it opened on 8 January 1917, with Lionel Atwill in the title role. Running in New York under the title of *The Lodger*, Vachell's version of Mrs Belloc Lowndes's work garnered some slight attention in the form of a mildly approving review in the *New York Times* and then folded after fifty-six performances.[6]

As tepid as the response had been to Vachell's adaptation of *The Lodger*, its appearance on stage nonetheless harbingered the many efforts that would follow. Mercifully, later versions would essentially eschew the ill-advised humour for a more fundamentally serious approach to the

Ripper phenomenon. In this sense, its first legitimate dramatization was
for the silent screen. Alfred Hitchcock chose, for his third directorial
effect, to re-work *The Lodger*, and his film would represent the first of
several screen versions of the celebrated novel.

Released in 1926 under the formal title of *The Lodger: A Story of the
London Fog*, the film represents Hitchcock's first screen immersion in the
suspense genre, and a viewing of it today reveals certain defining truths
of the Ripper legacy.[7] Although Hitchcock chose to remove his lodger
from the Victorian past and bring his character forward to the present,
certain social and historical truths were faithfully adhered to. William
Rothman, in *Hitchcock: The Murderous Gaze*, notes Hitchcock's perception of the public's reaction to the Avenger killings.

> In one of the most remarkable sequences of the film, Hitchcock dissolves
> from a radio announcer reading the story of the murder to one solitary lis-
> tener after another: a man who rolls his eyes, an angry woman who yowls
> like a cat, a man who listens taut with excitement, a woman so aroused that
> she runs her tongue sensually over her lips. Each listener appears less an
> individual than a representative of the London public.[8]

Hitchcock is able to depict the London public's perverse fascination with
the Avenger through powerful visual images. Marie Belloc Lowndes
implied the same self-absorbed reaction through the unforgettable spectacle of Robert Bunting squandering a precious penny in order to satiate
his appetite for news of the Avenger. Both Mrs Belloc Lowndes and
Hitchcock intuitively understood that the public's craving for word of
the Avenger was as great as the Avenger's seeming thirst for blood.
Ultimately, the story of Jack the Ripper is as much the story of society's
passion to voyeuristically follow in the Ripper's footsteps.

Mrs Belloc Lowndes and Hitchcock, each in their own way, contributed to the Ripper's mystical aura. But Hitchcock's insistence on the
ultimate innocence of his lodger, a favourite Hitchcock theme, contra-
venes the theme of Mrs Belloc Lowndes, who slowly built the case
against Mr Sleuth until there was no room left for denial. Hitchcock
prefers to explore a skein of false suspicions that ensnarl Jonathan Drew
(Ivor Novello) after he takes up residence in the Bunting household.
Although a departure from the original novel, Hitchcock's inquiry into
mistaken identities and mob vengeance was fairly rooted in the historical record of the Ripper murders. Early in the Ripper inquiry, for
example, suspicion fell upon a local figure, John Pizer, commonly
referred to as 'Leather Apron'. Pizer was later conclusively cleared of the
Ripper murders; however, false accusations vented in sensational press
accounts of the day apparently were never fully overcome. A significant

segment of the public apparently continued to believe in the guilt of Leather Apron.[9] As the hysteria intensified in Whitechapel, any man spied carrying a Gladstone bag or similar satchel fell immediately under suspicion. More than one man so encumbered was reportedly forced to flee for his very life from an aroused mob.

Generally overlooked is the fact that Hitchcock returned to *The Lodger* in the summer of 1940. Then working in America, Hitchcock was approached by CBS executives to participate in a series of experimental radio dramas. The concept, sheltered under the umbrella title of *Forecast* over an eight-week period, offered audiences fourteen studiously varied programme ideas. Hitchcock was asked to present his specialty – the suspense drama – which he directed on 22 July 1940.[10] Electing to present *The Lodger*, Hitchcock fell heir to the talents of Herbert Marshall, who performed the curiously dual roles of announcer and the mysterious Mr Sleuth, a device destined to be repeated in additional radio adaptations.

The shadowy figure of Jack the Ripper was ideal for radio, as Hitchcock must have understood, and as countless directors would later realize. But the horrific episodic murders perpetrated by the Ripper pushed the limits of radio's 'theatre of the mind'. Convention, public taste and the unwillingness of radio networks to offend the sensibilities of the nuclear family gathered around large console sets meant that the historical Jack the Ripper would have to undergo an assiduous re-editing. But Mrs Belloc Lowndes herself had started the process a generation before with the conversion of the Ripper to the Avenger and a blurring of the killer's motives. 'I am down on whores,' the Ripper allegedly noted in a letter dated 25 September 1888, but Mrs Belloc Lowndes's Avenger was down on young women whose fall from grace was less complete but nonetheless just as fatal. 'He 'ave got a down on the drink,' as a cabman summarized the Avenger's motives. Women who frequented public houses left themselves open to interpretation, and the Avenger acted on his own interpretation. But radio's interpretation would require considerable circumspection where the Ripper's motives were concerned if directors and playwrights expected to escape the blue pencils of the censors in the 'continuity acceptance departments'. Words like prostitute, whore, sex and harlot simply had no place on the radio; but since these terms represented the Ripper's reason for existence, changes in motive were decreed before such presentations would be allowed out over the airlanes. Hitchcock wryly caused the victims to be described as 'pretty, blonde' and 'light-hearted'; such descriptions obviously begged the question of the victims' social status in life but certainly met radio's need to sanitize the Ripper's real nature.

Hitchcock's *Lodger* was effective radio. Marshall, as narrator and lead character, dominated the play, tugging at listeners' emotions from two compelling directions, creating suspicion as the enigmatic Mr Sleuth while interpreting and insinuating the worst as the omniscient third-person observer of events, something that would find its ultimate effect in Robert Bloch's *Yours Truly, Jack the Ripper*.[11]

More or less following Mrs Belloc Lowndes's storyline, Hitchcock strategically breaks off adherence to the novelist's plot at the climax and reverts to the theme of his own screen version of *The Lodger* by reprising the lodger as an innocent man falsely accused. Fearing that their daughter, Daisy, is in immediate danger of becoming the Avenger's next victim, the Buntings burst unceremoniously into Mr Sleuth's room. At this point, in a masterful yet stylistic departure from standard radio form, Hitchcock is heard from the director's booth ordering 'cut'. This stops the scene and the forward movement of the play, depriving the listening audience of the expected conclusion. Hitchcock then explains to a perturbed cast and crew that the Bunting room is empty, that Mr Sleuth left that afternoon, not to be heard from again. Furthermore, Hitchcock wryly states that Daisy had merely gone out for a walk and is perfectly safe. In essence, Hitchcock's audience has once again been skilfully led to a conclusion of guilt which is ultimately unjustified, but Hitchcock's own ironic manner, reaching its pinnacle in his television series, makes the ending all too revealing: the Avenger/Ripper simply got away with it.

Mrs Belloc Lowndes's clever story underwent its next major screen reinterpretation under the auspices of Hollywood. In January 1944, Twentieth Century-Fox released John Brahm's *The Lodger*, featuring Laird Cregar in the title role with Merle Oberon, George Sanders, Sara Allgood and Sir Cedric Hardwicke.[12] Scriptwriter Barré Lyndon scrapped the illusion of the 'Avenger' altogether; here, the lodger *was* Jack the Ripper in name as well in fact. But for whatever creative reasons, Cregar's lodger became Mr Slade rather than Mr Sleuth; the Buntings become the Burtons; and the Buntings' daughter, Daisy, became their more worldly niece, Kitty Langley. In addition, Lyndon changed focus, like Hitchcock before him, from Ellen Bunting to the lodger, and this is what makes the film so memorable and effective. It is Cregar's characterization of the brooding lodger that strikes us; his 300-pound frame along with his rather plain features suggest a personality out of kilter with the rest of the universe. This is particularly apparent in Mr Slade's ruminations about the river. He laments that he sometimes goes down to the Thames, where the water will 'wash against your hands as you look down into ... [the] deep water [that] is dark, and restful, and full of peace'. Even more frightening are his ruminations about beautiful women, whom he sees as evil. He states that 'it's one thing if a woman is beautiful merely for herself, but when she exhibits the loveliness of her body upon the stage as a lure.' He later tells Kitty, 'you wouldn't think that anyone could hate a thing and love it, too', concluding that he knows 'that there is evil in beauty'. Later, when as the Ripper he confronts her, he malevolently tells her that 'I have never known such beauty as yours, nor such evil in such beauty! Men will not look at you again as they did tonight!' Gregory William Mank, in *Hollywood Cauldron*, asserts that Cregar's performance was motivated by his own sexual torment: 'That there was a strange garnish of sexual aberration in some of his performances was not surprising; a gay man himself, he was torn between acknowledging his sexual preference and hiding it'.[13] Maybe, but such an assessment – almost excuse – for an actor's talent denies the actor's rightful claim to genius. Personal problems or not, Cregar's performance remains unforgettable.

The Ripper's escape at the conclusion of the movie conforms to Mrs Belloc Lowndes's original tale. In a particularly poignant scene, the stoic Inspector Warwick (George Sanders) sees the river as sweeping a city clean, but Kitty, herself an intended victim of the Ripper, philosophizes about her assailant in the context of the river; she laments that the river 'carries things out to sea, and they sink in deep water', a reference to Slade's own demented personality finally at peace. Unlike Mr Sleuth in Mrs Belloc Lowndes's novel, Mr Slade here arouses our sympathy if only because of Cregar's masterful performance. Slade is not just presented as a maniacal misogynist hell-bent on murdering actresses; rather, Lyndon and director John Brahm turn Slade into a pathetic, introverted outcast, into one who is struggling against not just the world but with himself for no apparent reason other than that he seems to be so destined. For instance, Slade accepts the room from Mrs Burton by sighing that it is 'a refuge', and he entreats Mrs Burton to leave the Bible in his room because his 'problems [are] of life and death'. Here he is depicted as a lonely, melancholy figure who murmurs about late walks and empty streets, and prefers to be known as a lodger, not a guest; but a moment later Lyndon depicts the lodger as maniacal: Mrs Burton returns to the room to find the paintings of the dancers all turned toward the wall. Slade rages that 'wherever you went in this room the eyes of those women seemed to follow you about!'

Twentieth Century-Fox, in its 1954 remake of *The Lodger* titled *Man in the Attic*, virtually cannibalized Lyndon's original script to the point of giving him co-screenplay credit with Robert Presnell, Jr.[14] Director Hugo Fregonese elicited an exceptional performance from Jack Palance in the role of Slade, but the film lacks the intense psychological potency

4 The *Illustrated Police News* laments the poor luck of the police in
apprehending Jack the Ripper.

of the 1944 version, despite Freudian ruminations about Slade's mother,
who was an actress and a domineering spirit in this variation. Both
Palance and Cregar are large men with somewhat brutish features, but
whereas Cregar elicited a dark and deep melancholy to his portrayal of
Slade – reflective of the river – Palance remains merely aloof and reticent
in his portrayal. But this reticence is strangely appealing to Lily (previously Kitty and originally Daisy; played by Constance Smith, who was
also the Ripper's intended victim in *Room to Let*, discussed later), who
refuses to believe that Slade, despite his suspicious actions, could possibly be the Ripper. Also, in this variation, when Slade succumbs to the
dark waters of the Thames, as he inevitably must, there is no ambiguity
and no room for serious doubt: the Ripper is dead. What is also missing
is the magic of Lyndon's poetry in the final verdict. It is left to representatives of the relentless police force – not Lily – to summarize Slade's fate.

The officer remarks that 'it's too dark and it's too deep; we'll never get him now', at which point Inspector Warwick reassures the officer that it is 'not so dark and not so deep where he's going'.

It is worth noting here that *Man in the Attic*, like Lyndon's 1944 endeavour, drew upon the scientific method of fingerprinting for efforts to discover the Ripper's identity. Various critics have faulted the films, particularly the original 1944 version, for this obvious anachronism. In speaking of *Man in the Attic*, for instance, Tom Cullen states, 'This film contains a howler, incidentally, in that fingerprints are used to trap the killer; M. Bertillon's methods had not been adapted by Scotland Yard in 1888' (240).[15] True enough, but in fairness to Lyndon, Mrs Belloc Lowndes's novel was the original source of this temporal anomaly. As Detective Joe Chandler is conducting Daisy and her father on a tour of Scotland Yard's famed Black Museum, Chandler pauses in the entrance of a half-open door and says:

> Look in there, that's the Finger-Print Room. We've records here of over two hundred thousand men's and women's fingertips! I expect you know, Mr Bunting, as how, once we've got the print of a man's five finger-tips, well, he's done for – if he ever does anything else, that is.

Appropriate here is a look at an obscure British film produced in 1950 by Exclusive Films Ltd, the corporate predecessor to the celebrated Hammer Films. Godfrey Grayson's *Room to Let*, adapted from a BBC radio play by noted mystery novelist Margery Allingham, shares many characteristics with Mrs Belloc Lowndes's book.[16] The setting is London, a few years after the Ripper killings, and an elderly invalid named Mrs Musgrave (Christine Silver) and her daughter, Molly (Constance Smith), find it necessary to let one of the rooms in their home to a suitable boarder in order to make ends meet. Dr Fell (Valentine Dyall), a tall gaunt gentleman in cloak and top hat, applies for the room and is gratefully accepted by Mrs Musgrave. However, Dr Fell proves to be a strange fellow, who moves quickly and inexplicably to control the household. He dominates both women to such a degree that their wills are slowly given over to him; even the assertive Molly is unable to void his psychological stranglehold on the household. At one point, when Molly threatens to call the police, Fell merely asks rhetorically, 'Police calling on the house to arrest the lodger? Curious, isn't it, that I should be the lodger?'

The psychological horror, manifested by Grayson's frequent use of extreme low angles in framing Dr Fell, slowly builds as Fell inexorably extends his power over the Musgrave household to the point at which he gives approval and disapproval to Molly's suitors. Dr Fell's madness becomes morally certain when journalist Curly Minter (Jimmy Hanley), Molly's true love, believes that Fell escaped from a mental institution during a fire even though no-one from the institution will verify a missing patient. Dr Fell's other identity, that of Jack the Ripper, becomes obvious when he shows Mrs Musgrave his cherished map of Whitechapel, and mutters that maps are 'useful when you want to move about quickly'. He then tells her that he intends to pick up where he had left off after the Miller's Court murder in 1888, and at this point Grayson heightens the desperation of Mrs Musgrave by having her alone in a house with Jack the Ripper. At the moment of truth, however, Curly and Sergeant Cranbourne (Reginald Dyson) break into the house to find Mrs Musgrave alive on the floor near her overturned wheelchair. They are then forced to break into Fell's room through a window, where they find him dead, a bullet through the heart.

Grayson's *Room to Let* is told in flashback by an elderly Curly to his journalist friends, Harding (Aubrey Dexter) and James Jasper, or J. J. (J. Anthony la Penna). Curly describes the locked-room death of Dr Fell as a puzzle. The door was both locked and bolted from the inside, he says, and no gun was ever found; the only conclusion, of course, is suicide. J. J., however, sounding very much like Sherlock Holmes, explains to Harding what he believes to be the truth: that Mrs Musgrave shot the Ripper in self-defence, and that she locked the door and then slid the key underneath it into the room. J. J. says that Mrs Musgrave then descended the staircase ever so gently, until her feeble hands gave out and she crashed to the floor, where she placed the gun inside a book box for posting to her sister. When Harding points to the bolt inside the room, J. J. explains that Curly was the first one into the room, and that he bolted the door himself to save the Musgraves from potential scrutiny by press and authorities. J. J. adds that Curly's gentility is fixed, since he eschewed the scoop of the century for the love of a woman.

Viewed from a certain perspective, *Room to Let* might easily be taken as a sequel to Mrs Belloc Lowndes's *The Lodger*; indeed, Dr Fell's admission that he is 'the lodger' smacks of an in-joke by either Allingham or screenwriters John Gilling and Grayson. As a sequel, *Room to Let* explains what might have befallen the Whitechapel killer after he fled the Bunting household in 1888. The consistency of character is worth noting: the propensity for positioning himself in financially embarrassed families and the desire to kill certainly parallel major motifs of *The Lodger*. Moreover, Dr Fell's *over*concern for the welfare of Molly echoes Mr Slade's own anxiety about Kitty in Brahm's *The Lodger*. The explanation for Dr Fell's need to kill, however, is much less obvious than the religious fanaticism ascribed to Mr Sleuth or to Mr Slade. Dr Fell's need to dominate women leads him to the act of murder as the final and inevitable step in controlling women.

Contextually, radio, like film and television, tended to focus upon the emotional storytelling aspects inherent in the Ripper saga rather than on any historical analysis, which seemed the province of books and magazine articles (although such works were not without a significant body of fictional narratives constructed from Ripper lore). But radio was a near-perfect medium for Jack the Ripper and his various incarnations. From the start, the public had taken to endowing this monster with personal touches, filling in the horrific details to meet some private emotional needs. Radio, by its very nature, permitted – in fact encouraged – audiences to colour details to personal taste, and in so doing it significantly contributed to the lengthy ongoing process which was radically transforming the original Ripper into an archetypal figure. The confluence of desire and means significantly accelerated the process.

On 19 May 1946, radio's *Hollywood Star Time*, a series that saw itself in the mould of *Lux Radio Theatre* and *The Screen Guild Players*, both being prestige radio offerings which produced versions of popular movies, presented a half-hour version of *The Lodger* based on the Twentieth Century-Fox production.[17] Like its competition, *Hollywood Star Time* brought to the microphone top screen names to perform in lead roles. To assume the role of the mysterious lodger, director Robert L. Redd selected Vincent Price, whose association with horror roles had not yet been sealed. The opening narration skilfully and succinctly set the stage for the drama:

> This is the story of a scourge that broke upon the City of London in the year 1888. It is the story of a man who moved in the shadows, beyond the flickering gaslights of that era and who wrote his name upon the scroll of infamy with a knife, and his name was murder!

Within the constraints of a thirty-minute aural production, *Hollywood Star Time* attempted to adhere basically to the Twentieth Century-Fox outline, and certainly the essential elements remained intact. The one key exception was the concluding moment, at which the Ripper is dimly perceived swimming away through cold dark waters to freedom after a revealing confrontation in Kitty's dressing room. The *Hollywood Star Time* broadcast suggested, through Kitty's final speech and an absence of any evidence to the contrary, that Price's Ripper had, indeed, drowned in the river. We are told by Kitty that, 'The river killed him, even at the last.' She then reiterates, for the most part, Lyndon's melancholic farewell: the river 'carries things out to sea and they sink in deep, dark water, in dark peaceful water forever'. But radio's cautious use of public airwaves necessitated a sort of Victorian compromise all its own; indeed, a plethora of station, network and broadcasting codes in strict force at the time of *Hollywood Star Time*'s presentation precluded the Ripper's escape. Justice and inevitable retribution, an integral part of the National Association of Broadcasters code, demanded a re-writing of the screenplay to fit such constraints, and accordingly the addition of the key phrase that 'the river killed him, even at the last' sustained the broadcast standards, but it also subverted Kitty's final sentiments, which, as noted, were more ambiguous and, in the context of the moment, made more sense.

The following year yet another version of *The Lodger* was presented, this time on a short lived yet expertly conceived and acted anthology series titled *Mystery in the Air*. This rendering of *The Lodger* was broadcast on 14 August 1947, and featured radio veteran Agnes Moorehead as Ellen Bunting and series host Peter Lorre as Mr Sleuth.[18] Free from respecting the Twentieth Century-Fox account, *Mystery in the Air* tied its version much closer to the novel, and hence the Ripper was once again vaguely disguised as the Avenger. The Buntings' daughter, Daisy, was once more a secondary figure, all but inviting the attention of the Avenger. Moorehead's Ellen Bunting again served as the moral focal point, struggling with her fears, suspicions, sympathies and misplaced loyalties – just as Mrs Belloc Lowndes had conceived the character. Lorre's Mr Sleuth was as intense as Cregar but at times overly hysterical in his religious fervour that 'everything wicked and sinful should be purged from the earth'. Nonetheless, as closely as this rendering strove to adhere to the novel, once again the demands of the broadcasters' codes necessitated a significant change in denouement. While Ellen Bunting and her husband beat frantically against a locked door, on the other side an insane and ranting Avenger prepares to make Daisy his seventh and final victim. As he raises his knife to strike, the Buntings succeed in forcing their way into the room, and in the ensuing confrontation the Avenger falls on his own knife, delivering his own succinct epitaph, which could easily have been that of Cregar's melancholic figure: 'It is burning in me like a fire. It purges me and consumes me. All sin and evil are falling away. Praise, praise and glory, for it is I who am the seventh. Yes, the vengeance is fulfilled.'

Hitchcock's 1940 *Forecast* production of 'The Lodger' led two years later to the première of *Suspense*, one of the longest-running and most critically acclaimed mystery anthologies to appear on American radio.[19] Defining itself as 'radio's outstanding theatre of thrills', *Suspense* played for twenty years, consistently drawing upon the principles of fear and horror so skilfully articulated by Hitchcock in the pilot broadcast. Indeed, *Suspense* provided some of the most consistently frightening moments in radio drama, including the often reprised 'Sorry, Wrong Number', which was specifically written for the series.

On 14 December 1944, *Suspense* presented one of two adaptations of *The Lodger*. This time Robert Montgomery performed the twin assignments of narrator and lodger. The play was an essentially faithful translation of the novel, but the one significant dissimilarity was the final climactic moment when the Avenger holds Daisy at knifepoint, a scene that does not take place in the novel. In this instance, the Avenger does not die from his own hand, nor from the hand of the police or from the intervention of the Buntings rescuing their daughter, but rather succumbs to an act of God. The Avenger's fanatical rage is more than matched by a raging storm which has newly descended over London. Miraculously, the Bunting house is struck by lightning, and the terrible shrieking screams of the dying Avenger ring in listeners' ears. This *deus ex machina* solution to the case, while perhaps lacking credibility, nonetheless offers the attraction of poetic justice: God punished the crimes committed in His name.

Four seasons later, on 14 February 1948, *Suspense* had shifted to an hour format, and again *The Lodger* was its subject. Coincidentally, Robert Montgomery was serving as host that season and found himself again playing the mysterious Mr Sleuth. The radio adaptations, in both instances, were by veteran radio dramatist Robert Tallman, with the 1948 script essentially an expansion of Tallman's 1944 play. Another radio veteran, William N. Robson, directed the hour-long version, which featured Jeanette Nolan as Ellen Bunting and Peggy Webber as Daisy. The same *deus ex machina* convention was employed and the Avenger perished through God's wrath. Or did he? In both the 1944 and 1948 presentations, Montgomery, in his role of host, closes with something of a teaser which once again demonstrates our reluctance to permanently say goodbye to the Ripper.

> There were those at Scotland Yard who were never quite sure that the charred remains of a man they removed from the ashes of the Bunting home were, indeed, those of the Avenger any more than Mrs Belloc Lowndes, who novelized the case, was ever quite convinced. And there are those who will tell you that the real Avenger, a tall man clad in an Inverness cape, a man almost exactly like Mr Sleuth, left England and came to America to live in a town near your town.

One of the last substantive employments of Mrs Belloc Lowndes's narrative was the 1960 opera by British composer Phyllis Tate, which, together with Alban Berg's *Lulu* (1936), forms the foundation upon which all musical adaptations of the Ripper and his crimes are made. Tate's opera, which was first presented at London's Royal Academy of Music on 14 July 1960, and was televised by the BBC in 1964, is faithful to the thrust of the original but concentrates its tragic narrative more on the ambivalent relationship between the sympathetic Mrs Bunting and the deranged yet surprisingly 'good hearted' lodger than on the murders. Following the tradition of tragedy, the crimes were all committed offstage.

On the other hand, Berg's *Lulu*, adapted from the plays *Erdgeist/Earth Spirit* (1893) and *Die Büchse der Pandora/Pandora's Box* (1904) by Frank Wedekind, both of which had been adapted into a film by G. W. Pabst (*Pandora's Box*), centred its narrative on a cabaret dancer named Lulu and her various love affairs, which led to her moral ruin; in the end, she was reduced to a London prostitute who became a victim of Jack the Ripper.[20]

Ironically, the most celebrated musical version of the Ripper and his crimes actually bears little resemblance to the Victorian murderer and his reign of terror. Kurt Weill and Bertolt Brecht's *Die Dreigroschenoper/The Threepenny Opera*, first presented at the Theater am Schiffbauerdamm in Berlin on 31 August 1928, remains foremost in musical adaptations of the Ripper story, if only for the tremendous popularity of one of the play's songs, 'Mack the Knife'. The song, which is heard in the prelude as an introduction for the character MacHeath, recounts a string of Ripper-like murders and warns that their perpetrator – MacHeath – is yet on the prowl. The play itself, however, and its subsequent film versions including an expressionistic interpretation by G. W. Pabst in 1931, deal more with Brechtian ideology than murder. In this respect, the narrative offers the notion that the seedy political manoeuvring of underworld criminal organizations is analogous to the mundane operations of capitalist democracy. Brecht writes that the criminal mastermind MacHeath is an embodiment of capitalist greed in the sense of one who 'takes the greatest care that all the boldest or, at least, the most fear-inspiring deeds of his subordinates are ascribed to himself'. Such a view could be applied to the oppressed economic and social conditions of Whitechapel itself; but it remains the song 'Mack the Knife', whose popularity soared after Marc Blitzstein's Broadway revival of the play premièring on 10 March 1954, that keeps the eponymous figure of the Whitechapel killer alive, even if MacHeath himself is more like Dr Mabuse than Jack the Ripper.

Notes

1 Donald Rumbelow, *Jack the Ripper: The Complete Casebook* (Chicago: Contemporary Books, 1988), p. 236; Paul Begg, Martin Fido and Keith Skinner, *The Jack the Ripper A–Z* (London: Headline, 1994).

2 Marie Belloc Lowndes, *The Lodger* (Chicago: Academy Chicago, 1988).

3 Chris Steinbrunner and Otto Penzler (eds), *Encyclopedia of Mystery and Detection* (New York: McGraw-Hill, 1976), p. 252.

4 Susan Lowndes (ed.), *Diaries and Letters of Marie Belloc Lowndes, 1911–1947* (London: Chatto and Windus, 1971), p. 97.

5 Lowndes, *Diaries and Letters*, pp. 97–8.

6 For a review of the New York première of Ainsley's play as well as a history of this obscure and nearly forgotten play, see ' "The Lodger" Proves Highly Amusing', *New York Times*, 9 January 1917, p. 14.

7 *The Lodger: A Story of the London Fog*, *Production* Gainsborough, *Director* Alfred Hitchcock, *Producer* Michael Balcon, *Screenplay* Alfred Hitchcock and Eliot Stannard, *Based on the novel by* Mrs Marie Belloc Lowndes, *Director of photography* Baron Ventigmilia, *Editor and titles* Ivor Montagu, *Art direction* C. Wilfred Arnold and Bertram Evans, *Distribution* Unknown. CAST: Ivor Novello (The Lodger), June (Daisy Bunting), Marie Ault (Mrs Bunting), Arthur Chesney (Mr Bunting), Malcolm Keen (Joe Chandler). A British production in black and white; silent; released 1926; US distribution uncertain; 88 minutes.

8 William Rothman, *Hitchcock: The Murderous Gaze* (Cambridge, MA: Harvard University Press, 1982), p. 10.

9 Begg, Fido and Skinner, *The Jack the Ripper A–Z*, p. 253.

10 *Forecast* 'The Lodger', *Network* CBS, *Director* Alfred Hitchcock. CAST: Herbert Marshall as The Lodger. *Airdate* 22 July 1940.

11 Robert Bloch, *Yours Truly, Jack the Ripper: Tales of Horror* (New York: Belmont Books, 1962).

12 *The Lodger*, *Production* Twentieth Century-Fox, *Director* John Brahm, *Producer* Robert Bassler, *Screenplay* Barré Lyndon, *Based on the novel by* Mrs Marie Belloc Lowndes, *Music* Hugo J. Friedhofer, *Director of photography* Lucien Ballard, *Film editor* J. Watson Webb, Jr, *Art direction* James Basevi and John Ewing, *Distribution* Twentieth Century-Fox Film Corporation. CAST: Merle Oberon (Kitty Langley), George Sanders (John Warwick), Laird Cregar (Mr Slade), Sir Cedric Hardwicke (Robert Burton), Sara Allgood (Ellen Burton), Aubrey Mather (Superintendent Sutherland), Queenie Leonard (Daisy), Doris Lloyd (Jennie), David Clyde (Sergeant Bates), Lumsden Hare (Doctor Sheridan), Frederic Worlock (Sir Edward), Colin Campbell (Harold), Olaf Hytten (Harris), Harold de Becker (Charlie) with Billy Bevan, Forrester Harvey, Skelton Knaggs, Edmond Breon, Gerald Hamer, Montague Shaw and Cyril Delavanti. A US production in black and white; released 7 January 1944; 84 minutes.

13 Gregory William Mank, *Hollywood Cauldron: Thirteen Horror Films from the Genre's Golden Age* (Jefferson, NC: McFarland and Company, 1994), p. 245.

14 *Man in the Attic*, *Production* Panoramic Productions and Leonard Goldstein, *Director* Hugo Fregonese, *Producer* Robert L. Jacks, *Screenplay* Robert Presnell, Jr. and Barré Lyndon, *Based on* The Lodger *by* Mrs Marie

Belloc Lowndes, *Music* No credits, *Director of photography* Leo Tover, *Film editor* Marjorie Fowler, *Art direction* Lyle Wheeler and Leland Fuller, *Distribution* Twentieth Century-Fox Film Corporation. CAST: Jack Palance (Mr Slade), Constance Smith (Lily Bonner), Frances Bavier (Helen Harley), Rhys Williams (William Harley), Lillian Bond (Anne Rowley), Isabel Jewell (Katy), Lisa Daniels (Mary Lenihan), Byron Palmer (Paul Warwick), Tita Phillips (Daisy), with Harry Cording, Leslie Bradley, Lester Matthews and Sean McClory. A US production in black and white; released December 1953; 84 minutes.

15 Tom Cullen, *Autumn of Terror: Jack the Ripper: His Crimes and Times* (London: The Bodley Head, 1965), p. 240.

16 *Room To Let, Production* Exclusive Films Ltd, *Director* Godfrey Grayson, *Producer* Anthony Hinds, *Screenplay* John Gilling and Godfrey Grayson, *Based on the BBC feature by* Margery Allingham, *Music* Frank Spencer, *Director of photography* Cedric Williams, *Film editor* James Needs, *Art direction* Denis Wreford, *Distribution* Exclusive Films Ltd. CAST: Jimmy Hanley (Curly Minter), Valentine Dyall (Dr Fell), Christine Silver (Mrs Musgrave), Constance Smith (Molly Musgrave), Merle Tottenham (Alice), Charles Hawtrey (Michael Atkinson), Reginald Dyson (Sergeant Cranbourne), Aubrey Dexter (Mr Harding), J. Anthony la Penna (James Jasper). A British production (1950) in black and white; US distribution uncertain; 68 minutes.

17 *Hollywood Star Time* 'The Lodger', *Network* CBS, *Director* Robert L. Redd. CAST: Vincent Price as The Lodger. *Airdate* 19 May 1946.

18 *Mystery in the Air* 'The Lodger', *Network* NBC, *Director* Cal Kuhl. CAST: Peter Lorre as The Lodger and Agnes Moorehead as Ellen Bunting. *Announcer* Harry Morgan, *Airdate* 14 August 1947.

19 *Suspense* 'The Lodger', *Network* CBS, *Director* William N. Robson, *Writer* Robert Talman. CAST: Robert Montgomery as The Lodger, Jeanette Nolan as Ellen Bunting and Peggy Webber as Daisy. *Airdate* 14 December 1944.

20 Pandora's Box, *Production* Nero-Film, *Director* G. W. Pabst, *Producer* George C. Horsetzky and Seymour Nebenzahl, *Screenplay* Ladislaus Vajda, *Based on the plays* Erdgeist *and* Die Büchse der Pandora *by* Frank Wedekind, *Director of photography* Günther Krampf, *Film editor* Joseph R. Fiesler, *Art direction* Andrei Andreiev, *Distribution* Moviegraph Inc. CAST: Louise Brooks (Lulu), Fritz Kortner (Dr Peter Schön), Franz Lederer (Alwa Schön), Carl Goetz (Schigolch/Papa Brommer), Alice Roberts (Countess Anna Geschwitz), Daisy D'Ora (Marie de Zarniko), Siefried Arno (the stage director), Gustav Diessl (Jack the Ripper). A German production (1928) in black and white; silent; 131 minutes but some sources say the film was cut to 120 minutes; some sources say the film was released in the USA in 1929.

5

Blood and ink: narrating the Whitechapel murders

Alexandra Warwick

'Our story's written, Netley, inked in blood long dry, engraved in stone.'[1]

This sentence is the simplest summary of the fictions of the Whitechapel murders, but one that perhaps indicates why 'our story' continues to be told. The Whitechapel murders have always been 'our story'; Jack the Ripper has been a collective and collaborative invention since the moment of the murders taking place, and 'we' are the people of Whitechapel, the Victorian press, the readers, writers and filmmakers of the twentieth and twenty-first centuries. Alan Moore's phrase also captures the paradox: the story is over, past tense, written, inked, engraved, yet always unfinished. Other essays in this volume explore the manifold reasons why the story took such immediate root in the popular imagination. This piece will look at storytelling itself, and at questions of narrative in two of the most interesting fictional texts in Ripper literature: Iain Sinclair's *White Chappell, Scarlet Tracings* (1987) and Alan Moore and Eddie Campbell's graphic novel *From Hell* (1989–99).

Storytelling

There is little doubt that there is a profound textuality about serial killing. As Mark Seltzer notes: 'in such cases, the boundaries come down between private desire and public life, along with boundaries between private bodies and the public media. Letters and bodies, word counts and body counts, go together from the inception of serial murder'.[2] Arguably, the connections between murder and fiction go back even further, to the novel's earliest form and the influence of publications like the *Newgate Calendar* and the criminal confessions sold at public executions. The figure of the serial killer is invented in the shape of Jack the Ripper in the century that could be described as inventing seriality itself. From the forms of mechanical production and reproduction that are the product of industrialism to the serial mode that dominated nineteenth-century publication, Victorians were deeply familiar with the rhythms of repetition and instalment and, as Seltzer and others have suggested, the serial killer is industrial process applied to murder, a killing machine.

Jack the Ripper's crimes fit the motion of serial publication: sequential events recognizably part of the same work, varying enough to maintain interest, provoking the expectation of additional episodes, unfinished yet ultimately promising a conclusion. Diana Fuss notices this legacy in contemporary media; she says that 'tales of serial killers have become our new serial literature, with regular instalments, stock characters, behavioural profiles, and a fascinated loyal readership'.[3] Moore and Campbell's graphic novel mimics this seriality in its original publication in parts. In this, and in the juxtaposition of text and line-drawing, it resembles quite closely the original forms of the reporting of the murders. The press, and particularly the more sensational publications, carried many illustrations and, as was common at the time, these often took the form of a page or a strip of drawings with captions. In fact, the drawing style of *From Hell* seems deliberately similar to that found in the graphic periodicals, and the weekly *Illustrated Police News* actually appears in *From Hell* with the 8 September issue shown breaking up into autumn leaves.[4]

Serial killing is a relatively rare phenomenon, but the serial killer is a familiar figure in popular culture in novels, television drama, films and 'true crime' accounts. The relations between the true and the fictional are circuitous. As Seltzer says, 'the designation of the serial killer as a type of person has had ... a sort of switchback or looping effect: public knowledge about kinds of people has a way of interacting with the people who are known about and how these people conceive of themselves'.[5] The 'knowledge' here is of uncertain status, and Seltzer is suggesting that real killers continue to be a kind of collaborative and collective invention, one that is participated in by the killers themselves. The slippage between the real and the fictional extends to the professional sphere in the strange acknowledgement of the roots of modern detection methods. A psychological profiler for the FBI has written, 'our antecedents actually do go back to crime fiction more than crime fact', and he spends some pages discussing the invention of profiling by Edgar Allan Poe, Wilkie Collins and Arthur Conan Doyle.[6] Despite, or perhaps because of this blurring an appearance of the separation of fact and fiction is maintained, and almost no real serial killers have been directly fictionalized. Jack the Ripper is the obvious exception, with parallel strands, equal in volume, of 'true' accounts and fictions running through the twentieth century and showing little sign of diminishing in the twenty-first. The true-crime accounts make great efforts to establish themselves as reliable providers of information: Rumbelow and Begg begin with historical chapters on nineteenth-century

London, Sugden with a detailed discussion of the condition and availability of the archival record.[7] All are voluminously footnoted and characterized by a welter of dates, times, distances, names and locations. Some attempt to dispense with a narrative altogether, and present just the remaining documentary records. The effort is to banish stories and to fix the events as fact, but the problem is that the events are uncertain in status; it is difficult to be authoritative about a series of murders when even the number of those murders is in doubt.

Even in these documentary accounts the events are very small nodes of information in the much longer discourse of their telling, and the complex distinction between events and the telling of them is at the heart of the study of narrative. Narrative theory recognizes the crucial question of the relationship between the events referred to (which the Russian Formalists called *fabula*) and the events as presented in the narrative (which they called *sjužet*).[8] Jonathan Culler expands:

> we isolate a level of structure, call it *fabula*, which we treat as something given, a constant, a sequence of events, which the narrative presupposes and which it could describe in various ways. By identifying this sequence of actions as what the text is describing, we make it possible to treat everything else in the text as ways of viewing, presenting, valuing or ordering this non-textual sub-stratum.[9]

The fabula acquires something like the status of the real or true, in contrast with the storytelling, which is a subjective recounting of the events. Culler goes on to question the apparent clarity of the distinction made by the Formalists, as do many later narratologists. Peter Brooks, in his book, *Reading for the Plot*, summarizes it thus: 'we must, however, recognize that the apparent priority of *fabula* to *sjužet* is in the nature of a mimetic illusion, in that the *fabula* – "what really happened" – is in fact a mental construction that the reader derives from the *sjužet*, which is all that he ever knows'.[10]

While Brooks does not dismiss the Formalist distinction between events and the telling of them, he is interested in the nature of the relation between them, and proposes the term 'plot' as describing 'the interpretive activity elicited by the distinction between *sjužet* and *fabula*, the way we *use* the one against the other ... plot is the thus the dynamic shaping force of the narrative discourse'.[11] In his reading of Arthur Conan Doyle's Sherlock Holmes story, 'The Musgrave Ritual', he writes of the semantic range of the term 'plot' and reduces it to these four categories:

1. (a) A small piece of ground, generally used for a specific purpose.
   (b) A measured area of land; lot.

2. A ground plan, as for a building; chart; diagram.
3. The series of events consisting of the outline of the action of a narrative or drama.
4. A secret plan to accomplish a hostile or illegal purpose.[12]

Brooks suggests that there may be a subterranean logic connecting these different meanings, but it seems that in the detective story this logic is made a great deal more explicit. Brooks's reading shows Doyle constructing the revelation of 4 through 3, with 3 consisting of Holmes accomplishing the solution through the mapping of 4 on to 1 and 2 as he paces out the cryptic code on the lawn of the Musgrave house. This retreading is crucial: Brooks says that 'the work of detection in this story makes particularly clear a condition of all classic detective fiction, that the detective repeat, go over again, the ground that has been covered by his predecessor, the criminal'.[13]

Detective fiction has an important place in narratology, and particularly in the question of the relation between events and events as they are told. Tzvetan Todorov makes it clear that he regards detective fiction as something like the narrative of all narratives. He asserts that in each detective novel there are two stories, 'the first – the story of the crime – tells "what really happened", whereas the second – the story of the investigation – explains "how the reader (or the narrator) has come to know about it". But these definitions concern not only the two stories in detective fiction, but also the two aspects of literary work which the Russian Formalists identified.'[14]

For Todorov, the story of the crime is analogous to the fabula, (the 'real' events), and the story of the investigation to the *sjužet* (the telling of them). This very cursory sketch of some elements of narrative theory indicates why it might be useful in considering the Whitechapel murders. The events are there (the murders of Nichols, Chapman, Stride, Eddowes and Kelly), but so were many other crimes, including the murders of other women, in 1888. Most of these other events have little or no second story; the perpetrators were discovered almost immediately. The Whitechapel murders as events have no order, no characterization, no protagonist and no solution. As events they demand to be told, to be produced as narrative. As Todorov says: 'The first [story], that of the crime, is in fact the story of an absence: its most accurate characteristic is that it cannot be immediately present'.[15] If, as Todorov suggests, detective fiction is the narrative of narratives, then the Whitechapel murders represent both the inaugural event in serial killing and the narrative accounts of it. The two novels examined here are produced in a highly informed self-consciousness of the mass of previous writing on the

Whitechapel murders. As such, they are as much about the nature of plot and narrative as they are about the murders themselves.

Detecting fiction

All of Iain Sinclair's work is detective fiction of a kind. There is constant allusion to crime in his writings, sometimes obviously, as in *White Chappell, Scarlet Tracings*, or in his use of the Kray brothers or the Moors murderers in the earlier *Lud Heat* (1975) and *Suicide Bridge* (1979). Sometimes the crime is petty acts of violence, theft and vandalism, at others it is larger and more vague, as with the implied political criminality of Thatcherism in *Downriver* (1991) and *Radon Daughters* (1994). These crimes are, in Todorov's terms, what really happened, and Sinclair's writing is his work of detection; the accounts of his investigations foreground their status as narrative: 'The second story is not only supposed to take the reality of the book into account, but is precisely the story of that very book.'[16]

White Chappell complicates the relations further in having several sets of first and second stories. The novel is made up of three strands: the nineteenth century of the murders, the 1970s of the narrator's work in Truman's brewery in Whitechapel and the 1980s of his experiences as a book dealer. The 1970s and 1980s sections are thinly disguised autobiography, and thus refer to events as real as the murders of 1888, but in themselves are also Todorov's 'second story', the account of how the events of the first come to be known. Moore and Campbell's *From Hell* is ostensibly a rather different production, most obviously in the juxtaposition of text and image, but it shares a great deal with Sinclair. In the extensive notes on the chapters of *From Hell*, Sinclair and his work are referred to, and the two texts are very loosely based around Stephen Knight's 1976 book, *Jack the Ripper: The Final Solution*.

Knight's now familiar thesis is that the murders were masterminded by the Freemasons and carried out on their behalf by Dr William Gull, Queen Victoria's physician, in order to eliminate the evidence of her grandson's clandestine marriage and fathering of a child with a Catholic shopgirl. Gull was assisted by a coachman, John Netley, and committed to an asylum by his fellow masons after the murder of Mary Kelly. Sinclair and Moore depart from Knight in their interest in James Hinton, a figure who very rarely appears elsewhere in Ripper literature, possibly because he died in 1875 and therefore could not have committed the crimes himself. Had he still been alive it is hard to see how he would not have been arrested immediately, given his familiarity with the area and his pronounced views on prostitution and the sacrificial killing of women. Knight mentions Hinton briefly as a man afflicted with a 'divine despair' about prostitutes, and as Gull's closest friend, with whom he walked about the streets of Whitechapel.[17] James Hinton is a curious figure, and his attraction as a character in relation to the killings is very obvious, as he seems to display in anticipation a number of ideas that have come to be part of the popular and professional image of the serial killer. He saw prostitution as the main obstacle to a 'purified' relationship of love between men and women, and said that 'the cure of prostitution is to be in a great woman-sacrifice, nothing else or less'.[18] He wrote also of the 'genius', asserting that he is a man defined by an 'act'. Hinton gives among the characteristics of the act that 'it must be a thing in some respects the same as what "bad" persons do for their mere pleasure ... a thing he hates to do ... it must be a thing in its form new, and not a conscious repetition of a thing done before, and accepted as right to do'.[19] Further to this, Hinton's son Howard was a mathematician who wrote a number of speculative essays on the existence of the fourth dimension and on the possibility of perceiving or moving to it, effectively travelling through time.[20] Both Sinclair and Moore fuse James Hinton's violent obsessions with the theoretical work of his son, to suggest that the murders are in fact James's legacy. As Sinclair has him say: 'Will my friends try it after I am dead, for I cannot do it by myself.'[21]

Mapping the plot

In both texts the means by which the nineteenth-century story is known is through walking or moving through the streets. In *From Hell* the appearance of the text in strip form emphasizes the narrative process in the deliberate move from one panel to the next, and the control of the narrative flow comes through the variations in size of panel: smaller panels carry the movement forward, the larger panels slow it down. *From Hell* produces more closely, in visual terms, the mapping that Sinclair seeks verbally: in the motion of the figures through the lines and squares of the strip the reader's sense is of a telescopic eye that dissolves space and time to see the movements through the streets of Whitechapel. The grids of the text mimic a street map, where the smaller panels appear as crowded terraces, and the blind yards like Miller's Court, Dutfield's Yard and Mitre Square are places where the action expands suddenly in larger panels, yet bounded as dead ends by solid lines. In *From Hell* almost the whole of Chapter 4 consists of Gull directing Netley through London, explaining its ancient history and symbolism and the eternal struggle of male and female principles that he believes it embodies: 'Maps have potency; may yield a wealth of knowledge past imagining if properly divined.'[22] Although no murders have yet been committed, Gull begins by stating that the murders will be his 'work' and then effectively leads Netley through the plot, the explanation of the reasons why they will happen. The story, as he concludes, is already written, both foretold and recorded by the material environment of London itself. Walking is also absolutely central to all Sinclair's work. In his walking, Sinclair/the narrator becomes the Holmesian detective, going over the ground and reading that ground for the occluded evidence it holds. *White Chappell*, in its title, directly delimits its ground, and within that a still smaller demarcation is made: 'the zone was gradually defined, the labyrinth penetrated. It was given limits by the victims of the Ripper: the Roebuck and Brady Street to the East, Mitre Square to the West, the Minories to the South, the North largely unvisited.'[23] The repeated movement over this ground is not, in Sinclair's novel, proceeding towards a solution, at least not to a solution of the murders that would be recognized by those seeking the identity of the murderer. In fact the text appears explicitly to deny the generic conventions. The Sinclair character says:

This is to reverse the conventions of detective fiction, where a given crime is unravelled, piece by piece, until a murderer is denounced whose act is the starting point of the narration. Our narrative starts everywhere. We want to assemble all the incomplete movements, like cubists, until the point is reached where the crime can commit itself.[24]

Despite seeming to deny narrative convention, Sinclair's remarks actually come closer to the more complex understanding of the relationship between events and their telling articulated by narratologists after the Formalists. Paul Ricoeur, for example, defines plot as 'the intelligible whole that governs a succession of events in any story ... the plot's connecting function between the events and the story. A story is *made out of* events to the extent that plot *makes* events *into* a story'.[25] What Ricoeur, like Brooks, is asserting is a more dynamic conception of plot as giving shape and direction to narrative, and assigning a more active role to the reader than the Formalist analysis allows. For Sinclair the crimes do not happen on the ground as much as *through* it; the ground demands it: 'There were no instructions or whispers from secret masters: no sealed orders. A plot of ground in St. Patrick's Cemetery, Leytonstone, was unfulfilled'.[26] The 'plot' is simultaneously Mary Kelly's grave and the dynamic of the movement of the narrative towards and away from her death. The further sense of 'plot' as conspiracy is explicitly denied, but the master plot remains the piece of ground.

HORRIBLE LONDON : OR, THE PANDEMONIUM OF POSTERS.

5 *Punch* imagines the Whitechapel murders as a chaotic intermingling of
advertising, newspaper sensationalism and popular fiction.

In Sinclair's work, writing arises from the two activities of walking and reading. For him, to walk is not only to move wilfully between one point and another, but also to be walked, to be drawn along the lines of the streets and landscape. Reading enacts the same process: 'Beneath the narrative drive is a plan of energy that can, with the right key, be consulted'.[27] Sinclair's phrase here is almost exactly the same as Moore's statement about maps quoted earlier. It could be argued that the 'energy' is the narrative drive itself, not something that is beneath or separate from it, if narrative is conceived of as a more or less willing collaboration between reader and text, or indeed between walker and ground. The psychogeography that Sinclair has become identified with is the activity of the hypersensitive, even paranoid, reader/walker for whom the cacophonous multiplicity of significance must be ordered into intelligibility. In this there is another clear parallel with serial killing. In the practice of forensic detection and geographical profiling, it is again the ground that can be read for its significance, for the material and psychological evidence of the criminal. One of the best-known geographical profilers, David Canter, persistently describes both the killer and the map of his murders as having or being 'narratives', and implies that it is his task to read and interpret them. His self-identification as something like a literary critic is so strong that in his book *Mapping Murder* he uses as epigraphs quotations from Northrop Frye's classic work of literary analysis, *Anatomy of Criticism*.[28] In *Mapping Murder* there is a scientifically framed echo of Sinclair and Moore's more esoteric psychogeogeography in his chapter on Jack the Ripper, where he presents a mathematical formula for locating the centre of the murders, which, when fixed on a map, gives a point close to Christ Church.[29] In geographical profiling the zone defines the criminal as surely as it does for Sinclair and Moore, though in both of the latter there is also the strong sense that the zone does not simply stand in for the murderer, it *is* the killer, responsible for the crimes. The plot kills its characters; Whitechapel kills its women.

The allegory of plot

Brooks's commentary on 'The Musgrave Ritual' identifies Conan Doyle's story as an allegory of plot, with something like the status of 'narrative of narratives' that Todorov claims for the detective story. *From Hell* and *White Chappell* (and particularly the latter) could be seen as similar allegories of plot. The title of Sinclair's novel describes it as this – the white (page) written upon in red, the palimpsest of all its tracings, the ways in which story becomes discourse. Brooks claims that the result aimed at by plotting is the restoration of the possibility of the transmission of meaning, and describes narrative as 'the acting out of the implications of metaphor'. In his reading he stresses:

> how the incomprehensible metaphor of transmission must be unpacked as metonymy, literally by plotting its cryptic indications out on the lawn [of the Musgrave house] ... If we take metaphor as the paradigmatic axis that marks a synthetic grasp or presentation of a situation, the terminal points of a narrative offer a blinded metaphor of transmission and an enlightened metaphor of transmission.[30]

White Chappell opens with a description of 'an interesting condition of the stomach', afflicting Nicholas Lane, one of the book dealers. The language of the description betrays it immediately as just such a blinded metaphor: communication between the zones is blocked, narrowed to a tiny passage. Transmission itself is almost blocked, relief can only be obtained through the vomiting of the stomach's semi-digested contents, along the route through which they entered. The blindness of the metaphor is emphasized in the 'shady receptacle' with its 'secret tides' that nevertheless 'pass visibly'. There echoes faintly, too, the murders to come; the 'interesting condition' is a Victorian euphemism for pregnancy, the elimination of the evidence of which is, in Knight's thesis, the reason for the murders. The abdomen is the bodily centre of the Whitechapel murders, it is the site of the mutilations, the locus of the extracted organs, the place that hovers on the edge of respectable articulation in the newspaper reporting. In contrast to the opening, the end of the novel is the clearest image of enlightenment and transmission. The final paragraph opens with 'I recognise it' and closes 'the connection will be made, the circuit completed'. The narrator's wife will be 'released'; he will return with his family, his children will stand on the wreck: all that is required is that he fulfil the compulsion to 'write my way back to this moment'.[31]

From Hell opens with the image of a dead gull on a beach and closes with the gull floating out to sea. On the simplest level this is a reference to William Gull, whose dead body is the guarantee of the non-transmission of the secret. In the opening panels there are also oblique references to blindness: Robert Lees, the clairvoyant who claimed to have had psychic insight into the murders,[32] confides to retired Inspector Abberline that his visions are not real, he cannot 'see'. The end is more equivocal, much more broken than Sinclair's expansive confidence in telling the story. Chronologically, the prologue is actually long after the murders: Lees and Abberline's conversation on the beach takes place in 1923, and in the construction of the graphic novel there are in fact a number of endings. In the last chapter the ending is the asylum attendant pronouncing 'He's gone' over Gull's body.[33] The end of the epilogue returns to Lees and Abberline

on the beach and to Abberline's statement 'Now there's just us, knowin'
what we know, both washed up 'ere. Can't send a message, can't tell
anybody',[34] which is the flattest denial of the possibility of the transmission of meaning. The final image in the epilogue is the floating dead gull
against a black sky, like a message in a bottle that is uncertain of reception. But there follow two appendices, the first composed of very extensive footnotes which end with a suggestion that Mary Kelly escaped her
death, and the second, 'Dance of the Gull Catchers', a mocking and self-
mocking commentary on 'Ripper-hunting' which closes with a mourning
for the loss of Spitalfields in contemporary development. The text reads
'It's going. It's all going', and the last image is of a gull in flight, with the
text 'We were looking at a naked woman dancing when it flew away'.[35]
The 'it' that flies away is syntactically uncertain; 'it' appears no longer to
be the original quarry, Jack the Ripper, but the authentic life of
Whitechapel, of London itself, threatened by refurbishment.

At the end of *White Chappell*, the burned and buried hulk that
Sinclair's narrator recognizes is the barge of Hinton's father's funeral
pyre, the moment of the original loss of meaning for Hinton, and therefore, by extension, the origin of Jack. Its return in the text, like the return
of Moore's gull, is not as the same object, but as the object the-same-but-
different, decoded, meaningful. As Sinclair has said earlier in his text:

> We can't just carry on repeating the same myths: until we arrive at a fresh
> version. An authentic replica of our own making. We must use what we have
> been given: go back over the Ripper text, turn each cell of it – until it means
> something else, something beyond us. Otherwise we never over-reach our
> obsessions. We're doomed not to relive the past, but to die into it.[36]

The effort of unpacking the metaphors seems to be, for Sinclair at least,
a kind of exorcism that allows us to accept our own passing. The solution to be sought is not of the crime, but of larger questions of human
existence. What can finally be transmitted is not the identity of the murderer, but only the possibility of further narrative.

Story-time

Both Sinclair and Moore are deeply concerned with the nature of time
and the place of human consciousness within it, and neither appears convinced of anything like an acceptance of conventional linearity. In his
analysis of Conan Doyle, Brooks suggests that, 'if the plotting of a solution leads to a place ... this opens up temporal constructions which redi-
rect attention to the object of [the] search, which then in turn opens
up a new temporal recess, onto history'.[37] In straightforward terms,

the manifestations of this in *White Chappell* and *From Hell* are quite clear. The plotting of the solutions, such as they are, always leads to a place, or rather to a series of places. The sites of the murders are minor points on lines that point to the more significant nodes, principally Hawksmoor's churches and most important among those, Christ Church, Spitalfields. The temporal recess that is opened in visiting the sites is, at its simplest level, the past in the form of the autumn of 1888 and the recollection of those events. In the novels, however, the recesses appear to open in directions that include the future. The echoed actions and characters in *White Chappell* indicate this more obliquely, but *From Hell* renders it explicitly. In one panel, we see from the perspective of Gull (that is, we see as if *we* are in 1888) as a man opens his curtains and a television is visible in the room behind him.[38] Later, in a whole-page image, we again see from behind Gull as he raises his bloody knife in front of a towering modern office block (8, 40). The sequence of the mutilation of Kelly's body occurs simultaneously in Gull's past, his future and the twentieth century. Events, such as murder, are produced not only out of a past, but also out of a future. For example, both Moore and Sinclair notice Brady Street in Whitechapel and make a connection to Ian Brady, the Moors murderer. They read it not just as the future murders in some way being produced from the past, but as the murders of 1888 somehow being impelled from the future. What both narratives make clear is that the temporal recesses are not just the past, but time itself.

Questions of time are again central to narrative theory and are, to some extent, issues of the relation of spatiality and temporality and of the relations of different kinds of time. Shlomith Rimmon-Kenan claims that 'text-time' – the time of the novel – is a 'spatial, not a temporal dimension' because it has no time other than that taken to read it.[39] Text-time is inescapably linear, one-directional and irreversible because we read one word after another. Story-time, on the other hand, is multi lineal. The earlier quotation from Sinclair which speaks of assembling all the incomplete movement is revealing in this respect, but his and Moore's novels arrive at the disruption of temporal and spatial expectations through an element that is also part of both stories: Howard Hinton's theory of the fourth dimension.[40]

This is the description of it from *White Chappell*, which paraphrases Hinton's own writings:

[a] system of lines, nearly upright, sloping in different directions, connected to a rigid framework. He proposed that this framework be passed through a horizontal fluid plane which stretched at right angles to the direction of the motion. There would be the appearance of a multitude of moving points in the plane, equal in number to the straight lines in the system. We have

got to imagine some stupendous whole wherein all that ever came into being or will come co-exists.[41]

It seems that both writers conceive of the text as a time machine in the fashion of Hinton's description, in which the text is the rigid framework that passes through the fluid plane of reading, its motion being in the inevitable single direction that Rimmon-Kenan refers to. The moving points that are apparent to the reader during the process of reading are flickering indications of the lines that make up the stupendous whole, the totality of all events and experiences. The definition of 'text' is important here. It is fundamental to both Moore and Sinclair that landscape and architecture are also texts that function as time machines in the same fashion as writing. Sites are similar rigid frameworks that move in one direction (forward in time), but that are rendered multiply significant by the process of reading.

Sinclair's texts are a good deal more opaque than Moore's, tending to deliver the flickering points of the stupendous whole with the minimum of explication. Moore, through his writing and Campbell's drawings, gives a more easily accessible version of the same idea. The best example is Chapter 14 of *From Hell*, in which we witness Gull's death in an asylum. In 'text-time' it is twenty-five pages long and takes perhaps ten minutes to read. The duration of the action is also only a few minutes, intended to produce a sense of a 'real time' in reading. What is depicted, though, is 'an invisible curve, rising through the centuries'[42] that shows William Blake encountering the soul of a flea, the Moors murderers as adults, Ian Brady as a child, Robert Louis Stevenson's dream of Jekyll and Hyde, Peter Sutcliffe at work in a cemetery, Netley's death and Mary Kelly alive in 1905. As much as it reveals the notion of narrative as time machine, this section also makes clear something more problematic in the two novels: a sense of the presence of evil as an eternal force. In the context of Jack the Ripper, Brady, Myra Hindley and Peter Sutcliffe this comes close to suggesting that the sexual murder of women and children is somehow a metaphysical inevitability that has always happened and will always happen, refusing any social or cultural accountability for such events. This is a position fiercely resisted by feminist critics particularly,[43] and despite some self-conscious gestures in *White Chappell* and *From Hell*, it is not a problem that the novels resolve.

The use of Hinton's fourth-dimensional theory is one of the ways that the novels simultaneously tell and reflect upon their plots, but they also reflect upon the plots of others. Both novels are crowded with other texts. Principal among the numerous named and unnamed books in Sinclair's pages is Conan Doyle's first Sherlock Holmes story, *A Study in Scarlet*, published in December 1887. It is Nicholas Lane, the vomiting book dealer, who discovers a unique variant of the novella in the opening chapter of *White Chappell*. Its discovery is foreshadowed in one place by the narrator's description of himself as 'the Late Watson', but it is always about to arrive, presaged by the nesting of Doyle's title inside Sinclair's. *A Study in Scarlet* is always about to arrive in another sense too: the inescapable tie of Holmes to Jack the Ripper. If the victims are 'locked together like a famous football team',[44] so are Jack the Ripper and figures of fin-de-siècle fiction. Sinclair articulates a reason for this:

> certain fictions, chiefly Conan Doyle, Stevenson, but many others also, laid out a template that was more powerful than any local documentary account – the presences that they created ... became too much and too fast to be contained within the conventional limits of that fiction. They got out into the stream of time, the ether; they escaped into the labyrinth. They achieved an independent existence.[45]

These texts are being proposed as ones that function in something like Hinton's fourth dimension, propelling their characters beyond any fixed temporal or spatial location. Moore also shares the conviction of the ability of certain fictional figures to escape into the ether; another of his works, *The League of Extraordinary Gentlemen*, releases a group of *fin-de-siècle* characters – Mina Harker, Jekyll and Hyde, Allan Quatermain, the Invisible Man and Captain Nemo – into a densely intertextual, reimagined, 1890s London.

The narrative machine

The density of the loops of intertextuality and repetition increases as the novels proceed, particularly in *White Chappell*. The hovering sense in reading Sinclair's novel is an anxiety of the possible short-circuiting of narrative, of it collapsing into stasis under the weight of its circulations, the temptation to over-sameness that will slow the story into quiescence. Sinclair's text pulls strongly in this direction because it constantly draws people and places into analogy, the literary space where difference is reduced and restricted. For example, the imagined copy of *A Study in Scarlet* is destroyed in one of the many acts of violence against books in the novel. Nicholas Lane, whose damaged abdomen has already marked him as a proxy for the victims, is further identified with them: as the book is shredded he too is assaulted and his kidney detached. The gesture is clear: in the so-called 'double event' of 30 September 1888 Elizabeth Stride's body was identified by her partner, Michael Kidney, and Catherine Eddowes's kidney was removed and later, as the writer claimed, enclosed with the infamous 'From Hell' letter, sent to the chairman of the Whitechapel Vigilance Committee.

Books and dealers are interchangeable as victims in the novel, and their relationship also has the perverse intimacy of murderer and victim. The pursuit of *A Study in Scarlet* mirrors the pursuit of Mary Kelly, and both the book and the body are ultimately destroyed beyond recognition. The gang that destroys the book and assaults Lane is a twentieth-century version of the Old Nichol gang, generally believed to have carried out the fatal attack on Emma Smith in April 1888. One of the dealers is described as 'book ripper, bladesman, rapidly slicing', another as liking nothing better than 'to cleave ... to slash ... like a blade', and a third as exacting a terrible revenge in the secret razoring of volumes.[46] The licensed violence of surgery is overlaid with the illegitimate violence of the murders; Dr Gull is juxtaposed with Dr Treves and the latter's exhibition of John Merrick, the Elephant Man, with the spectacle of the prostitutes' ruined bodies. Thus the analogies spiral: the dealers are like the streets, which are like the books, which are like the victims, which are like the dealers, which are like the killers, which are like the streets, and so on. The pull of analogy towards stasis threatens the possibility of reaching an end, the prospect of the proliferation of likeness becomes infinite and there begins to seem no likelihood of the movement beyond it.

The frustration or anxiety of these dilatory middle sections is, however, necessary. The middle is the space of transformation. It is 'an operation in two directions: it affirms at once resemblance and difference; it puts time into motion and suspends it ... it allows discourse to acquire meaning without this meaning becoming pure information; in a word, it makes narrative possible and reveals its very definition'.[47] The transformation that is taking place is of the opening blinded metaphor to the closing moment of the possibility of transmission of meaning. What becomes apparent is that meaning acquired is not the 'pure information' of who might or might not be Jack the Ripper. That question becomes less and less important as the texts proceed, and the desire that is revealed is the desire for narrative itself. The transformation of the middle in *White Chappell* and *From Hell* produces meaningfulness because it casts 'Ripper hunting' as the desire, not for the name of the Ripper, but to tell the story. As Brooks observes, 'there is simply no end to narrative on this model, since there is no solution to the crime. The narrative plotting in its entirety is the solution'.[48] Ultimately, we can see Jack the Ripper not just as a killing machine but as a narrative machine that can only produce more versions, more stories and more narratives of writing itself.

Notes

1 Alan Moore and Eddie Campbell, *From Hell* (London: Knockabout, 2000), ch. 4, pp. 37–8. *From Hell* came out intermittently and under various imprints between 1989 and 1998. It was published in a complete edition in 1999. All subsequent references are to the 2000 reprint and are given as chapter and page numbers.

2 Mark Seltzer, *Serial Killers: Life and Death in America's Wound Culture* (London: Routledge, 1998), p. 9.

3 Diana Fuss, 'Monsters of Perversion: Jeffrey Dahmer and The Silence of the Lambs', in M. Garber, S. Matlock and R. Walkowitz (eds), *Media Spectacles* (London: Routledge, 1993), p. 199.

4 Moore and Campbell, *From Hell*, ch. 6, p. 25.

5 Seltzer, *Serial Killers*, p. 15.

6 John Douglas and Mark Olshaker, *Mindhunter: Inside the FBI's Elite Serial Crime Unit* (London: Arrow Books, 1995), pp. 32–3.

7 Donald Rumbelow, *The Complete Jack the Ripper*, rev. edn (London: Penguin, 2004); Paul Begg, *Jack the Ripper: The Definitive History* (London: Pearson, 2003); Philip Sugden, *The Complete History of Jack the Ripper*, rev. edn (London: Robinson, 2002).

8 This distinction appears in Boris Tomashevsky, 'Thematics' (1925) in *Russian Formalist Criticism: Four Essays*, ed. and trans. L. T. Lemon and M. J. Reis (Lincoln and London: University of Nebraska Press, 1965), pp. 61–98.

9 Jonathan Culler, 'Fabula and Sjuzet in the Analysis of Narrative', *Poetics Today*, 1:3 (1980), p. 28.

10 Peter Brooks, *Reading for the Plot* (Cambridge, MA: Harvard University Press, 1984), p. 13.

11 Brooks, *Reading*, p. 13.

12 Brooks, *Reading*, pp. 11–12.

13 Brooks, *Reading*, p. 24.

14 Tzvetzan Todorov, *The Poetics of Prose*, trans. Richard Culler (Oxford: Blackwell, 1977), p. 45.

15 Todorov, *Poetics*, p. 46.

16 Todorov, *Poetics*, p. 45.

17 Stephen Knight, *Jack the Ripper: The Final Solution* (London: Harrap, 1976), p. 208.

18 Mrs Havelock Ellis (Edith Lees), *James Hinton: A Sketch* (London: Stanley Paul & Co., 1918), p. 102.

19 Ellis, *James Hinton*, pp. 215–16.

20 One of these books, *What is the Fourth Dimension?*, was published in 1887.

21 Iain Sinclair, *White Chappell, Scarlet Tracings* ([1987] London: Granta, 1998), p. 111.

22 Moore and Campbell, *From Hell*, ch. 4, p. 19.

23 Sinclair, *White Chappell*, p. 35.

24 Sinclair, *White Chappell*, p. 61.
25 Paul Ricoeur, 'Narrative Time', in W. J. T. Mitchell (ed.), *On Narrative* (Chicago: University of Chicago Press, 1981), p. 167.
26 Sinclair, *White Chappell*, p. 151.
27 Sinclair, *White Chappell*, p. 59.
28 David Canter, *Mapping Murder* (London: Virgin, 2003).
29 Canter, *Mapping Murder*, p. 89.
30 Brooks, *Reading for the Plot*, pp. 26–7. In his usage of the terms metaphor and metonymy Brooks is following Roman Jakobson, where metaphor depends upon the juxtaposition of things not normally found together and metonymy is the substitution of a part, attribute, cause or effect of a thing for the thing itself. See Roman Jakobson, 'The Metaphoric and Metonymic Poles', in David Lodge and Nigel Wood (eds), *Modern Criticism and Theory*, 2nd edn (London: Longman, 2000).
31 Sinclair, *White Chappell*, p. 210.
32 Although, according to his diary, Lees certainly offered his psychic assistance to the police, there is no evidence that the offer was taken up. The story that he led police to a physician's house in the West End, where blood-stained clothing was found and the physician admitted to loss of memory, seems to have been the creation of enterprising journalists, appearing first in the *Chicago Sunday Times Herald* in April 1895. See also Rumbelow, *Complete Jack the Ripper*, pp. 221–3.
33 Moore and Campbell, *From Hell*, ch. 14, p. 25.
34 Moore and Campbell, *From Hell*, Epilogue, p. 9.
35 Moore and Campbell, *From Hell*, Appendix 2, p. 24.
36 Sinclair, *White Chappell*, p. 198.
37 Brooks, *Reading*, pp. 26–7.
38 Moore and Campbell, *From Hell*, ch. 7, p. 24; ch. 8, p. 40; ch. 10, pp. 9–22.
39 Shlomith Rimmon-Kenan, *Narrative Fiction: Contemporary Poetics* (London: Routledge, 1983), p. 44.
40 See Rudy Rucker (ed.), *Selected Writings of C.H. Hinton* (New York: Dover, 1980).
41 Sinclair, *White Chappell*, p. 112.
42 Moore and Campbell, *From Hell*, ch. 14, p. 17.
43 See, for example, Jane Caputi, *The Age of Sex Crime* (London: The Women's Press, 1988); Deborah Cameron and Elizabeth Frazer, *The Lust to Kill: A Feminist Investigation of Sexual Murder* (Cambridge: Polity, 1987).
44 Sinclair, *White Chappell*, p. 50.
45 Sinclair, *White Chappell*, p. 128; p. 9.
46 Sinclair, *White Chappell*, pp. 15, 68, 99.
47 Todorov, *Poetics*, p. 75.
48 Brooks, *Reading*, p. 33.

Part II
Culture

6

The Ripper writing: a cream of a nightmare dream

Clive Bloom

Jack of Hearts, Jack O'Lantern, Jack the Giant-Killer, Jack the Lad, Jack Sheppard and Springheeled Jack; 'Jack', a common name that represents ubiquity: the nomenclature of the ordinary. In the late nineteenth century, as in the late twentieth, there was only one Jack – *the Ripper*; of the famous nineteenth-century criminals this one alone has endured into legend. Of Charlie Peace, Neill Cream or Israel Lipski little is remembered; of other famous murders only the victim is recalled: Maria Marten offering herself to melodrama and Fanny Adams to a coarse joke. Jack survives, but not merely because he was not caught.

This chapter is an attempt to consider the determinants and the progress of the Ripper legend as both text and history and to consider the constellation of historico-psychological notions that have gathered around the name of the Ripper.

Jack, it seems, timed his murders at a correct psychological moment, for almost immediately, not least for their ferocity, his deeds became the stuff of legend. He instantly became both a particular and a general threat, a focus for numerous related fears among metropolitan dwellers across Europe and America. One newspaper late in 1888 declared:

> The Whitechapel murderer, having been arrested all over the metropolis and in several provincial towns, is now putting in an appearance in various foreign countries, and also in the United States of America. ... [He is] a Russian with a religious mania ... murdering Magdalens in order that their souls may go to heaven, or [on New York advice] ... [He is] a butcher, whose mind is affected by changes of the moon.[1]

Already, only one month after the murders had ceased, Jack has an international 'appeal'. His ubiquitous nature allows him appearances on both sides of the Atlantic and he is claimed by or accused of being a variety of nationalities. The article is already in light-hearted mood and Jack has taken on the serio-comic aspects of Sweeney Todd, himself a type of 'butcher'. Not only may he be both a Russian religious and sexual fanatic, but he may also be a New Yorker under biblical delusions (which the paper places under the 'Ezekiel Theory'). The Russian is not merely a religious fanatic but also a 'nihilist' and a member of a 'secret society' – Russia (the paper tells its readers) being notorious for secret societies. Thus, Jack becomes the focal point for an attack on foreigners (in particular Russians) and especially foreigners who are bent on undermining society in secret via covertly ritualized murder.

This mixture of grim charnel humour, political and religious fear, xenophobia and sexual innuendo (those journalistic 'Magdalens') partook of the atmosphere during the murders. At one end of the spectrum *Punch* (13 October 1888) dedicated a doggerel verse to the Ripper around a cartoon of Jack as a Mephistopheles bill-posting London with his latest exploits. This lampoon of the recent 'pennydreadfuls' and 'Ripperana' was matched more seriously by the upsurge of anti-foreign agitation fanned by phantom messages (supposedly by the Ripper) accusing 'the Juwes', and by the Assistant Metropolitan Police Commissioner's claim that 'in stating that he [Jack] was a Polish Jew [he was] merely stating a definitely established fact' (which nearly started a pogrom in the East End).

On 13 February 1894 the *Sun*, a sensationalist newspaper, began printing a piece of popular investigative journalism about the 'real' Ripper, traced by 'WK', one of the staff reporters, to Broadmoor, 'a living tomb of a lunatic asylum' where the 'greatest murder mystery of the nineteenth century' was about to be solved by Jack the Ripper's 'confession'. This further accretion to the legend attempted to locate Jack in the world of 'debased' humanity in Broadmoor where inmates (and especially Jack) showed no moral awareness of the import of their deeds. In linking his home life to 'Camden Town' and his criminal insanity to Broadmoor the paper ably accused middle-class prudery of responsibility for Jack's upbringing. Nevertheless, the paper absolved that same class from blame by accepting that, in contrast to Jack, the paper's readers obviously possessed moral awareness. Curiosity was thus legitimized by a veneer of morality.[2]

Unlike the clippings of the 1880s, this series put together insanity and the middle class. The murders were already thought of as the work of a depraved doctor. Nevertheless, the linking of 'the greatest murder mystery' and a 'living tomb' put together mysteriousness and living death in a way guaranteed *not* to reveal the killer's identity and certain to increase sales of the *Sun* for the duration of the series. Moreover, the paper could congratulate itself and its readers on tracking down the perpetrator without undoing the 'edge' of fear they wished to create – for, as the paper clearly stated, this lunatic had *escaped* in order to kill. So horrible was he, so morally unaware, that armed guards stood about his bed. Jack's ubiquity is therefore reinforced by his unnamed status (he is identified only by initials) and by the hints of his origins and his ability to vanish from the lunatic asylum at will if not guarded. The lunatic asylum was represented by the paper as a type of purgatorial doom from which the 'living dead' returned to reap vengeance on the twilight world of the living (twilight, precisely because the victims were prostitutes). One mysterious world preys on another. Indeed, by returning from Broadmoor the journalist literally returns from the dead to tell his tale.

Medical and criminological science are used in this series to reinforce secrecy and threat; commercialism dictates the possibility of other (and) endless articles on the Ripper.

However, even during the season of the killings in the autumn of 1888, papers quickly realized the value of Jack's exploits, conducting their own post-mortems and reporting coroner's verdicts at length. *The Times*, for instance, ran articles in its *Weekly Edition* from September 1888 to November 1888. On 28 September 1888 it gave a full page to the social background of Spitalfields and the poverty endured there by Annie Chapman, the Ripper's first victim. *The Times* was quick to guess the direction in which police might look. They thought a post-mortem surgeon's assistant might be the culprit because of 'his' specialized knowledge of the uterus, which was removed from the victim's body.

The Times further noted the curious circumstance of an American surgeon who wished to include real uteri with a journal he was mailing to clients. Could this bizarre surgeon, whose name was not known, have prompted the killer to get 'a uterus for the £20 reward?' asked the paper. In a later issue, next to the report of other Ripper murders, a clergyman protested in a long letter at the condemnation of the destitute by the middle classes, at their hypocrisy over prostitution and at their ignorance of the conditions prevailing in the East End. He concluded that this had 'blotted the pages of our Christianity'.[3]

The freakish, of which the nineteenth century was inordinately fond, found itself beside the missionary, which in its guise as Mayhew, Engels or Booth consistently restated the ordinariness of the 'freak' (the destitute, the prostitute, the opium addict, the derelict). 'Body snatching' (and the notion of a uterus as a 'free gift' with a new journal) then weirdly allies itself with murder for greed (the reward offered of £20) and murder as the act of the desperately destitute. Jack becomes the focus for the bizarre in the ordinary misery of everyday life in the metropolitan slums. Jack the murderer becomes Jack *the missionary* who focused on problems other investigators were unable to bring to such a wide audience. Murder allowed for social reform. The newspapers, by keeping Jack the centre of attention, ironically kept the slum problems central too.

After reports covering three months by *The Times* and *The Times Weekly Edition*, the newspaper concluded that 'the murderer seems to have vanished, leaving no trace of his identity ... with even greater mystery'.[4] Jack the Ripper, given his *nom de guerre* by Fleet Street, was the first major figure to offer himself to, and to become a creation of, journalism. By the 1880s newspapers commanded audiences large enough to make Jack a major figure of international interest rather than a local folktale figure for the East End of London.[5] The power of journalism and the crowded warrens of the central city of the Empire together provided ground for the dissemination of the legend, a legend based upon both fear *and* curiosity – a terrible ambivalence. The possibilities for the dissemination of *rumour* could never be more fortuitous, and letters from 'Jack' fed interest and added to the atmosphere of uncertainty.

Indeed, Jack's letters themselves may have been the work of an entrepreneurial journalist providing 'copy' for himself. These letters, conveying a black humour and a certain 'bravado',[6] may be read not merely as the realization of the power (for the first time) of the mass media but, whether authentic or fake, as yet another accretion to the fictionalizing of the Ripper and the self-advertizing and self-confidence of an entrepreneurial murderer (acquiring kudos by self-advertisement).

These letters convey a music-hall atmosphere and a self-important theatricality through which the Ripper's letters create an imaginary persona for the perpetrator. Addressed to 'the Old Boss', and signed (at least once) 'from Hell', Jack goes into his music-hall act for the bewildered audience – appalled, amazed (and applauding) the virtuoso performance. 'He' tells us that:

> I was goin' to hopperate again close to your ospitle – just as i was goin to drop my nife along at er bloomin throte them curses of coppers spoilt the game but i guess i will be on the job soon and will send you another bitt of innerd.

In another letter he finds the search for his identity a source of amusement: 'They say I am a doctor now. Ha! Ha!'

Each letter becomes a performance put on by an actor assuming a part. The letter-writing gives a self-importance to the writer, and a grandeur and status which is uncompromised by capture and identification. Hence, this letter activity becomes, for the legend at least, as important as the deeds themselves – just as Davy Crockett or P. T. Barnum were to make legends of their own lives by writing their 'autobiographies' and adventures.

The Ripper letters are a form of *true-life confession* heightened to the level of a fiction which embraces a 'cockney' persona, a sense of black humour, a melodramatic villain ('them curses of coppers') and a ghoul (sending 'innerds'), and mixes it with a sense of the dramatic and a feeling for a rhetorical climax. In these letters life and popular theatre come together to act upon the popular imagination. The Ripper (now possibly many 'Rippers' all reporting their acts) autographs his work as a famous artist (death as creativity) – anonymous and yet totally well known. Here, confession only adds to confusion (even Neill Cream claimed to be the Ripper). Jack's letter 'from Hell' concludes 'catch me when you can', adding a sense of challenge and a stronger 'hint' at the frustration of authority in its quest to identify the murderer.[7]

By the time of these letters Jack has ceased to be one killer but has become a multiplicity of performing personas for the popular imagination. The possibility of copycat crimes (although finally dismissed from at least two other 'torso' cases) lent to Jack the amorphous ability to inhabit more than one physical body (a point which I shall develop later).

Consequently, for the late nineteenth century, the Ripper became a type of 'folk' character whose exploits spilled into the twentieth century via cinema, theatre and fiction. The Ripper has been tracked and traced by numerous writers after a positive identity. Writers have named a Russian doctor called Konovalov (Donald McCormick), the Duke of Clarence (Thomas Stowell), William Gull (Stephen Knight), Montague Druitt (Daniel Farson) and J. K. Stephen (Michael Harrison) as possible candidates. Each, in his turn, has been refuted – the 'royal theory' being denied by Walter Sickert's son Joseph, who dismissed it as a hoax that he had played on an over-receptive author. The 'debate' heats up every few years with new flushes of theory and further refutations, while works such as Stephen Knight's *Jack the Ripper: The Final Solution* added to the growing heap of books searching for scandal in suburbia or in the Freemasons, in highest government or the royal family.[8] Knight, himself a journalist, stated that 'the evil presence of Jack the Ripper still seems to haunt ... the imagination of crime investigators', and he noted that in the 1970s letters were still arriving from people claiming knowledge of or claiming actually to be 'the Ripper'.[9] In the twentieth century Jack became the centre of a conspiracy debate. Indeed, so vast is the volume of literature to date that Alexander Kelly was able to write an article for *The Assistant Librarian* about his compilation of a bibliography of 'Ripperana and Ripperature'.[10]

The Ripper literature, however, is far from confined to the work of amateur sleuths (and they are a study in themselves) but extends to both fiction and film. Such fictionalization began almost immediately in 1889 with J. F. Brewer's *The Curse upon Mitre Square* and has continued in a steady stream of writers including Frank Wedekind (1895),

Marie Belloc-Lowndes (1911), Robert Bloch (1943) and many others. The Ripper has also made appearances in science fiction and fantasy tales, has been a staple of thriller movies and has appeared in opera (Alban Berg's *Lulu*) and pop music (a single by 'Lord Sutch').[11] As Kim Newman points out, 'The Ripper' is a type of *given* of a certain landscape – a required designation or focus for a number of traits.[12] Jack the Ripper is a name for both a necessary fiction and a fact missing its history. Here fiction and history meet and mutate so that the Ripper can be searched for by 'historians' of crime at the very same moment that he can appear in a Batman comic. Separable from his origins, the Ripper is a strange historicized fiction, a designation for a type of murderer and his scenario (for the game is to give 'Jack' his real name and collapse fiction into biography), while also being a structural necessity for a type of fictional genre: the author of the 'Dear Boss' letter, etc. The Ripper is never quite the same person as the slayer of several prostitutes:

> Whereas popular heroes ... usually have their origins in a particular work or body of fiction, they break free from the originating textual conditions of their existence to achieve a semi-independent existence, functioning as an established point of cultural reference that is capable of working – of producing meanings – even for those who are not directly familiar with the original texts in which they first made their appearance.[13]

This dual movement and reciprocity can be seen clearly in the parallel claims made on the Ripper by the latest 'biographer' and by the artists and scriptwriters of Batman. As has been said of Adolf Hitler, that other bogy man of the twentieth century, the figure overshadows the circumstances and as with Hitler so the Ripper acts as 'a dark mirror held up to Mankind'.[14] It was indeed the appearance and exposure of the Hitler diaries that were uppermost in researchers' minds when the 'Diary' of the Ripper was itself published in 1993.[15] Apart from the simple matter of authentication, the 'Hitler' and 'Ripper' diaries are curious mirror images: the Hitler diaries represent a scandal of celebrity while the Ripper diaries represent a scandal in the ordinary; the Hitler diaries were needed as proof of innocence (of the persecution of the Jews and of warmongering) while the Ripper diaries were needed as proof of guilt (of a psychopathic personality); both sets of diaries purported to be major documents authenticating the narrative and nature of historical process. Whatever the two sets of documents actually represent, they both attempt to put a *face* and fix a character on to two historical figures whose evil actions are at once ambivalently symbolic and legendary and yet specific and located. This ambivalence seems irreconcilable with the nature of the facts of either case as the facts are themselves transmogrified into symbolic co-ordinates for the transmission of the two legends; in this way authentication acts as a means of refictionalizing the subjects under scrutiny. Each stage is simply more authentic (less fictional) than the last in a chain of never-ending speculation.

In chasing the identity of the Ripper and in placing his personality upon numerous more or less well-known historical characters (the latest being James Maybrick), investigators acknowledge the bizarre silence at the heart of the tale, a place where history has closed in upon itself and refused its *fact*. History becomes an abyss antagonistic to its own determinants and played upon by conspiracy in the fiction of the secret of Jack's identity. Scanning the grim, grainy, obscure picture taken of Mary Kelly's eviscerated body as if in search of clues we become dabblers in the oracular and the occult. In her photo the Ripper steps out of Victorian history to become the *epitome* of Victorian history, its embodiment and spokesman.

It is hardly surprising that Jack the Ripper has passed so easily into the world of fiction. Jack's most recent incarnation has been in the pages of DC Comics' *Gotham by Gaslight* as the opponent of Batman himself.[16] Dedicated to 'Elsa Lanchester, the Bride of Frankenstein' and with an introduction by Robert Bloch, Jack the Ripper travels across the Atlantic to Gotham City for his final showdown. The comic treats Batman with the same seriousness as the Ripper, and Bruce Wayne's own biography is rewritten and reauthenticated during the story (indeed is integral to the Ripper's identity). In such a context, Batman is as 'real' as the Ripper and using a 'what if' scenario he is placed not in 1940s or 1950s America but back in time – the 1880s. Who else would the greatest comic crime fighter confront in a steam-driven Gotham but the Ripper, only worthy opponent of the Bat? (Just as Sherlock Holmes had been pitted against the Ripper in the film *The Seven Per Cent Solution*.) Both Batman and Jack the Ripper become designationary loci for a scene and a moment. As such, Batman is every bit as real as the Ripper, inhabiting a location every bit as real and as distant as the foggy streets of London. New York/Gotham City or Victorian London, Jack the Ripper and Batman are the locations and the inhabitants of a certain modernity. As Robert Bloch points out (writing as the Ripper), 'Batman? Yes I know the name'.[17] Batman's authenticity (*the* Batman as he has now become) and the status of his myth are reaffirmed in our ability to accept the migration of his character into a historical past. That Jack the Ripper awaits him is confirmation of his status; that there is parallel publication of Ripperological works and comic books only heightens the reciprocity between the production methods of two different yet dependent forms of publishing. As Geoffrey Fletcher commented, 'hence it is that Jack belongs not only to the criminologist, but also to folklore'.[18]

The first part of this chapter dealt with the rapid dissemination of the Ripper legend and its endurance in popular publishing. I now wish to turn to the constellation of possibilities around which this publishing industry revolved and upon which the legend was built.

It is obvious that any legend requires a small and possibly spectacular fact to unleash a great deal of 'fiction'. Before turning to the legend as a type of 'fictional' genre it is necessary to consider the Ripper legend as revolving around (a) a series of bizarre and ferocious crimes, (b) an impotent and mocked authority (the Criminal Investigation Department being left totally in the dark and being criticized from Windsor), (c) a mysterious and unapprehended felon, and (d) the power of fiction and the use of the human sciences.[19]

The murders of autumn 1888 allowed for the appearance of a new urban dweller, a dweller on the limits of society and yet fully integrated into it – the homicidal maniac, *the psychopathic killer.* Unlike de Sade, the psychopath is always *in disguise*; his intentions and his secret actions are on another plain from his social responsibilities. Consequently, the psychopath delineates that absolute psychological and mental 'deterioration' that Kraepelin had considered as a form of dementia praecox and that was not defined as schizophrenia until 1911. The Ripper, however, was seen as split not merely in personality but in *morality* as well. The case of the psychopath is a case not of deterioration of mental power but of a demonic engulfing of the egotistic soul by a monstrous and sensuous will. Here the psychopath unites theology and science, unites the lowest and the highest impulses in his society. The psychopath is ill and yet suffers only from an overwhelming need to impose his will on his surroundings. The psychopath 'lets go' only in order to secrete his lost personality more fully in those daylight hours of responsibility. The demonic had not yet lost its force in the 1880s, reinforced as it was by scientific research.

In order to explore the paradox of the psychopath more fully we can turn to the popular fiction of the 1880s. Robert Louis Stevenson's *Dr Jekyll and Mr Hyde* was published in 1886, two years before 'Jack' made his own spectacular appearance.

Stevenson's story deals specifically with split personality – split between the sensual and the socially and morally responsible. Jekyll is the epitome of middle-class propriety, living in a street described as having houses with 'freshly painted shutters, well polished brasses and general cleanliness', while Hyde is a monstrous and 'ape-like' maniac who lives amid the sexual depravity of Soho: 'that dismal quarter of Soho seen under these changing glimpses, with its muddy ways, and slatternly passengers, and its lamps, which had never been extinguished or had been kindled afresh to combat this mournful reinvasion of darkness, seemed, in the lawyer's eyes, like a district of some city in a nightmare'.[20]

This duality of personality and class (the more working-class the more depraved) is considerably complicated by Stevenson's own mixing of Darwinism and pseudo-science. Degeneracy for Stevenson (as for Edgar Allan Poe in 'The Murders in the Rue Morgue') is a decline into an animal state – the noble savage has become the sex-crazed ape. However, this motif (repeated by Rider Haggard in *She*) is interrupted by a 'psychological' study of Jekyll from whose dark side Hyde is generated. Jekyll has always been aware of his dual nature:

> Hence it came about that I concealed my pleasures; and ... I stood already committed to a profound duplicity of life ... that made me what I was and, with even a deeper trench than in the majority of men, severed in me those provinces of good and ill which divide and compound man's dual nature. In this case, I was driven to reflect deeply and inveterately on that hard law of life which lies at the root of religion, and is one of the most plentiful springs of distress. Though so profound a double-dealer, I was in no sense a hypocrite; both sides of me were in dead earnest; I was no more myself when I laid aside restraint and plunged in shame, than when I laboured, in the eye of day, at the furtherance of knowledge or the relief of sorrow and suffering. And it chanced that the direction of my scientific studies ... led wholly towards the mystic and the transcendental.[21]

Indeed, it is Jekyll's very aspirations toward the ideal that have caused his degeneracy. Such a duality makes Jekyll tell his friend that 'if [he is] the chief of sinners [he is] the chief of sufferers too'.[22]

Highlighted here is not schizophrenia as illness but Jekyll's schizoid nature as showing signs of *moral* degeneracy. Mental decay is seen as a consequence of original sin lurking in the hearts of all men of whatever class – the more denied (by the respectable) the more virulent its final outburst. Stevenson makes this quite plain in his description of Hyde's manic progress during the opening narrative. He lets his narrator tell us that 'then came the horrible part of the thing; for the man trampled calmly over the child's body and left her screaming on the ground. It sounds nothing to hear, but it was hellish to see. It wasn't like a man; it was like some damned Juggernaut'.[23]

Hyde becomes an abominable *it*, a desecration of the sanity of the human causing revulsion even in the doctor who witnesses the deed. Equally this combines with fear at the bizarre and freakish appearance of the culprit: 'There is something wrong with his appearance; something displeasing, something downright detestable. I never saw [a man] I so disliked, and yet I scarce know why. He must be deformed somewhere; he

6 The *Illustrated Police News* summarizes the investigation of the
Whitechapel murders.

gives a strong feeling of deformity'. Hyde combines animality and the
terror of the 'troglodytic' with fear of evil, for he has 'a kind of black
sneering coolness ... really like Satan'.[24]

This mixture of the animal and the devilish comes from the perverse
idealism of Jekyll, a scientist and pillar of society who is bent on unlock-
ing his *own* potential for experiencing the limits of perception through
the power of his own will. His science is therefore put to the cause of
metaphysical speculation. He tells us: 'it chanced that the direction of
my scientific studies ... led wholly toward the mystic and transcen-
dental'.[25] Here, then, the scientist manipulates the soul in order to
reorganize the nature of the body, for in destroying the 'fortress of identity' Jekyll employs science as if it were magic: 'man is not truly one, but
truly two'.[26]

Stevenson's short story became a massive popular hit when published.
In it he summed up the pseudo-science of the popular imagination as well
as the confused state of the emergent psychological sciences which were
'treating' schizophrenic patients. The psychopath (Mr Hyde is such
through his maniacal killing for killing's sake and the enjoyment he
gains) crosses the border of scientific discourse and acts as its limit,
beyond the rational explanations of form and natural function. Instead,
the psychopath takes us beyond science and before it into theology, into
the analysis of *sin*.

In picking up on this duality, Stevenson made repeated statements about the nature of evil and its relationship with insanity. He tells us:

> The pleasures which I made haste to seek in my disguise were, as I have said, undignified; I would scarce use a harder term. But in the hands of Edward Hyde they soon began to turn towards the monstrous. When I would come back from these excursions, I was often plunged into a kind of wonder at my vicarious depravity. This familiar that I called out of my own soul, and sent forth alone to do his good pleasure, was a being inherently malign and villainous; his every act and thought centred on self. ... The situation was apart from ordinary laws, and insidiously relaxed the grasp of conscience. It was Hyde, after all, and Hyde alone, that was guilty. Jekyll was no worse; he woke again to his good qualities seemingly unimpaired; he would even make haste, where it was possible, to undo the evil done by Hyde. And thus his conscience slumbered.[27]

Here the 'monstrous' connects with metalaws that organize consciousness but cannot escape from it, for will (according to Jekyll's philosophy) and the drive to power dominate the consciousness of mankind. According to Stevenson, from the socially responsible, the morally restrained and the intellectually ideal come anarchy, moral degeneracy and perversity dominated by a Calvinistic notion of predestined sin.

As with Jekyll and Hyde so Jack the Ripper too was seen as an inhuman, if not non-human, monster who combined possible middle-class respectability (a doctor or a surgeon) with lower working-class savagery (an immigrant, 'Leather-Apron', a mad butcher). The Ripper united both classes inasmuch as he was excluded by his acts from both (just as were his victims). The Ripper was both a technician (a post-mortem surgeon, a doctor, a butcher) and an insane lunatic (incapable of finesse). He was supposedly at once able to focus his aggression in anatomical detail and yet unable to curb its force. Thus, the forensic nature of the Ripper's 'work' (his 'job') provided a focal point for popular fears and prejudices against those professions dealing in the limits of the 'decent' (psychologists, doctors, post-mortem surgeons, forensic experts). The Ripper's supposed anatomical expertise suggested all sorts of horrible possibilities about the life of the 'expert' and the specialist. His ability with a knife united him to the very professionals paid to track him down.

Like Hyde, he was the *alter ego* of the police force, and the letters clearly demonstrate him showing off his expertise to them and the vigilante forces operating in Whitechapel. Later his dual nature as criminal and enforcer-of-law became explicit when reports of his deerstalker gave one attribute to the occupier of 221b Baker Street, whose business was forensic science, whose other real-life model was a surgeon and whose friend was a doctor.

Thus the Ripper was not merely a murderer but the catalyst for a series of psychological and social reactions. He combined the supposed popular idea of the expert as well as the darker side of the madman, lunatic, animal degenerate. As a median point between middle-class respectability and a debased Darwinian proletariat, the Ripper became the invisible man; like Jekyll he might well have said that 'for him in his impenetrable mantle, the safety was complete. Think of it – he did not exist!' The Ripper's letters acknowledge the pretence of cockney patois while pointing directly towards a middle-class author – but the author of what: a letter or the murders? The Ripper is both murderer and social 'reformer', both scientist and magician.

In the previous section of this chapter we saw that the combination of popular prejudice and fiction produced a character and a rationale for the Ripper *qua* murderer *and* respectable member of society. His split nature (if such it was or presumably had to be) was completed by a hypocrisy concerning the very people he killed (the 'Magdalens'). For these people were themselves invisible, acting as a certain outlet *and* limit to urban society. The psychopath and the prostitute were two ends of a society that refused to acknowledge their presence. Invisibly, they provided their services on the edge of the rational, morally degenerate as both supposedly were.

Yet Jack the Ripper's threat is one that spills back into 'ordinary' society and threatens that society. In the period when the legend of 'the Ripper' begins, the psychopath becomes an urban reality but as a character-type is not quite part of a mental spectrum and yet is not fully freed from being a theological problem either. Jack combines notions of evil, insanity and moral justice at the moment when the nineteenth century saw itself as the century of progress, enlightenment and escape from 'moral' prejudice. The Ripper's name denotes a certain consequent frontier for the human sciences at this time.

At the culminating point of the human sciences came the science of legitimized 'murder'. James Berry, the public executioner at the time of the 'Ripper' murders, wrote his autobiography in the 1890s and in it we see combined Jack's role as breaker and upholder of the law and of natural justice.[28] Berry, who became an abolitionist (he decapitated one of his clients because of an incorrect 'drop'), viewed his work as 'a job like any other'[29] and H. Snowden Ward in his appraisal called Berry 'tender-hearted'.[30] This businesslike and tender-hearted man carried out public executions and gave his rope to Madame Tussaud's. His contribution to the human sciences was to calculate the proportion of rope needed relative to body weight, in order to cause death without mutilation of the victim. He also endeavoured to 'understand' the mind of a murderer, whom, unlike the general public, he viewed as neither a 'fiend' nor a 'monster'.[31] He commented that he hoped he could 'advise his readers to consider that a murderer has as much right to judge the state as the state has to judge him',[32] which is an oddly radical comment for the ultimate enforcer of the state's law. Indeed, Berry saw quite clearly the anomaly of his position.[33] Hence he becomes both killer and killed, both culprit and revenger, both state appointee and state victim. Within Berry's own person these ambiguities were traced.

James Berry and Jack the Ripper are joined by the technology of death. This unites and yet ultimately separates their purposes, for Berry participates in the oddly humanitarian enterprise that Michel Foucault sees as a movement from torture to the timetable in dealing with miscreants. Berry, working in secret, takes on the onus of the executioner's task as a duty as well as a job. His book portrays a deep ambivalence as well as pride in work well done. The business of death puts professionalism at a premium. Berry's expertise is, however, the expertise of an almost defunct craftsman, for, although hanging remained for another eighty years, its power was severely limited and its function debilitated by secrecy and humanitarian concern. The acknowledged schizoid nature of the executioner begins to crack open in James Berry and his autobiography in his constant justifications and special pleading. The Ripper takes pride in his particular executions, for Jack belongs to another *older* tradition of execution.

Michel Foucault, quoting eighteenth-century sources, gives the grisly details of the form of public execution then required in France:

> The executioner, who had an iron bludgeon of the kind used in slaughter houses, delivered a blow with all his might on the temple of the wretch, who fell dead: the mortis exactor, who had a large knife, then cut his throat, which spattered him with blood; it was horrible sight to see; he severed the sinews near the two heels, and then opened up the belly from which he drew the heart, liver, spleen and lungs, which he stuck on an iron hook, and cut and dissected into pieces, which he then stuck on the other hooks as he cut them, as one does with an animal.[34]

We may compare this to Jack's own 'private' (but very public) methods. His last victim, 'Mary Kelly ... was lying on her back on a bed, where she had been placed after the murderer cut her throat ... he set to work mutilating the body, which was stabbed, slashed, skinned, gutted and ripped apart. Her nose and breast were cut off; her entrails were extracted: some were removed.'[35]

In the eighteenth century executions became a ritual in which the 'main character was the people, whose ... presence was required for the performance'.[36] By Jack's time public execution was long since over, but Jack took on the symbolic weight of a 'higher' justice operating beyond the arm of the law, exposing and cutting out the cancer of sexual commerce. His role was acknowledged in his instant fame and his ferocity in his attack on the condemned: the prostitute class. It appears that Jack represented the return of a social memory of the proximity of death (by violence, cholera, starvation) now distanced by the work of social and medical reformers.

In that latter half of the industrialized nineteenth century ceremonies about the integration of death had long ceased to be necessary. In a sense the body had gained utility value but lost its 'sacred' humanness (its 'mystery' that early Christians feared). Jack represents the unconscious of that society – a repression not yet exorcized; he forcibly reminded society (unable to speak of bodies without blushing) of the crudest function of that mass of organs. Jack clearly unites ideas about the mortification of the flesh and the technology that manipulates the body (the human sciences: biology, psychology, forensic science, medicine). One end of the spectrum acknowledges desire for and the power of the flesh while the other denies both and reduces the body to a mass of functions and utilities: an automaton. The body hence becomes ironically 'sacred' (as an object in religious devotion to be escaped *from*) and yet also machinic.

Yet the savagery of Jack's attacks suggests more. As the attacks became more savage, so the mutilation of the victim became more complete. Finally it took pathologists six hours to piece together the empty shell of Mary Kelly scattered around the room in which she died. For Jack this final attack meant more than an attempt to punish womankind for its sins and its tempting flesh. Here the body is emptied, turned into a shell into which the murderer could plunge his knife and hands. The emptying assumes the form of an attempt to 'go beyond' the boundaries of flesh in a 'new' and horrific way. This violence demolishes and liquefies the body, which flows away and takes with it its ego boundaries. The body is opened, penetrated, dissected, made totally possessable.

As the bodily boundaries vanish we are reminded of the search for the auguries at Rome, a desperate search for a stable and knowable destiny. As the uterus determines the growing foetus, so the 'innerds' of the female body offer themselves for decoding. But what do they signify? Nothing, or more properly, an absence, for the place of origin is missing. The quest carried out by the probing knife reveals only a mess of tangled 'innerds'. Jack's attack signifies a going beyond towards an otherness that is totally non-human. The object and the possessor mesh into one critical quest.

What did Jack search for? Inside the body, finally opened, the culprit used the technique of a manic autopsy in order to find the non-body: the beyond and yet absolute of his own existence – his soul perhaps? In finding this origin Jack may have been able to find his own significance unhindered by the body which forced him to kill. For Jack as for his public, these killings, graphically illustrated and documented in the popular press, may have signified, as they still may do, the final frenzied acknowledgement of the coming of the age of materialism.

The body of the 'Magdalen' signifies the absence of purity and the presence of sin; but what does each weigh – what atomic weight can be assigned to the soul? Can the significance of the Ripper's violence, which has fascinated readers and researchers for so long, be explained in this way – that his quest was for a lost and discarded origin and that his method was a repressed and supposedly outdated one? The object of Jack's killing is not to take on the power of 'the other' but to bypass 'the other' altogether in order to confront otherness itself.

This may be borne out perhaps in the nature and morbid (perhaps healthy?) interest of generations of readers. Jack's killing partakes of a deep substratum of cultural knowledge, a cultural awareness of the nature of sacrifice. If this appears far-fetched we can turn to René Girard's *Violence and the Sacred*, an anthropological work which appeared in 1972.[37]

First, though, let me briefly recapitulate the ideas outlined above. I have drawn attention to the dual nature of the popular notion of alienation – both demonic and machinic, with its consequent ambiguities over the relationship of victim to killer: social pillar and social pariah. At this juncture the psychotic killer, a product of urban life at the end of the nineteenth century, appears as both mentally defective and metaphysically gifted – both cancer and purgative. I have further suggested the possibilities and limits of Jack's 'quest' and the disturbance to identity that that caused. To further this inquiry let us now return to Girard's work on sacrifice.

Girard tells us that initially 'the sacrificial act assumes two opposing aspects, appearing at times a sacred obligation ... at others a sort of criminal activity'. He notes the 'ambivalent' nature of sacrifice but says this does not fully account for its 'value'.[38] In his view, 'sacrifice contains an element of mystery',[39] and it is this mystery that he wishes to penetrate. Quoting Joseph de Maistre, he adds, 'the sacrificial animals were always those most prized for their gentleness, most innocent creatures, whose habits ... brought them most closely into harmony with man'.[40] Indeed, we are told that 'sacrificial victims are almost always animals'.[41]

Here then we see that Jack the Ripper and James Berry share both a criminal and a 'sacred' (legitimized by the state) obligation. Berry acknowledged the ambivalence in his role. Moreover, in both cases, secrecy adds an air of mystery to the proceedings. The 'Magdalens' fit the role of sacrificial 'animals' through their own ambiguous position: both gentle, and aggressive in selling their wares; innocent and sexually aware; *and* in harmony with 'man' while in competition with and engaged in commercial transactions with him.

We may go further, for Girard points out that the very lowest (slaves) and the very highest (sacrificial kings) are the ends of the sacrifice spectrum.[42] But he concludes that 'in many cultures women are never, or rarely, selected as sacrificial victims',[43] because of the feuds this would cause between husbands and children and the class that claims them. However, these points can be easily met, for prostitutes are both 'animals' and 'Magdalens'; both subhuman and sacred. Moreover, in the culture of which we speak these women are precisely those that were forced (therefore to the popular mentality *chose*) to break all their ties with husbands, children, class. They became the sacrificial victims for that culture, without ties or kinsfolk to gain revenge on their behalf. At one end of our spectrum Jack does nothing illegitimate – but his act is illegal for he kills outside the *context* of the sacrificial system (long since forgotten, of course, in the nineteenth century). His act is both sacred and lunatic, bestial and totally 'sane'.

Moreover, Jack's acts of sacrifice/murder appeal to a deeply archaic level of human response – a response long since channelled elsewhere into 'humane' destruction for sane offenders and lunatic asylums for 'morally degenerate' offenders. In the 1880s these two conditions partook of a peculiar mixture of demonic ability and psychological disintegration neither properly disentangled from the other in either the popular imagination, literature or the human sciences.

Yet we must go deeper to fathom the legendary power of Jack (for structuralist approaches consider the action of legend and myth in too formalistic a way). We have seen the specific historico-psychological aspects of the Ripper's enduring fame. But we must return to Girard for our final formulation of his power over our imaginations.

Girard considers sacrifice an attempt by society to 'deflect upon a relatively indifferent victim ... the violence that would otherwise be vented on its own members, the people it most desires to protect'.[44] Consequently 'the sacrifice serves to protect the entire community from its own violence'.[45]

Let us return to *Dr Jekyll and Mr Hyde*. Jekyll *generates* from *his own* personality the characteristics of the psychopath. His dual nature partakes not of a ghostly *Doppelgänger* but of aspects from *within* himself. His violence is a hatred of his own class and its expectation of restraint and decorum – its understanding of order. Girard comments on the Bible story of Cain and Abel that 'Cain's "jealousy" of his brother is only another term for his own characteristic trait: his lack of sacrificial outlet'.[46] Right at the beginning of *Dr Jekyll and Mr Hyde* we are introduced to Mr Utterson the lawyer, the ultimate figure of respectability, who 'was austere with himself' and who says of himself, 'I incline to Cain's heresy'.[47] As with Jekyll, it is more than a psychological problem; it is 'deeper'. Like Jack, Jekyll crosses a profound border, a border that disturbed 'anthropologists' and theologians alike in the nineteenth century.[48]

Thus we see the truly ritualistic and 'psychological' nexus of Jack's violence, for his work dissolves boundaries, acts as a gaping maw into which perception of order and rightness are sucked. Jack's *name* as well as his deeds and the deeds in his name disturb our order, trangress boundaries, translate legitimacy into illegitimacy and the sacred into the bestial, and translate them back again. For Jack there is no 'other', only a gaping hole within self that is beyond reconciliation with laws of man or God.

Jack, like any legendary figure, represents this effectively because he steps out of historical circumstance and into the imagination of the future. As such, like King Arthur or Robin Hood or Count Dracula, he is the undead. Jack, however, bypasses the criminal underworld, for he does not belong to it. He is outside that underworld, which is itself defined within the comprehension of the living (the non-animal). Jack is demon/animal and therefore totally other, therefore unrecognizable (invisible), therefore the perfect criminal. He disturbs the human only to reinforce it. Indeed, this monstrosity embeds himself in the imagination of each generation that needs his presence. For that reason alone there is a smile on the face of the Ripper.

The historical details of the Whitechapel murders are nothing less than the facets of a scenario for a script about modernity itself. Reworked in fiction and film as well as the focus for true-crime books (of the solve-it-yourself variety), the Ripper's deeds are ever reworked to remain forever contemporary, and thus curiously emphasized by layers of nostalgia. The Ripper's script has violence, eroticism, sentimentality and the supernatural: a text to live out the sensationalism of the modern.[49]

Notes

1 *The Times*, 3 December 1888.
2 *Sun*, 17 February 1894.
3 *The Times*, 26 October 1888.
4 *The Times*, 10 November 1888.

5 'In appearance, a paper of the 1890s was a product substantially the same as our own ... the phrase "new journalism" was first used by the poet Matthew Arnold of the lively work of the *Pall Mall Gazette* and its competitors in the late 1880s. This was indeed the seedbed of the twentieth century commercial popular press ... There was also a new group of evening papers circulating in London and going out aggressively for new readers ... It was these evening papers which first educated the morning papers into editorial policies suitable for the masses. Kennedy Jones and Alfred Harmsworth (later Lord Northcliffe) worked out their ideas for mass journalism for there was a new generation emerging in the years after the Great Exhibition of 1851 which had curiosity but little education.' Anthony Smith, *The Newspaper: An International History* (London: Thames and Hudson, 1979), pp. 153–4.

6 *Stratford Express*, 7 May 1965.

7 Letters quoted by C. M. McLeod in *The Criminologist*, 9 (1968), pp. 120–7.

8 Stephen Knight, *Jack the Ripper: The Final Solution* (London: Grafton, 1976).

9 *East London Advertiser*, 7 December 1973.

10 Alexander Kelly, 'Ripperana and Ripperature', *The Assistant Librarian* (1973), pp. 3–6.

11 Kim Newman in *Million* (March/June 1993), p. 20.

12 Newman, *Million*, p. 20.

13 Tony Bennett and Janet Woollacott, *Bond and Beyond: The Political Career of a Popular Hero* (London: Macmillan, 1987), p. 14.

14 Robert Harris, 'Selling Hitler', in *The Media Trilogy* (London: Faber & Faber [1986], 1994), p. 579.

15 Shirley Harrison, *The Diary of Jack the Ripper* (London: Smith Gryphon, 1993), pp. ix and 178. For further discussion of the authenticity of the evidence see the *Evening Standard*, 13 March 1994, p. 12.

16 Brian Augustyn, Michael Mignola, P. Craig Russell and David Hornung, introduced by Robert Bloch, *Gotham by Gaslight* (New York: DC Comics, 1989).

17 Augustyn *et al.*, *Gotham by Gaslight*, p. 1.

18 *Daily Telegraph*, 9 October 1974.

19 T. A. Critchley, *A History of Policy in England and Wales* (London: Constable, 1978), p. 161.

20 Robert Louis Stevenson, *The Strange Case of Dr Jekyll and Mr Hyde and Other Stories* (London: Everyman, 1992), pp. 100, 113, 115.

21 Stevenson, *Jekyll and Hyde*, pp. 141–2.

22 Stevenson, *Jekyll and Hyde*, p. 154.

23 Stevenson, *Jekyll and Hyde*, p. 101.

24 Stevenson, *Jekyll and Hyde*, p. 103.

25 Stevenson, *Jekyll and Hyde*, p. 142.

26 Stevenson, *Jekyll and Hyde*, p. 142.

27 Stevenson, *Jekyll and Hyde*, p. 146.

28 James Berry, *My Life as an Executioner*, ed. Jonathan Goodman (Newton Abbott: David and Charles, 1972).

29 Berry, *My Life*, p. 1.

30 Berry, *My Life*, p. 11.

31 Berry, *My Life*, p. 66.

32 Berry, *My Life*, p. 95.

33 Berry, *My Life*, p. 95.

34 Michel Foucault, *Discpline and Punish*, trans. Alan Sheridan (London: Allen Lane, 1977), p. 53.

35 Gordon Honeycomb, *The Murders of the Black Museum, 1870–1970* (London: Hutchinson, 1982).

36 Foucault, *Discipline*, p. 57.

37 René Girard, *Violence and the Sacred*, trans. Patrick Gregory (Baltimore: Johns Hopkins University Press, 1977).

38 Girard, *Violence and the Sacred*, p. 1.

39 Girard, *Violence and the Sacred*, p. 1.

40 Girard, *Violence and the Sacred*, p. 2.

41 Girard, *Violence and the Sacred*, p. 9.

42 Girard, *Violence and the Sacred*, p. 12.

43 Girard, *Violence and the Sacred*, p. 12

44 Girard, *Violence and the Sacred*, p. 4.

45 Girard, *Violence and the Sacred*, p. 8.

46 Girard, *Violence and the Sacred*, p 4.

47 Stevenson, *Jekyll and Hyde*, p. 99.

48 René Girard, 'Myth and Ritual in Shakespeare: *A Midsummer Night's Dream*', in *Textual Strategies*, ed. Josué V. Harrari (London: Methuen, 1980), pp. 189–212.

49 See Stewart Evans and Paul Gainey, *The Lodger: The Arrest and Escape of Jack the Ripper* (London: Century, 1995) for the latest 'factual' accretion.

7

The Whitechapel murders and the medical gaze

Andrew Smith

London lies today under the spell of a great terror. A nameless reprobate – half-beast, half-man – is at large, who is daily gratifying his murderous instincts on the most miserable and defenceless of classes of the community. There can be no shadow of a doubt that ... the Whitechapel murderer, who has now four, if not five, victims to his knife, is one man, and that man a murderous maniac ... The ghoul-like creature, who stalks through the streets of London, stalking down his victim like a Pawnee Indian, is simply drunk with blood and will have more.[1]

The rowdy hobbledehoy is developing more and more rapidly into the savage of the slums. He in turn is becoming more and more akin to the monster – half-man, half-brute – who is now prowling round Whitechapel like the 'were-wolf' of Gothic fable. But where is this process of hideous evolution to stop? Are the resources of civilisation powerless against it?[2]

The murder of five prostitutes working in the East End of London between 31 August and 9 November 1888 attracted, as is well documented, considerable attention from the media, social commentators, the public and politicians. The fact that the murderer acquired an almost mythic status early on in the media discussion of the killings tends to obscure the reality of the murders, so that any discussion of them has to acknowledge both the complex web of social views which informed this process of mythologization, and make some attempt at disentangling the specific concerns which they articulate. Judith R. Walkowitz's superlative analysis of 'Ripper narratives' in *City of Dreadful Delight* (1992) attempts just such an analysis of the often incompatible narratives (which included anti-Semitism, hostility to the medical profession, anti-vivisectionism, the claims of radical feminism, support for class agitation, and anti-Americanism) which contributed to speculation on the murderer's identity.[3]
[...]
Dr George Phillips, who carried out the autopsy on Annie Chapman, claimed that the murder weapon could have been of the type 'used for post-mortem purposes' and that the killer evinced 'some anatomical

knowledge'.[4] *The Times* reported the coroner's belief that there was a purpose behind the incisions, although why the murderer removed the uterus was not clear. The lack of motivation was an obvious obstacle to the investigation. The coroner (Wynne E. Baxter) informed the jury that 'they were confronted with a murder of no ordinary character, committed not from jealousy, revenge, or robbery, but from motives less adequate than many which still disgraced our civilization'.[5]

The idea that a 'mad' doctor was responsible for the murders began to be widely discussed in the press and this, alongside some of the suggestions made at the inquest, meant that the police took this seriously. D. G. Halstead trained as a doctor at the London Hospital in the Whitechapel Road and noted of this period: 'Suspicion immediately turned upon my colleagues and myself, and I often had the feeling, especially when I was walking home late at night, that the inhabitants were shunning me and that the plain-clothes men were following my movements'.[6] Chief Inspector Donald Swanson, who was in charge of the Whitechapel investigation, wrote to the Home Office on 19 October and stated that 'Enquiries were ... made to trace three insane medical students who had attended London Hospital, two traced, one gone abroad'.[7] They were ultimately excluded from the inquiry, but the notion that an insane doctor was the culprit was considered throughout the police investigation.

In December 1888 one Dr Robert Stephenson (who was later entertained as a likely candidate for the killer) wrote to the Home Office concerning the behaviour of a Dr Morgan Davies, who was treating Stephenson as a patient at the London Hospital.[8] Stephenson recounted that after a discussion about the murders, Davies enacted a scene to illustrate how he thought they had been committed. For Stephenson, the frenetic display suggested the mental instability of Davies and a first-hand knowledge of the murders: 'He took a knife, "buggered" an imaginary woman, cut her throat from behind; then, when she was apparently laid prostrate, ripped & slashed her in all directions in a perfect state of frenzy'.[9] This strange, seemingly insane, re-enactment also resonates with a wider view of the medical profession at the time, a view which continued long after the murders had stopped. In October 1889, for example, an anonymous letter was sent to the Home Office relating to 'a Dr in practice' who was 'rather strange in his manners' and who was additionally suspicious because 'The last letter purporting to be written by Jack the R – was found ... within [a quarter] hours walking distance of Dr's lodgings'.[10] Although Swanson dismissed the letter as 'the product of an excited imagination', it does illustrate the degree of suspicion with which the public regarded the medical profession[11] – a suspicion which can be confirmed by a reading of the autopsy reports.

The politics of the autopsy

When looking at the autopsy reports on the victims we are to some significant degree moving beyond the kind of imaginative speculation to be found in the press. Elizabeth Bronfen has noted in *Over Her Dead Body: Death, Femininity and the Aesthetic* (1992):

> It seems as necessary to stress the fundamental difference between real violence done to the physical body and any 'imagined' one ... [because] it is necessary to explore the way in which these two registers come to be conflated and confused. Not because the latter can then be absolved of any responsibility towards the material of its depiction but because to collapse the two levels on which signification works might also mean not doing justice to the uniquely horrible violence that occurs when a body is used quite literally as the site for an inscription by another.[12]

The accounts of the autopsies bridge these two worlds of the real and the imaginary. They are both accounts of real deaths and textual performances which encode other, hidden 'realities' relating to the politics of the medical profession in general, and a peculiarly pathologized, strangely directed, male gaze in particular.

The autopsies indicate that what was at issue was not just the way in which the victims died, but how healthy they were at the time of death. That is to say that there was an additional narrative which was looking for signs of disease; typically venereal disease, alcoholism, malnutrition and general indicators of social deprivation which could, at least theoretically, render the victim complicit with their fate.

Martha Tabram, who may or may not have been the Whitechapel killer's first victim,[13] was described by Dr Timothy Killeen in his report to the inquest in these terms:

> Her age was about 36, and the body was very well nourished ... The left lung was penetrated in five places, and the right lung penetrated in two places. The heart, which was rather fatty, was penetrated in one place, and that would be sufficient to cause death. The liver was healthy, but was penetrated in five places, the spleen, which was perfectly healthy, was penetrated in six places.[14]

The emphasis is on Tabram's relative health at the time of her death, but this search for pathology reveals how an alternative narrative 'read' the signs of injury alongside the signs of health. Nothing incriminating can be learnt about Tabram from the state of her body; she is neither syphilitic nor alcoholic and so eludes any attempt to 'read' her body as pathologized.

The autopsy report on Annie Chapman contains the seemingly irrelevant comment that 'The front teeth were perfect, so far as the first molar, top and bottom, and very fine teeth they were'.[15] Later Dr Phillips notes:

> The deceased was far advanced in disease of the lungs and membranes of the brain ... The stomach contained a little food, but there was not any signs of fluid. There was no appearance of the deceased having taken alcohol, but there were signs of great deprivation, and he should say she had been badly fed. He was convinced she had not taken any strong alcohol for some hours before her death.[16]

This part of the autopsy brings together a range of issues relating to the moral and social standing of the victim. The signs of deprivation and malnutrition suggest Chapman's social context, although ultimately this passage represents a search for agency. Chapman's status as a 'genuine' victim is being evaluated in these claims about social context (malnutrition) and personal responsibility (the failed search for signs of alcohol abuse). The implicit question raised here is, to what extent was Chapman responsible for her death?

Alongside this search for visible signs of disease exists an alternative narrative concerning the identity of the killer which implicates the medical profession, because the cuts on Chapman's body appear to have been inflicted by someone who possessed anatomical knowledge. Dr Phillips was reluctant to give further details about how Chapman's body had been mutilated. Baxter cleared the courtroom of women and children and Phillips, according to the journalist from *The Times*, 'proceeded to give medical and surgical evidence, totally unfit for publication'.[17] That medicine and the press agreed that there existed a line beyond which disclosures could not be made indicates a shared cultural notion concerning 'taste'. However, it also served to conceal what came to be seen as important 'clues' about the likely occupation, and so identity, of the killer.

Narratives of social deprivation had already been widely discussed in accounts of London by social commentators and journalists. Such discussion, as in Phillips's search for the signs of alcoholism, had also nodded towards this debate about the moral status of the subjects living in the East End. Such narratives about London helped to make the dangerous, seemingly irrational, urban spaces explicable (at least in social terms), whereas the murders suggested the continuing presence of the irrational and the inexplicable (the murderer's actions being difficult to account for in terms of social context). And yet the murders had a proximity to medicine which was in its own way as troubling as the proximity of the West to the East. The hidden narrative at the Chapman inquest related to how the mutilation of the body after death resembled an autopsy. Dr Phillips informed the now partially emptied court room that:

> The abdomen had been entirely laid open: the intestines, severed from the mesenteric attachments, had been lifted out of the body and placed on the shoulder of the corpse; whilst from the pelvis, the uterus and its appendages with the upper portion of the vagina and the posterior two-thirds of the bladder, had been entirely removed.[18]

For Phillips, 'Obviously the work was that of an expert – of one, at least, who had such knowledge of anatomical or pathological examinations as to be enabled to secure the pelvic organs with one sweep of the knife'.[19] Indeed, in response to questions from the coroner, Phillips evinced some grudging admiration by indicating that it would have taken him around fifteen minutes to effect such an operation, and that if he had done it in a proper manner 'as would fall to the duties of a surgeon it probably would have taken ... the best part of an hour' (p. 350).[20] The killer had done this in a matter of minutes.

The question was whether this apparently pathologized autopsy indicated the signs of madness or implied something that was central, but concealed within, models of the 'norm'. The *Lancet* came down on the side of normalization when it suggested that 'It is most unusual for a lunatic to plan any complicated crime of this kind. Neither, as a rule, does a lunatic take precautions to escape from the consequences of his act; which *data* are most conspicuous in these now celebrated cases'.[21] The murderer's behaviour was atypical and so suggested sanity. Also, this normalization of the pathological is relevant to how the autopsies examined what looked like earlier autopsies, rather than murders. In this way there is an unusual moment of self-reflection in which the medical profession confronts a version of its 'normal' processes, although processes which are pathologized because they cause death rather than explain it. Nevertheless it was an encounter that challenged the distinction between 'normal' and 'pathological'. Sander L. Gilman in a commentary on the German expressionist Gottfried Benn's fictionalized account of an autopsy notes how 'the physician's eye is always cast to examine and find the source of pathology ... hidden within the woman's body', but that this search becomes reflected back on to the doctor who is rendered pathological in the process (in the cutting up of dead women).[22] Gilman's argument largely addresses the representation of 'Jack', but she also discusses this in relation to medicine and acknowledges the existence of a relationship in which 'Jack' actually represents a form of doctoring:

> Killing and dismembering, searching after the cause of corruption and disease. The paradigm for the relationship between Jack and the prostitutes

7 The eye-witness sketch of Jack the Ripper most closely resembling a middle-class doctor.

can be taken from the popular medical discourse of the period: *Similia similibus curantur*, 'like cures like,' the motto of C.F.S. Hahnemann, the founder of homeopathic medicine. The scourge of the streets, the carrier of disease, can be eliminated only by one who is equally corrupt and diseased. (p. 268)

In this way 'Jack' is really a synonym for 'doctor'. Although a coroner such as Baxter expressed considerable sympathy for the plight of the victims, D. G. Halstead referred to them as diseased purveyors of syphilis and claimed that 'it must have been ... an almost moral urge to purify the East End of these plague-bearing harpies' (p. 56). Halstead's reference to the second victim (Mary Ann Nichols) also dwelt, cruelly, on her alleged immorality: 'The victim was a slut of a woman who had been heard of in the Lambeth workhouse, and had stolen £3 from her employer when working as a servant' (pp. 46–7).

Anxieties relating to the conduct of the medical profession were expressed within the profession itself. The proximity of the killer's actions to 'normal' medical procedure also suggests this pathologization of medicine, a view which was quickly developed in the press, and which contributed to a widespread cultural distrust of doctors at the time.

Jekyll and Hyde and Hyde's apparent abnormality is relevant to this process of pathologization because it suggests the presence of an abnormality, a pathology, which is observed but which cannot be accounted for, precisely because it implies (as would the autopsies) that pathology is inherent to specific notions of the 'norm'. This is implicit in the demonization of medicine, but also reflects on the idea of criminal responsibility. The murders are not ordinary crimes because there is no demonstrable motivation for them (notwithstanding considerable press speculation about this), and paradoxically this suggests that 'abnormalities' in the guise of clues are not produced. The killer cannot be identified because, like Hyde, he becomes a kind of everyman and therefore, as suggested in The *Lancet*, normalized. What is truly horrific is that he represents a kind of male collective unconscious, which would also explain why so many different, frequently incompatible, suspects were entertained at various times. The point is that the killer does not appear as a special, specifically and clearly motivated, figure.

Crime and symptoms

One strange paradox was that the killer's extraordinariness emerged from his ordinariness. The lack of the usual motivations for his crimes distanced him from the typical criminal and thus rendered the crimes extraordinary. A report to the Home Office, dated 23 October 1888, by Robert Anderson, who took charge of the Whitechapel investigation from 6 October 1888 until the file closed in 1892, noted:

> That a crime of this kind should have been committed without any clue being supplied by the criminal is unusual, but that five successive murders should have been committed without our having the slightest clue of any kind is extraordinary, if not unique in the annals of crime.[23]

The signs of crime and the symptoms of disease were conflated at this time. To return to *Jekyll and Hyde* for a moment, we can see that the novella links Hyde with criminality *and* disease, although it is not clear what Hyde's crimes are. Hyde is not a sexually sadistic criminal but the associations made between sex crime and Hyde in the press (the West End gentleman preying on East End prostitutes) emphasized a link between pathology and sexual criminality. However, the demonization of doctors (as in media speculation and in *Jekyll and Hyde*) means that the 'norm', or a bourgeois professional middle-class construction of it, also becomes pathologized. Hyde, like the Whitechapel murderer, eludes attempts to interpret him because his pathologies are developed from within (in ways also suggested by Stead). Pathologies therefore produced symptoms which, within the context of the murder investigation, were then read as 'clues' about identity.

Crime also represents the presence of social disease, one which can only be made present through signs of explicable agency. An example of this is to be found in a domestic murder that took place in Whitechapel only a few hours before the murders of Elizabeth Stride and Catherine Eddowes. *The Times* carried a report on 1 October detailing how John Brown murdered his wife and then gave himself up to the police at Rochester-row, telling them that he had killed her 'in consequence of [her] unfaithfulness'. *The Times* also noted that 'the Police went to the house, where the woman was found lying dead on the floor with her throat cut. Several wounds had been inflicted in the shape of stabs and cuts'. Brown's actions were explicable because there was a suggestion of motivation, even though it appears as though he was suffering from some mental disturbance at the time; whereas two hours later the murder of Elizabeth Stride by the Whitechapel killer remained a mystery because of the lack of motivation.[24] There were therefore normalized murders, which are made sense of by the domestic context in which they occurred, and other murders which failed to produce evidence. Agency is the key issue here; as Baxter had commented at the Chapman inquest, 'There were no meaningless cuts', even though what they signified was unclear. Attention therefore turned to the bodies of the victims, as if they could generate the necessary clues.[25]

At this point narratives about London and degeneration become relevant, but the search for pathology was not just a search for signs of social depravity. There was always the implication that the victims were themselves responsible, at least potentially, for their plights. For this reason, as we have seen, a medical gaze subjected the bodies to an analysis of how healthy they were. We saw this in the Tabram and Chapman autopsy reports, and it appears again in Stride's, which includes the claim that 'the brain was fairly normal'.[26] The search suggests that the apparent mental instability of the killer is transferred to one of his victims; and yet, as the Brown murder indicated, mental instability did not in itself generate mysterious murders. Brown's apparently insensible, and manifestly misogynistic act could be rationalized (although not legitimated), but this merely indicates just how misogynistic such rationalizations could become.

As we have seen, the medical profession was seemingly confronted, at least as various authors of the autopsy reports saw it, with an image of themselves. The suggested medical knowledge, combined with the idea that they were essentially producing autopsies about autopsies, placed the medical gaze in a strange narcissistic moment in which everything is familiar but unfamiliar at the same time. This constitutes a moment of self-reflection which can be usefully explored through Freud's idea of the 'uncanny', because it provides an insight into the construction of the cultural anxieties which such an encounter generates. It also helps to reposition the debate about the 'normal' and the pathological which illuminates the dilemmas faced by medicine at the time.

Freud, the uncanny and medicine

At this juncture it is helpful to examine how the autopsy reports can be read through Freud's idea of the uncanny because it clarifies their cultural context (rather than sheds light on the psychology of their respective authors). In spirit this is a line of enquiry indebted to Peter Stallybrass and Allon White, who in *The Politics and Poetics of Transgression* (1986) explored how the body of the urban subject was, in the nineteenth century, read in terms of the body politic of the city. In this way noble thoughts corresponded to the presence of urban civilization whereas low bodily functions or urges corresponded to the slums and sewers of an outcast London.[27] In other words the prevailing models of urban subjectivity were formed through metaphors of the city, meaning that a psychoanalytical account of such subject formation also tells us something about the city (which also goes some way in explaining why *Jekyll and Hyde* became one of the dominant means of accounting for the murders in social *and* psychological terms).

For Freud the terms of the uncanny, *unheimlich* and *heimlich*, or uncanny and homely, slide into each other in an (uncanny) way; so that the everyday, the homely, also becomes the site of secrets, specifically defining family secrets which condition the self in certain Oedipal ways. The issue of secrecy and visibility is as central to this process as it is to the autopsies which are also trying to explain that 'which is obscure, inaccessible to knowledge'.[28] For Freud the double emerges as our conscience by 'exercising a censorship within the mind' and so represents the emergence of a moral sensibility (p. 357). However, at some stage in the development of the ego the double starts to take on a more sinister aspect as it goes through a transformation in which 'from having been an assurance of immortality, it becomes the uncanny harbinger of death' (p. 357). This model of psychological development becomes relevant to our enquiry at the point where Freud associates such a feeling of uncanniness with the dead: 'Many people experience the feeling in the highest degree in relation to dead and dead bodies' (p. 364). Such an encounter inevitably creates feelings of anxiety.

In the autopsy reports there is a literalized encounter with the dead: the sense of uncanniness that these bodies generate for the medical profession is in part related to how they appear to have been subjected to a particularly brutal (but in their own way 'skilled') autopsy. In this way the 'normal' and the pathological become conflated. However, this conflation is also subject to a particular diversion which displaces the pathological from the medical context back to the victim. The search for the signs of disease indicates this, whilst the failure to confirm their presence suggests that culpability is to be found elsewhere. The problem is that this 'elsewhere', the murderer, mimics normalized medical procedure and so indicates that such procedure is *already* pathological.

For Freud the self, in moments of uncanniness, is confronted with an unnerving, pathological experience, which is nevertheless commonplace (commonplace to the degree that it is a shared experience and so can be generalized). The pathological in this instance really does become the psychopathology of everyday life. In the autopsies the attempt to displace this on to the victim fails because the victim cannot generate an alternative narrative which directly involves them in the murder, and thus they cannot be held morally responsible for it. And yet, as in the uncanny, there is always the sense that knowledge is immanent, that understanding is only a moment away. This is apparent in the claims about how the wounds suggest deliberation, agency and purpose, and so the presence of the killer is manifested through a series of symptoms, or 'clues'. However, such 'clues' merely echo the supposedly normal medical procedure of the autopsy and as such they are familiar, but paradoxically unreadable because they do not identify a specific 'abnormal' culprit. Any knowledge which is produced is a secondary one which relates to medicine. Instead of the murderer becoming pathologized, it is medicine which becomes pathologized. The search for a 'mad' doctor in 'sane' places (such as the areas in and around the London Hospital) suggests this. The search is for the enemy within, not for an outsider. In this way the sense of *unheimlich* (uncanny) and *heimlich* (the home) become conflated in a way which Freud saw as one of the central characteristics of the phenomenon. Medicine is on the side of benevolent order (a caring profession, the 'home') but is also associated with secrecy. This is illustrated by the partial clearing of the courtroom at the Chapman inquest, but also in a wider, less specific sense, that the murderer was hidden, disguised, by the medical profession, which develops the sinister aspect of *heimlich:* 'Concealed, kept from sight, so that others do not get to know about it, withheld from others' (p. 344).

I am not suggesting that one should read the murders in psychological terms, indeed to do so would be to depoliticize the notion of derangement and take it out of its cultural context; rather it is the case that the notion of the uncanny enables us to unravel some of the complexities of that cultural context. This is principally because, as we have seen, displacement and transference characterize the way in which the murders were discussed in the press (as in their evocation of *Jekyll and Hyde*, for example) and the search for 'clues' of either criminality or moral pathology (which were displaced on to the victims). This process of displacement and projection also reflects the epistemic inability to generate 'truth' and consequently implicates medicine and the police in this failure. By extension, it also implicates a pathologized 'normalized' masculine gaze which was held responsible for the murders *and* for the failure to solve them.

What I am suggesting is that the medical profession was confronted by its pathologized Other in the sense that the 'otherness' of the cuts on the victims' bodies becomes familiar to the degree that they represent apparently 'normal' medical procedure. However, a sense of 'otherness', which is linked to this pathologization (indeed, it indicates the presence of the pathological), is transferred on to the victims' bodies by this search for 'disease'. The murderer of Elizabeth Stride, for example, may indeed have been insane, although in a strictly misogynistic way, but this, as indicated earlier, is transformed into an exploration of *her* brain.

At the Stride inquest Dr Phillips reiterated his view that the murderer possessed some surgical skills, claiming that 'there appears to have been knowledge where to cut the throat'. He also made an implicit comment about the moral health of Stride when, in response to a question, he indicated that there 'was no trace' of alcohol in her stomach.[29] The story was different with Catherine Eddowes (who was murdered shortly after Stride) because she had been arrested for drunkenness on the evening of 29 August and released by the Police at 1.00 a.m. on the 30th. The Corporation of London records contain the inquest report of the 4 October and the account of the autopsy made by Dr Frederick Brown, who was the surgeon of the City of London Police. Despite Eddowes's apparent reputation for drunkenness, Brown failed to find signs of pathology which reflected this, noting that the 'liver itself was healthy' and that 'the other organs were healthy'. He also looked for signs of sexual activity but notes that 'there were no indications of connexion'.[30] Brown intimated that the removal of the uterus and a kidney suggested some anatomical skill, although not necessarily a strictly medical one. He remarked, 'it required a great deal of ["medical" – deleted] knowledge to have removed the kidney and to know where it was placed, such a knowledge might be possessed by some one in the habit of cutting up animals'.[31] Aldergate slaughterhouse was in the area, although Brown's suggestion that the murderer could have been a slaughterman does not necessarily exclude the idea that it was a doctor. Indeed in the original report the word 'medical' had been deleted. The comparative health of the victim, I would argue, prompts this new diversion. This is not to suggest that this was deliberate or consciously strategic (after all, Brown may have been right), but rather that the failure to mention that it *could* have involved medical knowledge implicates the profession through omission.

In exploring these autopsies it is clear that there is both an account of the reality of the terrible crimes and a narrative process that operates alongside this, one which works within models of the pathological. It is in this adjacent narrative of pathology that complexities emerge. The victims' bodies do not generate 'clues' as to the identity of the killer, but in some instances (such as Chapman's) they do indicate the presence of social disease, although they do not produce the signs of moral pathology.

This is another way of saying that the autopsies were as much cultural as medical procedures, opening up the lives of the victims to a controlling male gaze which could generate the kind of knowledge on which a moral evaluation could be made. It is a process in which the identities of the victims actually become peculiarly obscured because they are rendered in terms of their suspect, latent pathology, one which tells us just how far such a medicalized, masculine gaze had itself become pathologized in its search for confirmation of the signs of depravity. As in Stead's notion of the commodification of young women in prostitution, the victims are ultimately reduced to a series of objects, things and internal organs. Catherine Eddowes succinctly captured this sense of depersonalization; when requested to give her name during her arrest for drunkenness (and shortly before she was murdered) she replied 'Nothing': an erasure of identity that was reaffirmed by the autopsy.[32]

We have seen how an examination of the pathologization of the medical profession implicates a particular model of middle-class masculinity. This specific male gaze articulates an anxiety about authority, one which was referenced through images of a threatened medical profession. Such a process works at a covert level and the issue of concealment and visibility in some way glosses this.

Notes

1 The *Star*, 8 September 1888, cited in L. Perry Curtis, Jr, *Jack the Ripper and the London Press* (New Haven: Yale University Press, 2001), pp. 122–3. All subsequent references are to this edition and are given in the text.
2 *Daily Chronicle*, 10 September 1888, cited in Curtis, *Jack the Ripper*, p. 128.
3 Judith R. Walkoitz, *City of Dreadful Delight: Narratives of Sexual Danger in Late-Victorian London* ([1992] London: Virago, 1998), pp. 191–228. All subsequent references are to this edition and are given in the text.
4 *The Times*, 14 September 1888, from Stewart P. Evans and Keith Skinner (eds), *The Ultimate Jack the Ripper Sourcebook: An Illustrated Encyclopedia* (London: Constable, 2001), p. 98.
5 *The Times*, 26 September 1888, from Evans and Skinner, *Ultimate Jack the Ripper*, p. 120.
6 D. G. Halstead, *Doctor in the Nineties* (London: Christopher Johnson, 1959), p. 51. All subsequent references are to this edition and are given in the text.
7 Quoted in Paul Begg, Martin Fido and Keith Skinner (eds), *The Jack the Ripper A–Z* (London: Headline, 1996), p. 383.
8 See Begg *et al.*, *Jack the Ripper A–Z*, for an account of Stephenson's colourful life, which included associations with the occult and the theosophical society, pp. 428–30.
9 Letter sent 26 December 1888, from Evans and Skinner, *Ultimate Jack the Ripper*, p. 670. There were also doubts about Stephenson's reliability as a witness because of his alcoholism.
10 In Evans and Skinner, *Ultimate Jack the Ripper*, pp. 600, 601.
11 Evans and Skinner, *Ultimate Jack the Ripper*, p. 601.
12 Elizabeth Bronfen, *Over Her Dead Body: Death, Femininity and the Aesthetic* (Manchester: Manchester University Press, 1992), pp. 59–60.
13 Tabram was certainly regarded by the police as a victim of the Whitechapel murderer, although more recent 'Ripperologists' such as Begg, Fido and Skinner tend to discount her on the basis that the manner of her death contrasts with that of some of the later victims.
14 *The Times*, 10 August 1888, from Evans and Skinner, *Ultimate Jack the Ripper*, p. 9.
15 *The Times*, 14 September 1888, p. 4, from Evans and Skinner, *Ultimate Jack the Ripper*, p. 96.
16 Evans and Skinner, *Ultimate Jack the Ripper*, p. 98.
17 *The Times*, 20 September 1888, p. 3, from Evans and Skinner, *Ultimate Jack the Ripper*, p. 109.
18 Quoted in Begg *et al.*, *Jack the Ripper A–Z*, p. 350.
19 Quoted in Begg *et al.*, *Jack the Ripper A–Z*, p. 350.
20 Quoted in Begg *et al.*, *Jack the Ripper A–Z*, p. 350.

21 Quoted in *The Times*, 14 September 1888, p. 4, from Evans and Skinner, *Ultimate Jack the Ripper*, p. 100.

22 Sander L. Gilman, ' " Who Kills Whores?" "I Do," Says Jack: Race and Gender in Victorian London', in Sarah Webster Goodwin and Elisabeth Bronfen (eds), *Death and Representation* (Baltimore and London: Johns Hopkins University Press, 1993), pp. 263–84, p. 267. All subsequent references are to this edition and are given in the text.

23 Quoted in Evans and Skinner, *Ultimate Jack the Ripper*, p. 149.

24 *The Times*, 1 October 1888, from Evans and Skinner, *Ultimate Jack the Ripper*, p. 134. The following day *The Times* discussed Brown's recent release from a convalescent home, see Evans and Skinner, *Ultimate Jack the Ripper*, p. 135.

25 *The Times*, 27 December, from Evans and Skinner, *Ultimate Jack the Ripper*, p. 118.

26 *The Times*, 4 October 1888, p. 10, from Evans and Skinner, *Ultimate Jack the Ripper*, p. 177.

27 Peter Stallybrass and Allon White, *The Politics and Poetics of Transgression* (London: Methuen, 1986), see pp. 144–5.

28 Sigmund Freud, 'The "Uncanny" in Jensen's "Gradiva", Leonardo Da Vinci and Other Works', Penguin Freud Library, trans. James Strachey, ed. Albert Dickson, vol 14, pp. 335–76, p. 346. All subsequent references are to this edition and are given in the text.

29 *The Times*, 6 October 1888, p. 6, from Evans and Skinner, *Ultimate Jack the Ripper*, pp. 182, 183.

30 From Evans and Skinner, *Ultimate Jack the Ripper*, p. 231.

31 From Evans and Skinner, *Ultimate Jack the Ripper*, p. 231.

32 Quoted in Begg *et al.*, *Jack the Ripper A–Z*, p. 123.

8

'Jonathan's great knife': *Dracula* meets Jack the Ripper

Nicholas Rance

The popular legend used to be that at supper in 1895, Bram Stoker had 'a too generous helping of dressed crab', and that the crab begot the subsequent nightmare which in turn begot *Dracula*.[1] This theory was nullified, however, by the discovery in the 1970s of Stoker's working notes in the Rosenbach Foundation library of Philadelphia.[2] Stoker, it seems, made his initial memorandum for the novel on 8 March 1890 while on holiday in Whitby, where Dracula was eventually to disembark in canine semblance. By February 1892, he had sketched out a plot, complementing a nod to the new technology – Kodak cameras, portable typewriters and recording phonographs – by situating events in the next calendar year, 1893. The retrospect over an interval of seven years in Jonathan Harker's 'Note' comprising the final pages of the novel would thus imply a date of composition of 1900; they were actually written, however, by Stoker, in July 1896, and one may wonder whether his official chronology was at this point to the forefront of Stoker's consciousness. Arguably, July 1889 would have been precisely among the candidates to have been a portentous date, epitomizing an epoch when 'we all went through the flames' (p. 378) so far as the inspiration of *Dracula* is concerned.[3]

If the origins of the novel were earlier than the publication date of 1897 might suggest, so also the ferment evoked by the crimes of Jack the Ripper in 1888 resonated long after the actual crimes. The five canonically accredited victims of the Whitechapel murderer were slaughtered in what was dubbed an 'Autumn of Terror', from 31 August to 9 November 1888, so that even if the uncanonical Martha Tabram, who died on 7 August is regarded as the earliest victim of the Ripper, his rampage lasted a bare three months. For several years, however, the spectre of the Ripper haunted the East End: news stories abounded, and the shock of any future unsolved murders was diluted by the expedient of attributing them to the same source. Moreover, there were two subsequent murders of prostitutes which were akin to the accredited Ripper murders, to the extent that police and officiating doctors, as opposed to a merely superstitious public, were

inclined to believe that the Ripper remained active. Alice McKenzie's mutilated corpse was found in an alley on 16 July 1889: 'I am of opinion that
the murder was performed by the same person who committed the former
series of Whitechapel Murders,' reported the forensic expert, Dr Bond.[4]
Since no one was charged with the murder, the popular mind remained
obdurate that it was the Ripper's handiwork. It was not until April 1890
that plainclothes patrols were finally withdrawn, and this seemed prema-
ture when, on 13 February 1891, the last real Ripper scare occurred, with
the murder of Frances Coles. As Benjamin Leeson – the constable who
would claim to have identified the victim – was to recall, 'There was
tremendous excitement now among the police engaged on the case, as it
really looked as though they were hot on the trail of the Terror'.[5]

Dracula has been much discussed in relation to the broad ideological
perplexities of the 1890s, and especially the controversies over issues of
gender; alternatively, however, a focus has been on specific events of the
period, perhaps as seeming to epitomize the general incitements to *Angst*,
so that *Dracula* has been argued 'really' to be about the career of Oscar
Wilde, for instance.[6] One inducement to proffer a late contender, the Jack
the Ripper case, as a crucial point of reference for *Dracula* is the scope
for confusion over issues of dating, as regards both Stoker's composition
of the novel and the duration of the impact of the case, which may have
helped to render such a connection the less obvious hitherto, though
inevitably the name of Jack the Ripper has cropped up in discussions of
Dracula. On a more forthright note, however, the ensuing argument will
be that the Jack the Ripper case was preoccupying Stoker as he contem-
plated writing *Dracula*, which is then duly permeated by impressions or
fantasies devolving from the case. The nature of Stoker's fascination with
the case seems to break down into two aspects, as Stoker perhaps was
bent on fissuring the popular image of Jack the Ripper. The Whitechapel
murders touched on some of the more exigent ideological conundrums
of the age, which have long been contended to find more or less disguised
expression in *Dracula*. The perception of the case was pertinent to constructions of the feminine; to the theory of racial degeneration; to the
presence of slum conditions in the midst of wealth; and to the rise of
socialist and Marxist popular politics, especially among the Jewish population of the East End.[7] As apart from the appeal of the Jack the Ripper
case to Stoker as a kind of quintessence of the times, however, the case
seems also to have been perceived by the novelist as intimating a solution
of sorts to at any rate some of the conundrums, even though one which
was unlikely to be enticing without some intrepid cosmetic surgery on
the popular image of Jack the Ripper. Arguably, such an operation is
comprised by *Dracula*.

Obviously, a prime reason for the contemporary (not to mention sub-sequent) fascination with the Ripper case was that it remained an enigma. 'Not a trace is left of the murderer, and there is no purpose in the crime to afford the slightest clue, such as would be afforded in other crimes almost without exception,' the *Times* observed.[8] By its very obscurity, the Ripper case served to focus a prevalent feeling of mystery and confusion in the late-Victorian period, encapsulated in George Gissing's phrase 'sexual anarchy'. The impact of the case cast an influence over a cluster of succeeding novels. In 1905, Edgar Wallace touched on the theme in his first bestseller, *The Four Just Men*. The sensation created by the public resolve of the Just Men to murder the Foreign Secretary, if he persists with his parliamentary bill to repatriate aliens, reminds a *maître d'hôtel* of the prior sensation of 'the atrocious East End murders'. Manfred, one of the Just Men, is taken aback: 'it never occurred to me that we should be compared with – him!'[9] There are sup-plementary echoes of the Ripper, from the mandatory resourcefulness of newspapers deprived of official information and striving to compensate – 'Every half-hour brought a new addition, a new theory' – to the bizarre mood of expectancy in the crowd, 'waiting for a man to be murdered', recalling a similar popular state of suspense in the wake of letters to the Central News Agency promising future events.[10] Parallels, however, especially function to underscore the differences. There may have seemed to be a case for regarding the indifference of the Just Men to the rule of law and the taboo against murder as subversive and shocking, so that the unwelcome comparison with the Ripper was merited. Nevertheless, not only the police but the Prime Minister concede the Just Men to be the salutary rough diamonds which the age demanded. It has to count in their favour, too, that unlike the police in 1888 they at least get their man.

The *East London Advertiser* remarked in 1888:

> It is so impossible to account ... for these revolting acts of blood, that the mind turns as it were instinctively to some theory of occult force, and the myths of the Dark Ages rise before the imagination. Ghouls, vampires, bloodsuckers, and all the ghastly array of fables which have been accumu-lated throughout the course of centuries take form, and seize hold of the excited fancy.[11]

If the Ripper case evoked vampires and vampirism for journalists, Stoker's vampire fantasy returns the compliment via allusion to Jack the Ripper. In his introduction to the 1993 Penguin edition of *Dracula*, Maurice Hindle draws attention to Lucy Westenra's report of the nervous lovemaking of Dr John Seward (known as 'Jack' to his friends), specifi-cally his 'playing with a lancet in a way that made me nearly scream'

(p. 56). As Hindle observes, one popular assumption was that Jack the Ripper was a doctor.[12] Barbara Belford's recent biography of Bram Stoker also buttresses the notion that Stoker had Jack the Ripper in mind when writing *Dracula*. Belford herself insists that 1888 was:

> a turning point for the theatre and Stoker. It was the year the Lyceum began the long awaited production of *Macbeth*, and the year Jack the Ripper terrorized Whitechapel, bringing evil into the drawing rooms of Mayfair and Kensington. At this time Stoker conceptualized a story that would intermingle Shakespeare's dark psychology with contemporary evils.[13]

She also quotes, however, from Stoker's introduction to the Icelandic edition of *Dracula*, published in 1901, where the author in puckish mood insists on the actuality of his events and characters, and links the Whitechapel murders of 1888 with the vampire killings: 'This series of crimes has not yet passed from the memory – a series of crimes which appear to have originated from the same source, and which at the time created as much repugnance in people everywhere as the notorious murders of Jack the Ripper'.[14]

This might seem to be no more than an opportunistic puff in retrospect; more imposing evidence is that the Ripper case was preoccupying Stoker as he conceived the novel. In the working notes for *Dracula*, Stoker refers to the league of Van Helsing and friends against the vampire as 'a vigilante committee' (and likewise as 'a necktie party'), suggesting to Christopher Frayling that the novel initially was proposed to co-opt features from the 'Western', with perhaps a more specifically involved role for the Texan, Quincey P. Morris.[15] A phrase which was a variation on 'vigilante committee', however, 'vigilance committee', was a crucial component of the vocabulary with which the Ripper case was fashioned in the popular imagination, possessing an aura rivalling that of the baleful medical 'black bag', an item carried by Van Helsing in the wake of a plethora of Ripper suspects. Various committees were spawned by the Whitechapel murders; however, the Mile End committee was the journalistic favourite, even before its president, George Lusk, was donated a human kidney through the post, apparently a token from the murderer. As a result of this whimsy, Philip Sugden remarks, the Mile End Vigilance Committee was to be guaranteed 'a kind of immortality by commanding space in every book that would ever be written about Jack the Ripper', having dominated the columns of contemporary newspapers prior to the proliferation of the books.[16]

According to *The Shorter Oxford English Dictionary* the term 'apprehend' had acquired two distinct meanings by the second half of the sixteenth century. 'To seize in name of law, arrest' is attributed to 1548, and 'to lay hold upon, seize' to 1572. By 1577, however, the term had also come to mean 'to lay hold of with the intellect'.[17] In the absence of a conclusive arrest during the 'Autumn of Terror' in 1888, it was irresistible to compensate by claiming 'to lay hold of' Jack the Ripper with the intellect, whether the culprit was proposed to be that tautological creature, a mad foreigner, or, as was hazarded by a lady on the Isle of Wight, writing to the *Star* and presumably influenced by 'The Murders in the Rue Morgue', an ape.[18] Otherwise, there were such spectres to contemplate as those raised by a correspondent to the *Times*, who was adamant that the killings should be blamed on society, which had sown the seed and must reap the harvest, rather than on the demented monster appalling the East End with its quest for blood.[19] To characterize the murderer as a mad monster would even here tend to let society off the hook.

Before the 1880s, and with the robust exception of Sunday newspapers, the modest ambition of the press arguably had been to convey the news, leaving readers free to opine as they would. The 1880s saw a new emphasis on diverting readers with conceivably minimal attention spans, so that a focus on crime and iniquity, to be duly deprecated, became the order of the day. In 1888, Alfred Harmsworth, the future Lord Northcliffe, launched *Answers to Correspondents* and his career as a newspaper proprietor which followed. One of his maxims would be that 'crime exclusives are *noticed* by the public more than any other sort of news. They attract attention, which is the secret of newspaper success'.[20] Like Harmsworth, W. T. Stead, his contemporary and the editor of the *Pall Mall Gazette*, was abundant in maxims: 'For the great public, the journalist must print in great capitals, or his warning is unheard'.[21] His own renowned piece of sensational journalism was the 1885 series, 'The Maiden Tribute of Modern Babylon', which exposed the widespread procuration of young females to be deflowered. As its tone persistently suggests, however, the series was yet more aimed to sell newspapers and so to make money: 'The maw of the London Minotaur is insatiable, and none that go into the secret recesses of his lair return again'.[22]

The public obsession with Jack the Ripper in 1888 is thus intimately associated with the 'new journalism' of the 1880s, and the incipient stages of the newspaper revolution which culminated in the founding by Harmsworth of the *Daily Mail* in 1896. As the *Bath and Cheltenham Gazette* remarked during what it stressed was actually a lull in the case, 'that the excitement has been great there is no denying, but it has been largely stimulated and fed by the great and unnecessary prominence given to the subject and by the many foolish rumors which have been published'.[23] One may not dismiss the furor, however, as being merely an effect of the 'new journalism'. The reporting of the case develops much of the popular sensationalism of the broadsheet tradition, exemplified by the widely circulated account of the confession and execution of William Corder, murderer of Maria Marten in the Red Barn.[24] Perhaps, for example, the murders had been committed by an archetypal melodramatic villain, such as was by now incessantly exemplified on the stage in the form of the Suffolk squire, William Corder. This is seemingly the burden of the highly spiced sketches of an early suspect in the Ripper case, 'Leather Apron', prior to his arrest: 'His expression is sinister ... His eyes are small and glittering. His lips are usually parted in a grin which is not only not reassuring, but excessively repellent'.[25] Such accounts abounded in the comfort that if villainy were so transparent, then capture could hardly fail to be imminent. Plausibly, too, the killer might be mad or foreign or both, and almost certainly not a Christian. Thus the impression of 'Leather Apron' continued, 'His name nobody knows, but all are united in the belief that he is a Jew or of Jewish parentage, his face being of a marked Hebrew type'.[26] Such an insistence arguably was a response to the influx of immigrants into the East End after the pogroms of 1881, whence 'foreigner' became a euphemism for 'Jew'. In the 1880s, after some initial sympathy, the Jewish population was resented twice over for supposedly spoiling the market with cheap goods and cheap labour.

Jack the Ripper may actually have been a foreigner, but such repeated assertions as that in the *East London Observer* that 'no Englishman could have perpetrated such a horrible crime as that of Hanbury Street ... it must have been done by a Jew', did not require to be buttressed by evidence.[27] Popular prejudices regarding Eastern European creeds or folklore could be ransacked with the cavalier eclecticism employed by Bram Stoker in *Dracula*. In the nature of things, however, as a correspondent wrote to the *Star*, an Englishman who could behave like a foreigner must be a mad Englishman, who 'would then loose all civilized restraint on such matters'.[28] Thus the faith of another correspondent that the mere celerity with which the crimes had been committed was inconsistent with 'ordinary English phlegmatic nature' was not impugned.[29]

Alternatively, the Ripper might be represented as a decorous if admittedly punitive moralist. The police were moved to visit Jewish abattoirs on the strength of the hypothesis of a ritual slaughterman inspired by the abhorrence in which prostitution was held in the *Talmud*. In *London Labour and the London Poor*, Henry Mayhew had adduced abundant evidence that the mass of prostitution was an effect of poverty.[30] Nevertheless, a popular and enduring version of Jack the Ripper was as a crusader against the inherent vice assumed to be encapsulated in prostitutes rather than their clients, who were subsequently likely to appear as injured parties.

From the mid-1880s it ceased to be plausible to blame the swelling ranks of the urban poor on personal failure, vice or improvidence. In Robert Louis Stevenson's *Dr Jekyll and Mr Hyde*, a bestseller in 1886, a cultural shift is evident from crediting personal irresponsibility as a source of urban poverty to theories of degenerate criminality, comprising an alternative distraction from an invidious hunt for social causes. There are recurrent allusions to Hyde's stunted growth or his proclivity to the subhuman: ' "Something troglodytic, shall we say?" ' muses Utterson.[31] Clubbing to death Sir Danvers Carew, Hyde proceeds 'with ape-like fury'.[32] Further, as Hyde's nature predominates over Jekyll's, the hand which Jekyll wakes to see on the bedclothes is 'lean, corded, knuckly, of a dusky pallor, and thickly shaded with a swart growth of hair'.[33] Stevenson's story is not dismissible as mere Gothic excess, since social commentators in the 1880s constantly reported seeing Hyde-like creatures on the streets of London. In 1886, Lord Brabazon advised: 'Let the reader walk through the wretched streets ... of the Eastern or Southern districts of London . . . should he be of average height, he will find himself a head taller than those around him; he will see on all sides pale faces, stunted figures, debilitated forms, narrow chests, and all the outward signs of a low vital power'.[34] As Gareth Stedman Jones has remarked, the phenomenon described by sociologists was no doubt a real one, which did not, however, imply that the theory of urban degeneration was 'an adequate explanation of London poverty'.[35] Rather, the theory smoothed the way for the middle classes to acknowledge that poverty was a problem of growing masses of the population, instead of being the consequence of the imprudence or bad luck of isolated individuals. The avowed dilemma was then, in the words of Max Nordau, author of *Degeneration* (originally published in 1892), one of 'the degenerate's incapacity for self-adaptation, and the resulting discomfort in the midst of circumstances to which, in consequence of his organic deficiencies, he cannot accommodate himself'.[36] The use of terminology borrowed from Darwin absolved the middle class of responsibility or blame for the crisis: to quote Nordau again in a slightly different context, it offered 'the possibility of scientifically cloaking' a 'mystic obsession'.[37]

The strategy was to insist that whatever might seem to expose deficiencies in the social structure was no more than the symptoms of atavism and an incapacity to adapt, so that the honour of the status quo was not diminished. A celebrated *Punch* cartoon of 29 September 1888, evoking the horror of the Ripper, 'The Nemesis of Neglect', promised via its title to deliver an unequivocally social message, with an emphasis on the slum conditions which governmental dereliction had fostered and which predictably had transpired to be a nursery for murderers, but this message is actually a diluted one, since the murderer is evinced as manifestly a throwback.[38] This was the context in which Stevenson's *The Strange Case of Dr Jekyll and Mr Hyde* acquired so much resonance in relation to the Whitechapel murders that moral force drove the dramatization from the stage during the Ripper scare. As the *Pall Mall Gazette* pithily reflected, 'There certainly seems to be a tolerably realistic impersonification of Mr Hyde at large in Whitechapel'.[39]

One may then regard *Dracula*, as arguably Stoker himself did, as a canny dismemberment of the perplexed popular image of Jack the Ripper, atavistic moralist. Evidently, at least the semblance of murderousness attaches not only to Dracula but to Van Helsing's party.[40] Officially, however, the Count bears sole responsibility for the death of Lucy Westenra, who expires after the sequence of attacks only to resuscitate as a vampire, and who must then for her own good succumb to 'the mercy-bearing stake' (p. 216). The essence of the idea of a vampire is to signify a more or less remote past declining to recede tactfully. There is no difficulty in associating Dracula with the degenerate version of Jack the Ripper, and no doubt a reason for Stoker's penchant for the new technology was to underscore the Count's degeneracy. Through Van Helsing's analogy of the Count as 'child-brain' and Mina Harker's subsequent elaboration, the text invokes Lombroso and Nordau to support the contention that the Count 'is a criminal and of criminal type': he is thus *ipso facto* a throwback, since a hallmark of the criminal was the inability to adapt to present conditions (pp. 341–2). Moreover, Dracula bears the marks of his degeneracy about him, again like Stevenson's Mr Hyde, whose hands anticipate those of the vampire: 'rather coarse – broad, with squat fingers ... hairs in the centre of the palm' (p. 18).[41]

Dracula's assault on his disciple, Renfield, is Ripper-like in effect, leaving the latter 'all covered with blood', with 'terrible injuries' and a face which eventually 'brightened *through its mutilation*' (pp. 274, 275, 277, my emphasis). On the other hand, 'mutilation' is a term to be invoked also in relation to Van Helsing's proposed treatment of Lucy: 'Not for the wide world will I consent to any mutilation of her dead body,' protests the unwitting Arthur (p. 206). The virtuous party's choice of weapons potentially evokes the Ripper. At Castle Dracula, Jonathan Harker has used a handy if humble shovel to slash at the encoffined vampire. At Dracula's house in Piccadilly, however, Harker 'had ready his great Kukri knife, and made a fierce and sudden cut at him' (p. 306). As Harker throws 'the terrible knife aloft again for another stroke', Dr Seward intervenes, substituting the more pacific weapons of crucifix and wafer (p. 306). In the concluding episode, 'Jonathan's great knife' consummately shears through Dracula's throat at the same moment that

THE NEMESIS OF NEGLECT.

" THERE FLOATS A PHANTOM ON THE SLUM'S FOUL AIR,
SHAPING, TO EYES WHICH HAVE THE GIFT OF SEEING,
INTO THE SPECTRE OF THAT LOATHLY LAIR.
FACE IT—FOR VAIN IS FLEEING!
RED-HANDED, RUTHLESS, FURTIVE, UNERECT,
'TIS MURDEROUS CRIME—THE NEMESIS OF NEGLECT!"

8 The neglected East End represented by a spectral Jack the Ripper wielding
the ubiquitous knife.

Quincey Morris's Bowie knife skewers the vampire's heart, and Dracula crumbles into dust (p. 377). This is not strictly against the tenets of vampire superstition, with which Stoker seems to have been quite familiar.[42] Nevertheless, it is suggestively at odds with the prevailing version of vampire lore in the novel.

As the institutional as well as popular suspicion of talmudic moralists suggests, the Whitechapel case mobilized the contemporary debate on the female as much as it did that on the degenerative male. This debate had its counterpart in fiction and reportage. For male novelists at least, the primary connotation of the phenomenon of the 'New Woman' was her disdain for custom in relation to sexual matters, as demonstrated in Grant Allen's *The Woman Who Did*, a bestseller of 1894, in which the heroine declines to marry her suitor, but as a consolation prize is in a hurry to live with him in what moralists must have regarded as 'sin'. In *Dracula*, the 'New Woman' is described by Mina as prone to emancipated proposals such as 'that men and women should be allowed to see each other asleep before proposing or accepting' (p. 89). Lucy, too, contrives her own utterances along similarly saucy lines: 'Why can't they let a girl marry three men, or as many as want her, and save all this trouble?' (p. 59). Lucy's blood transfusions symbolically fulfil this wild wish, so that Van Helsing is able to amuse himself with the irony that he himself is a bigamist and 'this so sweet maid is a polyandrist' (p. 176).[43]

Theoretically, female virtue was protected by an innate 'modesty': once this had somehow been vanquished, however, an inexorable sexual appetite was supposed to be released. Divested of this moral armour, any female would be prone to collapse into the nymphomania which was often assumed to be the impetus to prostitution. Alternatively, moralists among the experts at times objected to the idea of a prostitute enjoying not only the wages of sin but the sin itself. Hence, it was also frequently denied that prostitutes experienced sexual feeling, which had the drawback of being less than complimentary to the prowess of their male customers. The matron of a so-called Lock Hospital, for the treatment of venereal diseases, was quoted as insisting to W. T. Stead 'that the innocent girl once outraged seemed to suffer a lasting blight of the moral sense. They never came to any good: the foul passion from the man seemed to enter into the helpless victim of his lust, and she never again regained her pristine purity of soul'.[44] Theories about Jack the Ripper testify to the attenuation of the previous assumption that prostitutes and respectable women were worlds apart. In his medical persona, the Ripper was inferred to be conducting an anatomy of the sex as such: in a letter to the *Evening News* of 17 September 1888, for instance, he was hazarded to be a ' "medical maniac," investigating "the mysterious changes that take place in the female sex at about the age of these poor women" '.[45]

A heartless version of the Ripper murders was that they were predictably bloody encounters between the minimally evolved, with the Ripper evincing both symptoms of degeneration and a sexual obsession like that with which Nordau credited decadent modern writers such as Zola and Ibsen. If the Ripper was to be labelled a throwback, so, too, was the oversexed woman whose epitome was the prostitute: according to Lucy Bland, a leaflet issued by the Moral Reform Union, 'a feminist social purity organisation', claimed that 'Modesty and a chaste deportment are a young girl's birth right and her choicest adornment ... But when the beast and the harlot have taken the woman's place, there is no depth of shameful sensuality into which she is not prepared to sink'.[46] On the other hand, in *Dracula*, at least officially, the vampire is not lured by an atavistic affinity with his female victims, but wantonly infects Lucy and Mina with beastly sensuality.

The figure of Dracula is primed to evoke responses akin to some of the more artless reactions to Jack the Ripper. Both the vampire's mobility and flair for metamorphoses relate to the popular impression of Jack the Ripper moving wraithlike through the city, contemptuous of police cordons. The description of Lucy as a vampire returning to her tomb pertains to such a version of Jack the Ripper, as Van Helsing's party sees 'the woman, with a corporeal body as real at the moment as our own, pass in through the interstice where scarce a knife-blade could have gone' (p. 212). Dracula is also the epitome, however, of more brazenly tendentious constructions of Jack the Ripper. Evidently, he vindicates the intimations of vampirism in newspaper reports of the murders; to the extent that he has a terrestrial dimension, however, he is Eastern European and possibly Jewish.[47] In *Dracula*, then, it is not merely that a specific agent is to blame for what thus may be regarded as only a blip in the progress of English womanhood: such an agent is barely of this world, and conspicuously alien from England and hence English females in particular.

A stress both in Stoker's working notes and in the novel, however, is that it is in the nature of a vampire to be sufficiently polite to wait for an invitation. As Van Helsing remarks, 'He may not enter anywhere at the first, unless there be someone of the household who bid him to come; though afterwards he can come as he please' (p. 240). Conveniently, such a notion potentially dovetails with contemporary doctrines about female sexuality: with the wall of modesty once broken down, the next stop is nymphomania. In *Dracula*, Mina is newly married and Lucy is in the flush both of her engagement to Arthur and of her two other proposals. Mina herself opines of Lucy's propensity to walk in her sleep, the trance-like state in which she is vulnerable to Dracula, that it is the waiting for her fiancé 'which disturbs her; she will be all right when he arrives' (p. 72).[48] Such an ambivalence about whether there is something chronically wrong here, or whether there is merely a transitory infection, is barely unusual in Gothic fiction. If Gothic fantasy is seductive to readers in assuming to resolve a version of actual fears and conundrums, then the fears and conundrums have to be evoked in the first place. There seems to be a peculiarly nagging tension in *Dracula*, however, between a sense of indecorous behaviour as being uncharacteristic or alternatively as being all too predictable, as though the equivocating vampire metaphor were buckling under weight of an intimation of actual sexual mayhem.

Not only the skittish Lucy falls prey to Dracula, but the virtuous Mina, whose combination of a 'man's brain ... and woman's heart' renders her a source of anxiety (p. 234). Since woman's presumed role in evolution was to become more and more feminine and so to advance the cause of sexual differentiation, it was merely a mark of reversion to exhibit masculine qualities. Such a mark was ascribed to Jack the Ripper's victims, whose deficiency of femininity was assumed to be manifested in what was perceived as their sensuality rather than in their brains. One modern text on the Whitechapel murders, *The Jack the Ripper A–Z*, juxtaposes a mortuary photograph of one victim, Elizabeth Stride, with an 'artist's gratuitously unflattering impression'.[49] The more salient point, however, is that Stride is represented as hermaphroditic. (Her hair is styled in conventionally male fashion, with the one visible ear being entirely visible, except for the marginal concession to her femaleness of being slightly bushy and frizzy behind. She has a virile nose and jaw, while her mouth is a hybrid, ample but equipped with undulating and sensual lips. Her eyes seem to be focused sagaciously and equably on the mid-distance, evidently a flattering impression had the subject been male.) Moreover, in *Dracula*, a coyness tempers the vision of the worst that can befall, albeit at Dracula's behest, so that the aroused sensuality of Lucy has the relative grace of being monogamously inclined. If an adaptation of one version of Jack the Ripper, with Dracula infecting the women with his beastliness rather than his beastliness evoking the beast in women, seems to carry less than conviction, a rather more complimentary version of the Whitechapel murderer as embarked on a crusade against an atavistic womanhood infuses the depiction of Dracula's enemies.

On 17 November 1888, according to the Scotland Yard files on the Ripper case, 'Richard Watson turned in Oliver Matthews because the latter carried a black bag', and so much (or so little) cause for suspicion sufficed to lead dozens of men to police stations.[50] As one modern discussion of the case suggests, 'Almost overnight, the black bag, traditional accoutrement of the visiting physician, had become a badge of murder'.[51] Preparing for the disposal of Lucy as a vampire, Van Helsing relinquishes his customary 'little black bag' in preference for a more imposing item, 'a long leather one, something like a cricketing bag' (p. 213). The 'operation' on Lucy which follows vindicates her earlier apprehension in relation to Dr Seward and his lancet. With a stake being hammered into her heart, Lucy is to scream indeed: 'a hideous, blood-curdling screech came from the opened red lips' (p. 216). Officially, the text suggests, Lucy's condition is Dracula's fault. The evocation of Jack the Ripper, however, implies another scenario, since a gloss on the case had been that women merely were more or less as depraved as Lucy in her vampire state, so that sympathy was liable to accrue to a moralist turned 'avenger'.

Inevitably, there was an embarrassment about casting Jack the Ripper in such a role: however virtuous his cause, he resorted to desperate remedies, so that he was amiably conceded to be 'mad'. *Dracula* is haunted by a corresponding quandary, and Seward reports the mixed response as Van Helsing extracts his baleful paraphernalia from the enhanced version of the black bag: 'To me, a doctor's preparations for work of any kind are stimulating and bracing, but the effect of these things on both Arthur and Quincey was to cause them a sort of consternation' (p. 214). Van Helsing's moral ascendancy is bolstered in that he is an amalgam of two distinct myths about the Ripper. The 'medical maniac', striving to fathom the female condition, was not to be confused with the mad moralist, but Van Helsing is both medical *and* moral, so that the moral mission is endowed with the authority of 'science'. In 1926, Leonard Matters was to propose the pseudonymous Dr Stanley as being the actual Jack the Ripper, avenging his son, Herbert, who had fatally contracted syphilis from Mary Jane Kelly, the final victim, on Boat-race Night, 1886. Essentially, however, such a hypothesis predated *Dracula*. On 13 October 1888, the *East London Observer* reported an East End doctor as discerning the lineaments of the Ripper in his former assistant, whose prospects and sanity had been sacrificed to consorting with Whitechapel prostitutes.[52]

In *Dracula*, masculinity is menaced in complementary ways. The Count rescues the supine Jonathan Harker from the trio of female vampires at Castle Dracula with the insistence, 'This man belongs to me!', while in Whitby, properly passive women make wisecracks about the possibility of polyandry (p. 39).[53] Evoking an affinity between the Royal Academician and Jack the Ripper, however, Bram Dijkstra has stressed the peculiar resonance of dead women as a topic in *fin-de-siècle* painting, since 'Even those women whose "animal energies" made them threatening, active forces while alive could be brought back into the realm of passive erotic appeal by painters who chose to depict them safely dead'.[54] In *Dracula*, Lucy is duly dispatched, with Arthur 'like a figure of Thor as his untrembling arm rose and fell, driving deeper and deeper the mercy-bearing stake' (p. 216). Leonard Wolf, however, invokes the authority of the demonologist Montague Summers to suggest that Arthur is heedless of the rules of vampire-killing. According to Summers, 'it is highly important that the body of the Vampire should be transfixed by a single blow, for two blows would restore it to life. This curious idea is almost universally found in tradition and folklore.' Wolf himself then cites the case of Peter Kurten, 'the Düsseldorf Monster', who went on a murderous rampage in 1929, and whose custom was to 'continue to stab his victims until he experienced orgasm'.[55] Arguably, Stoker's ambition is to effect a divorce between the two most salient components of the Ripper's popular image, so that the Ripper in his relatively endearing aspect as a Nemesis visited on errant women would be free of the taint of what needed to be conceded as the beastly aspect. That Arthur has more affinity to a lust murderer than to a vampire killer, however, suggests the extent to which the Ripper's idiosyncratic display of sexual mastery was liable to elicit a less equivocal approbation from Stoker.

If the exorcism of Lucy breaks the rules of vampire folklore, so too, and much more brazenly, does the end of Dracula.[56] At least according to Van Helsing, one does not slay vampires with a Kukri and a Bowie knife. Rather, they need to be staked and have their heads cut off, the treatment which was meted out, even if in heterodox fashion, to Lucy, and to the trio of female vampires from Castle Dracula, and which Mina quotes Seward as advocating in the case of the Count: 'There must be no chances, this time; we shall not rest until the Count's head and body have been separated, and we are sure that he cannot reincarnate' (p. 354). It ought to be cold comfort that Dracula's body has 'crumbled into dust', when not only has Van Helsing warned but experience has testified that 'every speck of dust that whirls in the wind' may be 'a devouring monster in embryo' (pp. 377, 355). Perhaps to have staked Dracula may have seemed less than decorous, too reminiscent of the sexual innuendo which besets the disposal of Lucy, and so conceding to Dracula even as he is vanquished a chance to cast a slur on British manhood. Otherwise, one may suppose Stoker to have had a sequel in mind, but then to credit the dissolving Dracula with 'a look of peace' would be a mere imposition on the reader (p. 377).

There is a further possible reason for the anomaly, however. Stoker's virtuous characters may be seen also to have an affinity with Jack the

Ripper. This is potentially a source of embarrassment, as Jonathan Harker's choice of weapon, the Gurkha Kukri, a curved knife which broadens towards the point, might imply. Doughty defenders of the imperial cause though the Gurkhas were, they were not actually English, so that the Kukri knife has a function akin to that of the ubiquitous dagger in Agatha Christie's fiction, defining the act of murder as somehow quintessentially foreign, though occasionally committed by an Englishman. The queasy connotations of the scene of Arthur staking Lucy confirm that tact is requisite in differentiating the imputedly high-principled Jack the Ripper from the strictly seamy one, with necessarily an awkwardness about ascribing any kind of redeeming feature to the murderer. If 'Jonathan's great knife' evokes the Ripper, however, candidly avowing a kinship between the cause of virtue and his grisly exploits, at least one is allowed to infer that presumably it will be a relatively reputable Jack the Ripper to whom it falls to slay his beastly counterpart.

There was more of substance and less of commercial pragmatism than Icelanders may have appreciated in Stoker's prefatory invocation of the Whitechapel murders in relation to his fictional vampire killings. With Dracula as the embodiment of Jack the Ripper as a loathsome degenerate, the vampire now has more on his conscience than mere murder: officially, he initiates the licentiousness of his victims. At least, Dracula serves to accomplish the axiom that 'the wages of sin are death', so that disciples of Jack the Ripper as a moralist are licensed to kill the beast in women without the mission being compromised by the stain of murder. If the pertinence of the Ripper murders to *Dracula* turns out to be more than merely matter to inspire the odd casual allusion, a recent biographical revelation seems almost felicitous. The dedicatee of *Dracula*, 'My dear friend Hommy-Beg', alias the bestselling Manx novelist Hall Caine, transpires to have been erotically involved with the American quack doctor Francis Tumblety, who 'had such a powerful influence over him, it verged on the malign'.[57] This is the Tumblety who has also been unearthed as a prime candidate, according to contemporary police opinion, to have been Jack the Ripper.

The Strange Case of Dr Jekyll and Mr Hyde was invoked earlier in relation to the issue of Hyde's atavism, apparently an influence on conceptions of Jack the Ripper, so lending substance to the protest that the dramatization was too near the knuckle to be staged during the Ripper scare. If Dracula has hairy palms in common with Hyde, however, there is also a more radical affinity between the stories, and the suggestion here has been that the authorial project in *Dracula* is to segregate the morally uplifting from the less edifying images of the Ripper, in what amounts to a kind of emulation of Jekyll's experiment within the novella on the contending elements of his own personality. According to Jekyll's dream of a salutary state of moral apartheid:

> If each ... could but be housed in separate identities, life would be relieved of all that was unbearable; the unjust might go his way, delivered from the aspirations and remorse of his more upright twin; and the just could walk steadfastly and securely on his upward path, doing the good things in which he found his pleasure, and no longer exposed to disgrace and penitence by the hands of this extraneous evil. It was the curse of mankind that these incongruous faggots were thus bound together.[58]

Jekyll's venture is less than propitious, with the doctor 'slowly losing hold of my original and better self, and becoming slowly incorporated with my second and worse'; nevertheless, Stoker has a precedent for willing a divorce between the 'incongruous faggots' composing the popular reputation of Jack the Ripper.[59]

Dracula himself is close to a deprecatory version of the Ripper, though the idea of an affinity between atavistic murderer and his victims is discountenanced, only to rear its head in the display of Lucy's vivacity even prior to her encounter with Dracula. There was more empathy, however, with Jack the Ripper as an inferred 'moral avenger'. In *Dracula*, the virtuous Van Helsing evokes the Ripper, with his successive black bags and the idiosyncrasy of the mode of disposal of Lucy. The lineaments of the Whitechapel fiend are thus apportioned between Christian medic and medieval relic; the ineluctably repellent aspects accruing to the face of the Ripper are quarantined, so enabling homage with the less embarrassment to the alternative 'incongruous faggot' of his reputation, as being a crusader against depraved women. While behaviour prone to be construed as motiveless murder and mutilation is evidently beyond the pale, it is incumbent to accost the problem of the 'New Woman', whom Lucy and Mina in *Dracula* both asperse and emulate, so that perhaps even besmirched role models should not be frivolously jettisoned.[60] In Stoker's last novel of 1911, *The Lair of the White Worm*, and as regards the female protagonist, Lady Arabella, 'who, under the instincts of a primeval serpent, carried the ever-varying wishes and customs of womanhood, which is always old – and always new', a happy ending is sponsored by the solution of dynamite, as disposed to be ignited by at least somewhat providential lightning (p. 173).

Notes

1 Harry Ludlam, *A Biography of Dracula: The Life Story of Bram Stoker* (London: Foulsham, 1962), p. 99.

2 For a digest of Stoker's groundwork for *Dracula*, with an accompanying commentary, see Christopher Frayling, *Vampyres: Lord Byron to Count Dracula* (London: Faber & Faber, 1991), pp. 297–347, and also Joseph S. Bierman, 'The Genesis and Dating of *Dracula* from Bram Stoker's Working Notes' (1977) rept. in Margaret L. Carter (ed.), *'Dracula': The Vampire and the Critics* (Ann Arbor: UMI Research Press, 1988), pp. 51–5.

3 Page references to *Dracula* are to Bram Stoker, *Dracula*, ed. Maud Ellmann (Oxford: Oxford University Press, 1996), and are included in the text.

4 Paul Begg, Martin Fido and Keith Skinner, *The Jack the Ripper A–Z* (London: Headline, 1996), p. 50.

5 Colin Wilson and Robin Odell, *Jack the Ripper: Summing Up and Verdict* (London: Corgi, 1988), p. 97.

6 See Talia Schaffer, '"A Wilde Desire Took Me": The Homoerotic History of *Dracula*', rept. in Nina Auerbach and David J. Skal (eds), *Dracula* (New York: Norton, 1997), pp. 470–82.

7 It may not have been merely random that one victim was murdered in a yard next to the International Working Men's Educational Club.

8 Philip Sugden, *The Complete History of Jack the Ripper* (London: Robinson, 1995), p. 324.

9 Edgar Wallace, *The Four Just Men* (Oxford: Oxford University Press, 1995), p. 68.

10 Wallace, *The Four Just Men*, p. 92.

11 Sugden, *The Complete History*, p. 2.

12 Maurice Hindle, 'Introduction', in Bram Stoker, *Dracula*, ed. Maurice Hindle (Harmondsworth: Penguin, 1993), p. x.

13 Barbara Belford, *Bram Stoker: A Biography of the Author of 'Dracula'* (London: Weidenfeld and Nicolson, 1996), p. 202.

14 Belford, *Bram Stoker*, p. 272.

15 Frayling, *Vampyres*, p. 307. The character of Morris sometimes has been a crux for critics, as being so ineffectual as even to inspire speculation that the American is an agent of Dracula, i.e., a vampire; see Franco Moretti, *Signs Taken for Wonders: Essays in the Sociology of Literary Forms* (London: Verso, 1983), p. 95.

16 Sugden, *The Complete History*, p. 123.

17 *The Shorter Oxford English Dictionary*, vol. 1 (Oxford: Clarendon Press, 1975), p. 93.

18 Donald Rumbelow, *The Complete Jack the Ripper* (Harmondsworth: Penguin, 1988), p. 108.

19 Rumbelow, *Complete Jack the Ripper*, p. 52.

20 Tom Clarke, *My Northcliffe Diary* (London: Gollancz, 1931), p. 199.

21 Peter Keating, *The Haunted Study* (London: Secker and Warburg, 1989), p. 297.

22 W. T. Stead, *The Maiden Tribute of Modern Babylon* (London: Pall Mall Gazette, 1885), p. 2.

23 Begg *et al.*, *Jack the Ripper A–Z*, p. 15.

24 Matthew Engel, *Tickle the Public: One Hundred Years of the Popular Press* (London: Gollancz, 1996), p. 25.

25 Melvin Harris, *The Ripper File* (London: W. H. Allen, 1989), p. 42.

26 Harris, *Ripper File*, p. 42. Though less than amiable, 'Leather Apron' turned out to be a frail and diminutive man who spent much of his time in hospital.

27 Bruce Paley, *Jack the Ripper: The Simple Truth* (London: Headline, 1996), p. 62.

28 Rumbelow, *Complete Jack the Ripper*, p. 109.

29 Begg *et al.*, *Jack the Ripper A–Z*, p. 137.

30 Henry Mayhew, *London Labour and the London Poor*, vol. 1 (London: G. Newbold, 1861), pp. 412–13.

31 Robert Louis Stevenson, *'The Strange Case of Dr Jekyll and Mr Hyde' and Other Stories*, ed. Jenni Calder (Harmondsworth: Penguin, 1984), p. 40.

32 Stevenson, *Jekyll and Hyde*, p. 47.

33 Stevenson, *Jekyll and Hyde*, p. 88.

34 Gareth Stedman Jones, *Outcast London: A Study in the Relationship between Classes in Victorian Society* (Harmondsworth: Penguin, 1984), p. 308.

35 Stedman Jones, *Outcast London*, p. 151.

36 Max Nordau, *Degeneration* (London: University of Nebraska Press, 1993), p. 398.

37 Nordau, *Degeneration*, p. 353.

38 Judith R. Walkowitz, *City of Dreadful Delight: Narratives of Sexual Danger in Late-Victorian London* (London: Virago, 1992), plate 9.

39 Harris, *Ripper File*, p. 41.

40 Several critics have suggested the potential for an embarrassing equivalence in iniquity between Dracula and his officially virtuous enemies. Most intriguingly, perhaps, Rebecca A. Pope compares Arthur Holmwood as a stake-driving 'figure of Thor' to Othello, 'a man who perceives himself wronged by a passionate woman and consequently uses violence to reassert the patriarchal gender code', in 'Writing and Biting in *Dracula*', rept. in Glennis Byron (ed.), *'Dracula': Contemporary Critical Essays* (London: Macmillan, 1999), pp. 68–92 (p. 76). In 'Seward's Folly: *Dracula* as a Critique of "Normal Science"' rept. in Carol A. Senf (ed.), *The Critical Response to Bram Stoker* (London: Greenwood Press, 1993), pp. 73–84, John L. Greenway remarks that 'As we have only the narrators' sentiments, we overlook the contrast between their tedious moralizing and the violence of their behavior' (p. 83). On the other hand, Seward perhaps leads the way with a curious remark rebuffing sanctimony, and, aptly for the present argument, acknowledging that the moral crusade is strictly criminal: 'Again I felt that horrid sense of the reality of things, in which any effort of imagination seemed out of place; and I realized distinctly the perils of the law which we were incurring in our unhallowed work' (p. 200).

41 Dracula's Lombrosian affinities have been discussed in Leonard Wolf (ed.), *The Essential Dracula: Annotated Edition of Bram Stoker's Classic Novel* (New York: Plume, 1993), p. 300, and more comprehensively in Ernest

Fontana, 'Lombroso's Criminal Man and Stoker's *Dracula*', rept. in Carter, *Dracula*, pp. 159–65. The latter also registers the marks of criminal degeneracy in Dracula's victims, in inviting the vampire in the first place, so that what links Lucy 'to the epileptic criminal is her somnambulism, which, according to Lombroso, is a frequent characteristic of epileptics' (Fontana, 'Lombroso's Criminal Man', p. 162).

42 According to Paul Barber, *Vampires, Burial and Death: Folklore and Reality* (New Haven: Yale University Press, 1988), 'The Orthodox Gypsies of Stari Ras "consider that a sharp knife is as efficacious as a thorn stick for killing a vampire"' (p. 72). Nevertheless, the knife-thrust of the mate of the *Demeter* fails to harm Dracula.

43 It has been remarked of the apparently much more demure Mina that although she 'does not have an office career, her typing expertise moves her toward subversive – undomestic – ground'; see Auerbach and Skal, *Dracula*, p. 55. Pope piquantly compares Mina with Dorothea in George Eliot's *Middlemarch*, since 'in both instances traditionally male interests and prerogatives are taken up by a woman in the name of traditionally female duties and interests' (Pope, p. 85). To impute sexual symbolism to the blood transfusions in *Dracula* is a critical commonplace; Van Helsing, of course, sets the fashion.

44 Stead, *Maiden Tribute*, p. 50.

45 Walkowitz, *City of Dreadful Delight*, p. 209.

46 Lucy Bland, *Banishing the Beast: English Feminism and Sexual Morality 1885–1914* (Harmondsworth: Penguin, 1995), p. 116.

47 Jules Zanger has investigated Dracula's Jewish proclivities in 'A Sympathetic Vibration: Dracula and the Jews', *English Literature in Transition*, 34 (1991), pp. 33–43, as has Alexandra Warwick in 'Vampires and Empire: Fears and Fictions of the 1890s', in Sally Ledger and Scott McCracken (eds), *Cultural Politics at the Fin de Siècle* (Cambridge: Cambridge University Press, 1995), pp. 202–20. For briefer discussion, see Bram Dijkstra, *Idols of Perversity: Fantasies of Feminine Evil in Fin-de-Siècle Culture* (Oxford: Oxford University Press, 1986), p. 343 and Daniel Pick, ' "Terrors of the Night": *Dracula* and "Degeneration" ', rept. in Lyn Pykett (ed.), *Reading Fin de Siècle Fictions* (London: Longman, 1996), pp. 49–65 (p. 59).

48 As many critics have noticed, but Roth perhaps most pithily, 'Only when Lucy becomes a vampire is she allowed to be "voluptuous," yet she must have been so long before, judging from her effect on men and from Mina's description of her' (Phyllis Roth, 'Suddenly Sexual Women in Bram Stoker's *Dracula*', rept. in Auerbach and Skal, *Dracula*, pp. 411–21 (p. 414)). Warwick has remarked with similar crispness that 'the suggestion that they are "asking for it" is central to the vampire myth. Dracula makes it clear through Renfield that he has to be invited into a house, otherwise he cannot enter' (Warwick, 'Vampires and Empire', p. 207). As the editors of a recent collection of essays on Stoker note, the effect is that 'the challenged power and the disrupting force are at times almost identical in appearance in the

novel'; see William Hughes and Andrew Smith (eds), *Bram Stoker: History, Psychoanalysis and the Gothic* (London: Macmillan, 1998), p. 5.

49 Begg *et al.*, *Jack the Ripper A-Z*, between pp. 170 and 171.

50 Begg *et al.*, *Jack the Ripper A-Z*, p. 406.

51 Wilson and Odell, *Jack the Ripper*, p. 91.

52 Begg *et al.*, *Jack the Ripper A-Z*, pp. 425–6.

53 The editors of the Norton edition of *Dracula* remark of the claim in relation to Harker that 'This proprietary sentence recurs over and over in Stoker's working notes'; they further relate that 'in a passage published only in the 1899 American edition' Dracula 'announces that he will feast on Jonathan' (Auerbach and Skal, *Dracula*, pp. 43, xii). In one of the more celebrated essays on *Dracula*, Craft has argued that the novel proceeds via heterosexual mediation of its primary homoerotic concerns, so that, for example, 'Lucy receives the phallic correction that Dracula deserves' (Christopher Craft, '"Kiss Me with Those Red Lips": Gender and Inversion in Bram Stoker's *Dracula*', rept. in Auerbach and Skal, *Dracula*, pp. 444–59, (p. 457)).

54 Dijkstra, *Idols of Perversity*, p. 56.

55 Wolf, *The Essential Dracula*, p. 263; R. E. L. Masters and Edward Lea, *Sex Crimes in History* (New York: Julian Press, 1963), pp. 148–9.

56 The anomalous mode of the disposal of Dracula has often been noted by critics, though not to the exclusion of a recurring amnesia in relation to the circumstance of his not being staked.

57 Stewart Evans and Paul Gainey, *Jack the Ripper: First American Serial Killer* (London: Arrow, 1996), p. 260. Evans and Gainey derive their information about Hall Caine from the work of his biographer, Vivien Allan.

58 Stevenson, *Jekyll and Hyde*, p. 82.

59 Stevenson, *Jekyll and Hyde*, p. 89.

60 Johnson's remark is evidently percipient: 'One of the most striking characteristics of the considerable number of critical essays written about Bram Stoker's *Dracula* (1897) in the past thirty years is that, more often than not, they deny that Stoker really knew what he was doing as he wrote it' (Alan Johnson, 'Bent and Broken Necks: Signs of Design in Stoker's *Dracula*', rept. in Carter, *Dracula*, pp. 231–45, p. 231). Since the present essay's proposal of an authorial preoccupation with Jack the Ripper vies with what has become even more the trend since Johnson wrote (1987), I take comfort from the 'signs of design' which he adduces in *Dracula*.

9

Jack the Ripper, Sherlock Holmes and the narrative of detection

Martin Willis

The Whitechapel murders have offered numerous amateur (and some professional) detectives the opportunity to pit their deductive skills against both the Victorian London Metropolitan Police Force and the anonymous criminal known only as Jack the Ripper.[1] That these processes of detection have offered hugely varying interpretations of events and announced dozens of prime suspects suggest that many, at least, are more narrative fiction than fact. However, it is not only these stories of detection that have been given impetus by the Whitechapel murders. Detective fiction of the late nineteenth century – and Arthur Conan Doyle's Sherlock Holmes novels and stories in particular – responded specifically to the events of Whitechapel and its concomitant media coverage as well as to the ensuing mythologizing of Jack the Ripper as a representation of British degeneration, immorality and social fragmentation.

Conan Doyle never did write a story that involved both Jack the Ripper and Sherlock Holmes yet the Holmes canon has always seemed to inspire others to invent such a link. The 1965 film *A Study in Terror* was one of the earliest to offer a vision of Sherlock Holmes on the trail of the Whitechapel murderer.[2] This was followed by many other examples across a range of artistic genres, such as Ellery Queen's novel, *Murder by Decree*, or the satiric sketch 'Jock the Ripper' from celebrated British comedians Morecambe and Wise.[3] It is understandable that so many fictions of simultaneity have been created; as national icons of criminality and detection it would be unusual, in fact, if Jack the Ripper and Sherlock Holmes had not been set in direct opposition to one another. Nor is their convergence a twentieth-century phenomenon. In the 1890s – once his detective fiction had become popular – Conan Doyle was often invited to comment on how Sherlock Holmes would have investigated the Whitechapel murders. It is plausible that he would have given this some thought; Conan Doyle was as gripped by the murders as the rest of the population. Indeed he offered as a reason for the murderer's ability to remain hidden from detection that he was disguising himself as a midwife so as to move freely around Whitechapel while covered in blood.[4] Jack the Ripper remained in Conan Doyle's thoughts throughout the period in which he wrote the Sherlock Holmes stories. In 1892 he visited the Metropolitan Police's Black Museum, where aspects of the Whitechapel murders were exemplified by some of the physical evidence recovered from the murder scenes. Later, in 1905, the year of the book publication of *The Return of Sherlock Holmes*, he took a Whitechapel walk organized by the Crimes Club and including John Churton Collins, who recorded the event in his memoirs.[5]

Although Conan Doyle never did concur with the public view that Sherlock Holmes should investigate the Whitechapel murders it is clear that his own view of the murderer's modus operandi arose from the same imaginative rendering of criminal activity that coloured his detective fiction. The use of disguise, and of cross-gendered disguise in particular, plays a central role in several of the early Sherlock Holmes stories and novels. The first novel, *A Study in Scarlet* (1886), contains a male criminal disguised as a mature woman, while the first short story, 'A Scandal in Bohemia' (1891), reverses this structure by revealing the female protagonist in the dress of a male youth. The male criminal can also be found in disguise in two other early short stories, 'A Case of Identity' (1891) and 'The Man with the Twisted Lip' (1891). However, the use of disguise is not exclusive to the criminal. Sherlock Holmes also dons a series of disguises in the promotion of his detection. In *The Sign of Four* (1889), 'A Scandal in Bohemia', 'The Man with the Twisted Lip' and 'The Beryl Coronet' (1892) Holmes plays the parts of a seaman, a vicar, an opium addict and an unemployed working-class man as he seeks the evidence required to support his theories.

The similar methodology of Whitechapel murderer (as speculated), fictional criminal and fictional detective reveals not only that Conan Doyle saw a resonance between actual and imaginative crime – between Jack the Ripper and Sherlock Holmes – but that he also understood the similarity between criminal and detective. This may have been unproblematic earlier in the nineteenth century when the criminal was perceived as hero as often as villain but in the aftermath of the Whitechapel murders it was much more contentious to draw parallels between detective authority and criminal anarchy. After *A Study in Scarlet*, which of course was written before the Whitechapel murders, Conan Doyle attempted to eradicate the subtle associations to the criminal in both his heroic detective and his detective fiction. That it was only partially successful can be seen from the parallels that are still capable of being drawn between the detective and the criminal in the ensuing short stories. Nevertheless, it was Conan Doyle's project to disconnect the detective from the criminal and criminal pursuits from the Whitechapel murders. In doing this Conan Doyle subtly distanced his fictional world of crime from the horrors of Jack the Ripper while at the same time emasculating the many representations of Jack the Ripper (as foreigner and as misogynist, for example) and the methods of that representation (such as those found in the press) by continually stressing their powerlessness in the face of the deductive reasoning of Sherlock Holmes.

It is when we return to consider the descriptions and actions of Sherlock Holmes in *A Study in Scarlet* that the shift in characterization in the later novels and stories becomes so apparent. Describing Sherlock Holmes to John Watson, Stamford offers a rather neutral account of the detective's character. Holmes is 'a little queer in his ideas' and 'not a man that is easy to draw out' but 'a decent fellow' who 'can be communicative enough when the fancy seizes him'.[6] However, as Stamford becomes more expansive it is Holmes's strangeness that comes to the fore:

> 'It is not easy to express the inexpressible,' he [Stamford] answered with a laugh. 'Holmes is a little too scientific for my tastes – it approaches to cold-bloodedness. I could imagine his giving a friend a little pinch of the latest vegetable alkaloid, not out of malevolence, you understand, but simply out of a spirit of inquiry in order to have an accurate idea of the effects. To do him justice, I think that he would take it himself with the same readiness. He appears to have a passion for definite and exact knowledge.'
> 'Very right too.'
> 'Yes, but it may be pushed to excess. When it comes to beating the subjects in the dissecting-rooms with a stick, it is certainly taking a rather bizarre shape.'
> 'Beating the subjects!'
> 'Yes, to verify how far bruises may be produced after death. I saw him at it with my own eyes.'
> 'And yet you say he is not a medical student?'
> 'No. Heaven knows what the objects of his studies are.' (p. 17)

Holmes's similarity to a number of the representations of the Whitechapel murderer that were to become common in the media less than a year after the publication of *A Study in Scarlet* is striking.[7] Stamford describes a cold-blooded, amoral man of medical knowledge known to conduct violent experiments on fresh corpses. It may have been that Conan Doyle had based Holmes upon the Edinburgh Professor of Medicine, Dr Joseph Bell, but in the aftermath of the events of autumn 1888 it would be with Jack the Ripper that he would be more quickly associated.[8] The allusions to the Whitechapel murderer do not end with Stamford's depiction. As Watson begins to learn more of the man with whom he has agreed to share a suite of rooms his analysis of Holmes's habits and peculiarities only adds to the representation that Stamford has begun:

> Sometimes he spent his day at the chemical laboratory, sometimes in the dissecting-rooms, and occasionally in long walks, which appeared to take him into the lowest portions of the city. Nothing could exceed his energy when the working fit was upon him; but now and again a reaction would seize him, and for days on end he would lie upon the sofa in the sitting-room, hardly uttering a word or moving a muscle from morning to night. On these occasions I have noticed such a dreamy, vacant expression in his eyes, that I might have suspected him of being addicted to the use of some narcotic, had not the temperance and cleanliness of his whole life forbidden such a notion. (p. 20)

The addictive personality, the schizophrenia of his lethargic yet frenetic character and the mystery of his long periods of immersion in the 'lower' areas of London all combine to reinforce the similarity of Holmes to the composite Whitechapel suspect. Just as Jack the Ripper was – by various police, press and public sources – thought to be an addict made violent by drug use, a madman, or a medical man pursuing gruesome research, so Sherlock Holmes is, in turn, associated with violent medical investigations, significant personality change and addiction.

When Conan Doyle returned to detective fiction with *The Sign of Four*, almost a year after the Whitechapel murders and over three years since he had written *A Study in Scarlet*, his characterization of Sherlock Holmes was decidedly altered. Holmes's addiction is no longer a mysterious supposition of Watson's that might explain his changes in personality or his violent nature but has become a clear and common cocaine habit that Watson is able to contain and rationalize within his medical knowledge. Other aspects of Holmes's character that were unsettling in the earlier novel are also made safe, even assuring, for the reader. No longer is Holmes cold-blooded and violent, but is now 'cool [and] nonchalant' (p. 89). Holmes has become what Martin Priestman has identified as 'the completely different Holmes of *The Sign of Four*, an intellectual aesthete to his fingertips'.[9] The amoral Holmes who beat the dissecting-room corpses and poisoned a dog to prove a point of his thesis is now a scientific detective rightly concerned to maintain a level of objectivity: 'Detection is, or ought to be, an exact science and should be treated in the same cold and unemotional manner' (p. 90). These significant shifts in the rationalization of Holmes's character subdue any of the psychopathological traits that were available to the reader in *A Study in Scarlet*. Holmes is no longer mysterious and maniacal but learned, calm and precise.

Although Conan Doyle partially reinvents Holmes in order to remove any possibility of explicit comparisons with Jack the Ripper, the novels and stories after *A Study in Scarlet* still offer the potential for comparison with both the Whitechapel murderer and the generic criminal type. In *The Sign of Four*, for example, Watson reflects on Holmes's capacity for criminal activity as his subject investigates the evidence of a crime scene: 'So swift, silent and furtive were his movements, like those of a trained bloodhound picking out a scent, that I could not but think what a terrible criminal he would have made had he turned his energy and sagacity against the law instead of exerting them in its defence' (p. 112). This passage reflects a similar one in *A Study in Scarlet* where Holmes himself jokingly states that he is 'one of the hounds and not the wolf' (p. 35). Traces of Holmes's similarity to Jack the Ripper still exist in these assertions of both his predatory skill and his quick and quiet clandestine movements, all of which were necessary attributes – argue the various commentators on the Whitechapel murders – of whoever had committed the crimes. Yet these comparisons are not detrimental to Sherlock Holmes's status in the same way as the more mysterious and inconclusive hints at his behaviour found in *A Study in Scarlet*. The reason for this is twofold. First, it was a common trope of detective fiction in the nineteenth century for the criminal and the detective to be similar character types. The career of the French detective François Vidocq had given detective fiction its inspiration: Vidocq was a master thief who became the head of the Sûreté and published his *Memoirs* in 1829. Emile Gaboriau's series of detective novels in the 1860s continued the trend. His leading character, Lecoq, moved, as Martin Priestman points out, 'from a walk-on role as a reformed criminal to centre-stage as a master of deduction and disguise'.[10] By the 1880s and 1890s it was 'widely recognized', argues John A. Hodgson, that 'opposed though they may be, these characters ... have much in common'.[11] Second, drawing such a direct correlation between Holmes and the criminal highlights Holmes's unique understanding of criminal intention while at the same time reassuring the reader that such skills will be put to use in apprehending criminals rather than perpetrating criminal acts. Holmes's similarity to the criminal therefore becomes a strength of his detection rather than a fearful portent of his motives.

Conan Doyle's alterations to the character of Sherlock Holmes allow him to recalibrate what had been a misalignment of his detective with the most notorious criminal of the later nineteenth century to fit the more acceptable generic convention of the detective as a heroic investigator who carries with him the traces of criminality. This making safe of Sherlock Holmes was only one of several ways in which Conan Doyle's detective fiction recoils from both the reality and the perceived ubiquity of crime after 1888.

Another was his reimagining of the socio-geographic space of London as the setting for many of the Holmes narratives. The public perception of crime in London in the months and years after the Whitechapel murders was of an uncontrollable force against which the official police were impotent. The fire to fuel this view had been stoked by the popular press during the months of September to November 1888 when, as L. Perry Curtis reveals, law and order news took 'advantage of the growing dismay over the failure of the police to catch the killer' to claim that 'common criminals were thriving in central London' and that 'serious crimes were being committed by Englishmen in "the heart of the greatest commercial centre of the world"'.[12] The popular press was not alone in highlighting the general lawlessness of the nation's capital. Investigative journalists, ethnographers and other social activists used the public fascination with the Whitechapel murders to promote their own social reform agendas. In many of their reports and public statements areas such as Whitechapel are characterized as poverty stricken, diseased and dangerous. Although this was certainly true – and was intended to incite support for change – it also enhanced the impression of an anarchic metropolis pregnant with criminal danger.[13]

In *A Study in Scarlet* Watson rehearses what was shortly to become the prevailing view of London. Early in the narrative he describes the city as 'that great cesspool into which all the loungers and idlers of the Empire are irresistibly drained' (p. 15). This may have become a common view in reality but it was not to be the view of London that the Sherlock Holmes narratives followed. Indeed Watson's comment in this pre-1888 novel stands out as the only description of the capital that in any way coincides with public opinion. Even when Holmes observes that 'crime is commonplace' (p. 93) in *The Sign of Four* it is only to suggest that there is presently no criminal activity in London worthy of his investigation. Far more common is an imagined London in which the 'tranquil English home' (p. 116) dominates over the 'wild, dark business' (p. 116) of the unlawful act.

Nowhere is this more apparent than in the stories that appeared in the *Strand* magazine between July 1891 and June 1892 and which Conan Doyle published as *The Adventures of Sherlock Holmes*. 'The Adventure of the Blue Carbuncle' offers a fine example of London as a reimagined place of quaint events that have no criminal associations. As Holmes enacts his observational techniques upon a felt hat, Watson – acting as a synecdoche of the reader – is prompted to enquire after its significance:

9 Unofficial detectives investigate the Whitechapel murders.

'I suppose,' I remarked, 'that, homely as it looks, this thing has some deadly story linked on to it – that it is the clue which will guide you in the solution of some mystery and the punishment of some crime.'

'No, no. No crime,' said Sherlock Holmes, laughing. 'Only one of those whimsical little incidents which will happen when you have four million human beings all jostling each other within the space of a few square miles. Amid the action and reaction of so dense a swarm of humanity, every possible combination of events may be expected to take place, and many a little problem will be presented which may be striking and bizarre without being criminal. We have already had experience of such.' (p. 245)

Holmes's reference at the end of this speech to the previous cases that make up the *Adventures* makes clear Conan Doyle's determination to foreground the vibrancy and eccentricity of London rather than its villainy. Holmes laughs off Watson's assumption of criminality as though it were an unorthodox conclusion to have drawn. Watson's apparently haphazard opinions are again shown to be in error in 'The Copper Beeches', in which a contrast is drawn between London and rural England:

All over the countryside, away to the rolling hills around Aldershot, the little red and gray roofs of the farm-steadings peeped out from amid the light green of the new foliage.

'Are they not fresh and beautiful?' I cried with all the enthusiasm of a man fresh from the fogs of Baker Street.

But Holmes shook his head gravely.

'Do you know, Watson,' said he, 'that it is one of the curses of a mind with a turn like mine that I must look at everything with reference to my own special subject. You look at these scattered houses, and you are impressed by their beauty. I look at them, and the only thought which comes to me is a feeling of their isolation and of the impunity with which crime may be committed there.'

'Good heavens!' I cried. 'Who would associate crime with these dear old homesteads?'

'They always fill me with a certain horror. It is my belief, Watson, founded upon my experience, that the lowest and vilest alleys in London do not present a more dreadful record of sin than does the smiling and beautiful countryside.'

'You horrify me!'

'But the reason is very obvious. The pressure of public opinion can do in the town what the law cannot accomplish. There is no lane so vile that the scream of a tortured child, or the thud of a drunkard's blow, does not beget sympathy and indignation among the neighbours, and then the whole machinery of justice is ever so close that a word of complaint can set it going, and there is but a step between the crime and the dock. But look at these lonely houses, each in its own fields, filled for the most part with poor ignorant folk who know little of the law. Think of the deeds of hellish cruelty, the hidden wickedness which may go on, year in, year out, in such places, and none the wiser. (p. 323)

In this intriguingly counterintuitive argument of the places of criminality Holmes proffers a vision of London as a city of speedy justice where the criminal is under constant surveillance by a predominantly honest and lawful society. The London fog, which so many commentators on Conan Doyle's detective fiction take to be a representation of the transgressive acts hidden within 'the sprawling anonymous city perceived as virtually unknowable', hides, not crime but community.[14] This is London as judicial fantasy, London not as it was viewed by the media from 1888 but as they felt it would be if only, as L. Perry Curtis shows, 'more police, more surveillance of suspicious persons, and harsher sentences would stop the criminal element in their tracks'.[15] Conan Doyle, in a memorable phrase from the critic Stephen Knight, is attempting 'to draw the sting of the threats of city living' in his portrayal of London. Cleverly, though, it is a sting drawn by Londoners themselves; those residents whose watchfulness has made safe the 'lowest and vilest alleys'.[16]

The comforting knowledge of a decriminalized London was augmented by a failsafe mechanism that was brought into play whenever any criminal activity appeared to have eluded the scrutiny of the average Londoner. This guardian of observation was Sherlock Holmes himself.

Holmes's self-confessed 'exact knowledge of London' (p. 185) is further evidence that Conan Doyle's city is neither mysterious nor chaotic but known and regulated. In a remarkable moment of fantasy in 'A Case of Identity' Holmes says to Watson:

> 'We would not dare to conceive the things which are really mere common-places of existence. If we could fly out of that window hand in hand, hover over this great city, gently remove the roofs, and peep in at the queer things which are going on, the strange coincidences, the plannings, the cross-purposes, the wonderful chain of events, working through generations, and leading to the most *outré* results, it would make all fiction with its conventionalities and foreseen conclusions most stale and unprofitable.' (pp. 190–1)

This is surveillance made magical, the kind of sorcery that, to many of Holmes's clients, he seems able to perform.[17] Just as important, however, is the vision of Holmes and Watson's flight over a London that is fully understood by them, that has no secrets from them, no history that they cannot unravel, no future event that they cannot trace. Although the size and complexity of the city makes it implausible (as Conan Doyle recognizes) that crime will always be detected and curtailed by the communities in which it occurs, Holmes's unique knowledge places even the most inaccessible reaches of the city within his range of vision. As Watson perceptively notes in *The Sign of Four*, London crime is 'a labyrinth in which a man less singularly endowed than [Holmes] ... might well despair of ever finding a clue' (p. 116).

The fictional London Conan Doyle creates is firstly self-policing and voluntarily lawful, subduing, as Stephen Knight argues, the 'real threat to respectable life posed by the grim areas where the working-class and the "dangerous classes" lived'.[18] When criminal activity does circumvent the structures of security Conan Doyle has created – as it must do in detective fictions – Sherlock Holmes's mastery of the city in all its incarnations (geographic, botanical, geological, psychological, criminal) tracks, tames and makes safe the spaces of London that crime has temporarily upset. Holmes's knowledge of London may, ironically, provoke another similarity with the Jack the Ripper who was equally able to move without hazard through the labyrinthine streets of Whitechapel, but the vision of the city that the Holmes narratives offer to the reader is very different indeed from the London which the Ripper stalked.

If the Sherlock Holmes fictions made London safe by making it knowable they also contained and reduced the effects of crime by making it, too, known and understood. One of the key aspects of Conan Doyle's narratives of detection is the revelation of motive that almost always brings the plot to a conclusion. While Holmes uncovers the story of crime it is very often left to the criminal to retell that story in the presence of the reader, confirming Holmes's accuracy and making clear their motivation. This narrative structure – ordered as criminal event, gathering of information, speculative deductions, plausible conclusions, confirmation and unveiling of criminal and motive – responds particularly to the new media narratives given impetus by the Whitechapel murders.

Press reporting was fundamentally challenged by the case of Jack the Ripper. The gathering and representation of crime news (in the popular press) was normally a straightforward process which began with factual reporting of a given crime, imbued with a certain amount of sensationalism wherever possible, and concluded with 'many columns about the inquest and trial'.[19] However, the Whitechapel murders posed a problem: the failure to catch the killer or to know anything at all about their identity or motivations left an enormous gap in the predictable narrative of media coverage. L. Perry Curtis concisely details the difficulties journalists faced:

> Here was a series of shocking crimes without any closure. Instead of the customary sequence of arrest, indictment, trial, and execution, the public had to endure five gruesome inquests that shed no light on the killer's identity or motive. The long list of suspects brought the police no closer to their quarry, and complicated the journalists' tasks of narrating the crimes ... Instead of relying on tried and true formulas and familiar scenarios, reporters had to stretch their imaginations and create episodes as well as motives because they were just as baffled as the police by these attacks.[20]

The Whitechapel murders required a different kind of narrative structure: a narrative of crime fiction rather than of crime fact. Reporting the murders became a series of speculations as opposed to the more episodic relation of events and actions that characterized the coverage of other crimes. Analysis of evidence and suppositions on motive replaced the common fare of chronological narratives of event. In essence the reporting of the Whitechapel murders became self-performances of detection in action where they had once been summaries of detection already complete.[21]

Watson and Holmes offer their opinions on the difference between these two types of crime reporting in two short stories, 'The Engineer's Thumb' and 'A Case of Identity'. In the former Watson argues that 'the story [of the engineer's thumb] has, I believe, been told more than once in the newspapers, but, like all such narratives, its effect is much less striking when set forth en bloc in a single half-column of print than when the facts slowly evolve before your own eyes' (p. 274). For Watson it is the process of detection that captures the imagination of the reader. This is a reiteration of the conclusions already drawn by Holmes and Watson in the latter story:

> 'The cases which come to light in the papers are, as a rule, bald enough, and vulgar enough. We have in our police reports realism pushed to its extreme limits, yet the result is, it must be confessed, neither fascinating nor artistic.'
>
> 'A certain selection and discretion must be used in producing a realistic effect,' remarked Holmes. 'This is wanting in the police report, where more stress is laid perhaps upon the platitudes of the magistrate than upon the details, which to an observer contain the vital essence of the whole matter.'
> (p. 191)

Holmes and Watson's criticism of the style of crime reporting made inadequate by the Whitechapel murders highlights Conan Doyle's preference for the creative narrative of mystery and speculation that became so prominent in the journalism on Jack the Ripper. The narratives of his detective fictions repeat many of the techniques employed by that journalism in their efforts to maintain a reading public for Whitechapel murder news.

While *A Study in Scarlet* is episodic, sensational and more generically oriented toward the tale of adventure, from *The Sign of Four* onwards the Sherlock Holmes narratives become increasingly focused upon the observation of a body of evidence and the plausible conclusions to be drawn from it. In many of the stories appearing in the *Strand* in 1891 and 1892 the plot is more concerned to detail the processes by which Holmes draws inferences and supplies answers. Certainly in 'A Case of Identity', 'The Red-Headed League', 'The Boscombe Valley Mystery', 'The Speckled Band', 'The Engineer's Thumb' and 'The Noble Bachelor' Holmes requires nothing more than the testimony of his client and a study of the available evidence to come to a conclusion. Such narrative plotting is far removed from the episodic chronological rendering of events that dominated crime reporting before autumn 1888 and is much more closely allied to the innovative methods employed by journalists to make news of the Whitechapel murders.

However greatly Conan Doyle drew inspiration from the reporting of the Jack the Ripper case, it was not his project to copy it exactly. There was, of course, a key difference between the journalism of the Whitechapel murders and Conan Doyle's detective fiction: the journalistic narratives had no ending. The stories reporters had told their readers were never verified or completed. This had the effect of keeping a variety of stories in circulation, stories without power yet which could not be contained, understood or discarded. These stories are unsafe fictions – anarchic and dangerous narratives that exploit fears and vulnerabilities in their readers. Conan Doyle's detective fiction was designed to have the opposite effect: to placate and make comfortable the reader by offering solutions and resolutions. The importance of an appropriately resolved conclusion is verified by Watson, who, in 'The Five Orange Pips', offers as an explanation for his refusal to narrate more of Holmes's cases that: 'Some, too, have baffled his analytical skill, and would be, as narratives, beginnings without an ending, while others have been but partially cleared up, and have their explanations founded rather upon conjecture and surmise than on that absolute logical proof which was so dear to him' (p. 217).

Conan Doyle's dislike of narratives without conclusions is made apparent in many of the cases which make up the Holmes canon. In fact many of the stories and novels offer a doubled conclusion consisting of Holmes's explanation of the crime and the criminal's own story of their actions and motivations. The repetition of plot that this narrative structure demands has not always appealed to critics. John G. Cawelti, for example, believes that:

> The trouble is that once the detection has reached its goal, the story is effectively over. Even though the inner narrative [the story the criminal tells of himself] ostensibly provides a fuller explanation of the crime, it remains structurally tangential, an elaborate and frustrating digression from the main centre of interest.[22]

Cawelti is correct to note that the criminal's retelling of the crime is sometimes perceived as a digression, or at least as unnecessarily repetitive. This is certainly the case for many an enthusiastic reader of the Sherlock Holmes stories, who are far more likely to read through these sections rather impatiently since the resolution to the mystery has already been given. Nevertheless, Cawelti misses the significance of the criminal's own story in providing access to motive and offering corroboration of Holmes's explanations, both of which are important aspects of the placatory conclusions to Conan Doyle's fictional crimes.

That it is, at least in part, the reporting of the Whitechapel murders that leads Conan Doyle to place such emphasis on resolution and conclusion can be reinforced by comparing the narrative structures of *A Study in Scarlet* and *The Sign of Four*, the two important novels that fall before and after 1888. Although these seem similar to the extent that they both allow the perpetrator of the crime to tell his own story, the plotting differs significantly from one to the other. In *A Study in Scarlet* Holmes surprises Watson and the official police force by discovering the murderer without offering any explanation or providing forewarning. Only after this does Holmes invite the others 'to put any questions that you like to me now, and there is no danger that I will refuse to answer them' (p. 51). Yet the plot does not allow for any questions, leaping suddenly into a lengthy biography of the criminal. Only at the moment of its conclusion do we return to the present, where, briefly, Holmes can illustrate the reasoning that led to the criminal's capture. The structure of this narrative undermines Holmes's skilful deductions, first by relegating them to the end of the story and second by revealing them only after the reader is aware of all the facts and is thereby less impressed by Holmes's deductions because, in a narrative sense, s(he) has got there before him. *The Sign of Four* offers a different narrative sequence. Holmes's analyses and hypotheses are given throughout the story, before the crime is revealed to the reader. Only after Holmes's deductions have been explained to us and have proved successful in apprehending the criminal do we have access to the criminal's own story. Even then, Doyle makes explicit that it is Holmes who would like to hear the narrative of the crime, making the reader aware that the personal narrative of the criminal is also being listened to by the gathered actors in the story. This ordering of the plot may involve repetition but it is repetition that involves acknowledgement of Holmes's triumph. The reader is involved here in what Peter Brooks has called the 'verification of the fabula [story]', and it is this confirmation of Holmes's story, now embedded in the criminal's story, that makes the doubled conclusion a narrative structure offering security and solace to the reader.[23] Reading Holmes's deductive method and the motives of the criminal makes an apparently mysterious crime both detectable and understandable: two key elements of the Jack the Ripper case that the journalism of 1888 could never make available.

The new narratives of crime reporting that arose in response to the unique events of the Whitechapel murders therefore manifest themselves in Conan Doyle's detective fictions in two ways. First, Conan Doyle used the journalistic narrative devices of performance of detection, speculative inquiry and deduction of motive to create a new form of detective fiction that depended less on the episodic actions of the criminal and more on the reading of evidence and the creation of its 'story'. Second, Conan Doyle responds to the unsettling failure (or perhaps, inability) of the journalism to provide an ending to its narrative by substituting incompleteness for a robust closure that dispels doubt and instead gives certainty.

Add to this the safety of Conan Doyle's imagined London and the privileged position of the detective as criminal nemesis and the detective fictions of Sherlock Holmes become a reactionary series of narratives that elide the reality of late Victorian urban crime in order to give succour to a bourgeois readership. As Stephen Knight, always a perceptive critic of Conan Doyle's work, points out, 'the embarrassing success [of the Holmes stories] depended on the hero's power to assuage the anxieties of a respectable, London-based, middle-class audience'.[24] The inevitable consequence of this project was both an affirmation of 'the validity of the existing social order' and a moment of release from 'the guilty inner tension within the middle class' who felt in some ways responsible for the monstrous events of Whitechapel.[25] Very different from previous detective fictions, such as Edgar Allan Poe's playfully intellectual narratives or Wilkie Collins's uncomfortable domestic Gothic, Conan Doyle's Sherlock Holmes stories created a comfortable middle-class detective fiction which will always 'dispel magic and mystery' by making 'everything explicit, accountable, [and] subject to scientific analysis'.[26] In effect, these fictions, and the Whitechapel murders which had such an influence upon them, were instrumental in creating the classic forms and ideologies of English detective fiction.

Notes

1 From William Stewart, *Jack the Ripper: A New Theory* (London: Quality Press, 1939) to Stephen Knight, *Jack the Ripper: The Final Solution* (London: Treasure, 1984) and including the work of ex-policeman Stewart P. Evans and Paul Gainey, *The Lodger: The Arrest and Escape of Jack the Ripper* (London: Century, 1995).

2 *A Study in Terror* (1965), dir. James Hill.

3 Ellery Queen, *Sherlock Holmes Versus Jack the Ripper* (London: Gollancz, 1967); 'The Whitechapel Murders: A Tale of Sheerluck Holmes and Dr Witsend', *Morecambe and Wise Special*, 1977.

4 Conan Doyle's speculation on the disguised Whitechapel murderer has been connected to other theories in which the perpetrator is believed to be a woman, the so-called 'Jill the Ripper'. See L. Perry Curtis, *Jack the Ripper and the London Press* (New Haven: Yale UP, 2001), p. 279.

5 Laurence Churton Collins, *The Memoirs of John Churton Collins* (London: John Lane, 1912).

6 Arthur Conan Doyle, *A Study in Scarlet*, in *The Penguin Complete Sherlock Holmes* (London: Penguin, 1981), p. 16. All other references to Conan Doyle's detective fiction to be found in parentheses in the text.

7 *A Study in Scarlet* was written throughout March and April of 1886 but was not published until December 1887.

8 For Doyle's use of Joseph Bell as a template for Sherlock Holmes see Daniel Stashower, *Teller of Tales: The Life of Arthur Conan Doyle* (New York: Henry Holt, 1999), pp. 32, 76.

 9 Martin Priestman, *Crime Fiction from Poe to the Present* (Plymouth: Northcote House, 1998), p. 15.
10 Priestman, *Crime Fiction*, pp. 11–12.
11 John A. Hodgson (ed.), *Sherlock Holmes: The Major Stories with Contemporary Critical Essays* (Boston: Bedford, 1994), p. 338.
12 Curtis, *Jack the Ripper*, pp. 166–7.
13 See, for example, *The Times*, 'editorial', 10 November 1888 and *Lloyds Weekly Newspaper*, 9 September 1888.
14 Martin Priestman, 'Sherlock Holmes – The Series', in Hodgson, *Sherlock Holmes*, p. 315.
15 Curtis, *Jack the Ripper*, p. 167.
16 Stephen Knight, *Form and Ideology in Crime Fiction* (Bloomington: Indiana University Press, 1980), p. 95.
17 In 'The Beryl Coronet' Miss Mary Holder tells Holmes that he is 'like a magician' (p. 310) for his ability to make deductions from observations.
18 Knight, *Form and Ideology*, p. 94.
19 Curtis, *Jack the Ripper*, p. 91.
20 Curtis, *Jack the Ripper*, pp. 105–7.
21 The *Pall Mall Gazette* even gave a pastiche of such reporting at the end of 1888 in an untitled article written by 'one who knows' (*Pall Mall Gazette*, 1 December 1888).
22 John G. Cawelti, *Adventure, Mystery and Romance: Formula Stories as Art and Popular Culture* (Chicago: University of Chicago Press, 1976), p. 110.
23 Peter Brooks, 'Reading for the Plot', in Hodgson, *Sherlock Holmes*, p. 324.
24 Knight, *Form and Ideology*, p. 67.
25 Cawelti, *Adventure, Mystery and Romance*, pp. 103, 105. The Whitechapel murders were regarded as a product of the failure of Victorian middle-class philanthropy and efforts at social justice, and were thereby just as much the fault of the middle classes as they perhaps were of the other social groups (the working class, the criminal class, the police, the foreigner) who were blamed for the events.
26 Catherine Belsey, 'Deconstructing the Text: Sherlock Holmes', in Hodgson, *Sherlock Holmes*, p. 383.

10

Living in the slashing grounds: Jack the Ripper, monopoly rent and the new heritage

David Cunningham

He came silently out of the midnight shadows of August 31, 1888. Watching. Stalking. Butchering raddled drink-sodden East End prostitutes. Leaving a trail of blood and gore that led ... *nowhere*. Yes, something wicked this way walked, for *this is the Ripper's slashing grounds*. We evoke that autumn of gaslight and fog, of menacing shadows and stealthy foot-steps as we inspect the murder sites, sift through the evidence – in all its gory detail – and get to grips, so to speak, with the main suspects. Afterward you can steady your nerves in The Ten Bells, *the* pub where the victims – *perhaps under the steely gaze of the Ripper himself* – tried to forget the waking nightmare.[1]

Devised, and occasionally still guided, by veteran 'Ripperologist' Donald Rumbelow, the Jack the Ripper Tour, setting off at 7.30 p.m. from Tower Hill station – 'Children under 15 go free if accompanied by their parent(s)' – is the only one of those run by '*The Original* London Walks' company that is scheduled every day, '365 days a year, rain or shine' (with a bonus afternoon tour on Saturdays). Its special popularity is attested to by the fact that, unlike, say, '*The* Beatles Magical Mystery Tour' or 'Wren's London', this particular walk is plagued by impostors who attempt, every night, to 'steal' prospective customers from the '*bona fide* London Walks guide'. '*Don't let anyone pull a fast one on you*', warns the brochure, in its characteristic colloquial style, 'we <u>never ever</u> start the evening Jack the Ripper walk before 7.30 p.m.'.

Anyone who has lived in Whitechapel has encountered these groups. Making the walk back from the tube station or the supermarket, one has unexpectedly to negotiate a nervously paused pack of pedestrians, hud-dling around an often costumed man. Oblivious to the present-day passer-by, they stare fixedly at the pavement of some apparently unre-markable street, or squint in the direction of a 1960s building as if to see right *through* it to a lost landscape beyond. Drinking in the Ten Bells in the late 1980s, across the road from Spitalfields Market and near to the long-demolished building where the last of the Whitechapel murders took place, one would notice that at a certain regular time each evening, the bar would suddenly fill with Japanese or American tourists. Somewhat anxiously cradling half pints of lager shandy, they would soon file out again to enjoy more 'gory detail' down the road. The pub (which, for a brief, unhappy period in the 1970s actually changed its name to 'The Jack the Ripper', complete with lurid wall decorations) begrudgingly welcomed such invasions – an economic boost of a kind not much available then. Yet, despite the claims of the London Walks brochure, the groups of walkers who today still cluster outside the pub – made even more famous by the 2001 film adaptation of Alan Moore's graphic novel *From Hell* – will find themselves rather less welcome inside. What the brochure calls this 'spooky old Victorian pub' – where '*Here, the autumn of 1888 never ended*' – now has DJs playing most nights, and its young, affluent clientele offer considerably more profitable opportunities for its new managers than a nightly influx of tourists staying for less than half an hour. Spitalfields Market across the street is no longer home to London's sellers of vegetables and fruits, but to cafés and restaurants, and to artists and fashion designers promoting their wares.

Arriving at the site of the first murder, which took place on 31 August 1888, in Durward Street (then called Buck's Row), the walking tour will make one of its stops a few yards from a huge Victorian school building overshadowing the street. Back in the late 1980s this building was still derelict, damaged by fire, lying enigmatically abandoned just across from nearby Whitechapel tube station. Today, one of the renovated 'loft-style' flats that it incorporates is worth around a third of a million pounds. Making their way from here to the Ten Bells, the walkers will pass many more such real estate 'opportunities'. The eighteenth-century town-houses built by Huguenot silk merchants on Fournier Street, leading up to where the Ten Bells stands opposite Hawksmoor's imposing Christ Church, would set the prospective buyer back well over a million pounds. Of course, the walkers will also pass some very different buildings, inhabited by a very different population than that now installed in Fournier Street or the other streets linking Brick Lane to the outskirts of the City of London. At the point where Hanbury Street, site of the second murder, meets Vallance Road (childhood home of the infamous Kray twins), the tour will pass a cluster of 1960s tower blocks, now largely inhabited by Whitechapel's majority Bangladeshi community, which mark the continuing poverty of much of the area. Head up Vallance Road towards Bethnal Green Road and one passes many more, some in a nearly derelict state, yet often cheek by jowl with 'redevelopments' similar to that in Durward Street (like the old Bath House on Cheshire Street, cutting across Vallance Road).

At the same crossroads, towards the end of the evening or early in the morning, there will be the women engaged in the same work as the Whitechapel murderer's victims, albeit less likely to be 'drink-sodden' than addicted to heroin or crack. Driven out of the fashionable dining and clubbing destination that Brick Lane has become, they have moved further into the darker and quieter surrounding streets. In many ways, these women are the same as their nineteenth-century counterparts, being the visible street scene of capitalist exchange relations. Reflecting, as did their predecessors, the geographical structuring of such relations, they largely come from those Eastern European countries that have most recently lost out in the economic remappings of globalization; commodities trafficked to meet the demands of an affluent West's desires. Yet, intent on the ghosts of past crimes, the tour is unlikely to notice the conditions of such crimes in the present.

Tourist time and space

To the extent that the Ripper tours exemplify a generalized social phenomenon, a fairly obvious political and ideological critique would follow. Yet, if such a critique remains necessary, it is one that must itself be reviewed in light of the contemporary geographies of social division and capital accumulation. While, then, I shall pursue this in relation to some well-known problematics surrounding tourism, heritage and the 'spectacularization' of history, I also want to suggest the emergence of a historically *new* economics of space that may be theoretically mediated through the specific category of 'monopoly rent'. This, in turn, implies an emergent complication in our conventional conception of 'heritage' itself, as well as in the possible forms of resistance to its particular construction of 'history'. I will come to this soon, but first let us first revisit some more familiar ground.

In writings accompanying their installation piece, *Suitcase Studies*, Elizabeth Diller and Ricardo Scofidio elegantly make an oft-repeated point:

> In the heritage industry, histories and geographies are negotiable. Bypassing the limits of chronological time and contiguous space, touristic time is reversible and touristic space, elastic.[2]

Such reversibility and elasticity – figures of a dislocation in temporal and spatial experience that is definitive of commodity exchange – are apparent in the proliferation of images of Gothic London that satisfy a well-established tourist market. Some distance from the Ripper's actual 'slashing grounds', both Madame Tussaud's and the London Dungeon prominently feature Jack the Ripper displays. Neither includes a figure of the unknown murderer: his presence is implied by moving shadows and the sound of retreating footsteps. The victims, who *are* shown, appear in a compressed narrative: a living woman standing under a streetlamp, a dead woman lying on the ground. In an instantly recognizable stage set consisting of a narrow, dark Victorian street, each woman is safely abstracted from the specificities of *place*, in a way that is common to the contextless display of the theme park or museum reconstruction.

In more general terms, there is nothing new in such abstract representation of domestic or public space. Since the nineteenth century it has been a feature of exhibitions designed to edify, as well as of profit-driven spectacularizations of the aberrant or abhorrent. If the Ripper street itself only opened in 1980, Madame Tussaud's collection as a whole was based on wax models of guillotined French aristocrats. It began as a chamber of horrors long before it became a gallery of celebrity. Equally to the point, prior to the modern technological formations of spectacle, Londoners had for many decades been accustomed to viewing preserved mermaids and monsters of dubious provenance, as well as living examples of the manifold variations of the human body, in the upstairs rooms of coffee houses and pubs. It is far from surprising, then, that the Whitechapel murders were quickly assimilated into such spectacle. As Peter Ackroyd reports, even as the crimes were being committed 'a Whitechapel "peep–show" ... provided wax figures of the victims for the delectation of the spectators'.[3]

If therefore such 'show' already depends, to some degree, on the elasticity of touristic space – an abstraction of historical events that allows them to float free from their 'original' geographical coordinates – nonetheless the primacy of the 'authentic' site continues, simultaneously, to exert its own particular centrifugal pull; underwriting the economic value of the simulations. The forerunners of today's guided tours also began in 1888. What Ackroyd calls 'crime sightseers' were a common feature of the Whitechapel streets in which the murders took place, then as now. According to a report in the *Guardian* from 3 October 1893, even that great connoisseur of urban spectacle, Emile Zola, made sure to visit some of the places where *Jacques l'Eventreur* 'carried on his exploits' five years earlier. In this sense, the obviously 'mythic' fog-filled streets of Madame Tussaud's and the London Dungeon are predicated on their appeal to tourists' sense of historically conditioned *authenticity*. Multiplied many times over in films and fictions of various kinds, the frisson generated by the crimes' supposed 'origins' in 'real' time and space thus continues to give grounding to their spectacular circulation. Yet, at the same time, this brings the 'original' sites *themselves* into the realm of spectacle, becoming merely the projected image of that circulation 'elsewhere'.

Walking across thresholds

Albeit in a rather different context from the tours organized by the Original London Walks company, the benefits of walking are everywhere today advertised in our culture – not for the boost it provides to physical well-being, so much as to cultural health. From performance artists and filmmakers, to novelists like Iain Sinclair and W. G. Sebald, to legions of academic cultural theorists, the figure of the flâneur makes a contemporary comeback, mutated through his various progeny: Surrealism, Michel de Certeau, the Situationists. It is hard not to feel that this extraordinarily pervasive revival is itself the function of a certain negative relation to that figure (of 'inauthenticity' or cultural 'ill-health'), from whose shadow the contemporary flâneur can never truly extricate him- or herself: *the tourist*. Each of these figures is, in its own way, a distinct child of nineteenth-century capitalist modernity and its 'technologies' of vision. Connoisseur of urban spectacle, the flâneur – in whom the 'joy of watching is triumphant'[4] – stands, from the very beginning, as John Rignall observes, 'on the brink of the alienating system of commodity exchange into which he will eventually be absorbed'.[5] The contemporary flâneur is defined *against* the guided tour, as the subject of a 'psychogeographical' *dérive* (drift) that marks an 'authentic' engagement with a specific urban site. If the flâneur is customarily defined, then, in negative relation to his despised double, the tourist, by *how* he – for it is, of course, usually a 'he' – moves through the city, he is also defined by *where* he goes. The contemporary 'walker', as supposed figure of 'resistance' to a capitalist planned urbanism, is he who strays from the itinerary, from the spatio-temporal succession of sanctioned sites, in search of the forgotten, the marginalized, the occluded. Inevitably, this has always meant, above all, a movement across any boundaries drawn by the stratifications of class within the city.

Benjamin, theoretical patron saint of this contemporary fascination with the 'art of walking', locates a particular urban figure as the catalyst of a transgression by the inhabitant of a city's 'affluent quarter' into 'the exotic world of abject poverty':

> There is no doubt … that a feeling of crossing the threshold of one's class for the first time had a part in the almost unequalled fascination of publicly

accosting a whore in the street. At the beginning, however, this was a crossing of frontiers not only social but topographical, in the sense that whole
networks of streets were opened up under the auspices of prostitution ...
the places are countless in the great cities where one stands on the edge of
the void, and the whores in the doorways of tenement blocks and on the
less sonorous asphalt of railway platforms are like the household goddesses
of this cult of nothingness.[6]

The prostitute is of course a standard figure of metropolitan modernity,
one of the principal cast members of, among others, Baudelaire's metropolitan pageant; part of its 'feminine fauna', as Benjamin puts it elsewhere. It is in prostitution that women appear most clearly for the poet,
as for the flâneur, as 'subjects of his gaze, objects of his "botanizing" '.[7]
Discussing the figure of the labyrinth in the *Arcades Project*, Benjamin
writes: 'Whoever wishes to know how much at home we are in entrails
must allow himself to be swept along in delirium through streets whose
darkness greatly resembles the lap of a whore'.[8] Yet Benjamin also suggests something more, in the passage from *Berlin Childhood* cited
above, than this rather disquieting image itself implies: 'whores' are, in
a way, unconscious *travel guides*, leading the bourgeois customer
through 'whole networks' of previously unknown streets. As 'opened
up under the auspices of prostitution', such streets, and their inhabitants, themselves become objects of a spectacular consumption, as does
the body of the prostitute herself.[9] In this sense, prostitution can be
understood, both metaphorically *and* literally, as the basis for a kind of
tourism, just as much as the 'production' of 'objects' for the flâneur's
'botanising'. More generally, the passage across class thresholds, internal to the city, is conceived of as such from the nineteenth century
onwards. Not long after Zola's trip, Jack London, wanting to visit
the East End, in what became research for the book *The People of
the Abyss*, went first to the Cheapside branch of the travel firm
Thomas Cook: 'path-finders and trail-clearers, living sign-posts to all
the world'.[10]

Does this perhaps explain why, in 'Ripperology', the murderer himself
often appears in the guise of something like a tourist abroad: a West
End doctor, a bourgeois artist or even a member of the royal family?
The crimes themselves are intertwined with a particular construction
of the traversal of urban space as a transformation into spectacle.
Judith Walkowitz rightly notes that the murders operate as the 'centre
of a set of interwoven relationships, linking high and low, East and West
in class-divided London'.[11] This connects their symbolic functioning
to the desire for imaginary unification exhibited in the nineteenth-
century London novel generally, as exemplified by Dickens's 'family

romances'.[12] More specifically, it connects them to a nineteenth-century urban–Gothic fascination with the excitement and threat of transgressing thresholds. (Stevenson's *Dr Jekyll and Mr Hyde* or Stoker's *Dracula* would be exemplary here.) Benjamin's explicit linkage of the figure of the prostitute to such transgression suggests a social and spatial dimension to this that is not always acknowledged. Moreover, if the murders are *able* to operate as the 'centre of a set of interwoven relationships, linking high and low, East and West', this is because, *at the time*, prostitution already appears as a component of a proto-touristic space, 'guiding' the murderer, as tourist or (his twin) flâneur, into the 'whole network' of Whitechapel's streets.[13] Following his mythicized footsteps, crossing 'frontiers not only social but topographical', the contemporary tourist appears as a kind of unknowing descendant of the murderer himself.[14]

Myth and murder

If they are themselves ones in whom the 'joy of watching is triumphant', what is it that the walkers on the Ripper tours, just as much as the visitors to Madame Tussaud's, actually go to *see*? Who knows, or would have the arrogance to presume? But, to borrow Patrick Wright's felicitous distinction, explored in his 1985 discussion of the heritage industry, both the murders and their sites would certainly seem to (re-)present themselves as part of a reified and replete 'past' rather than of 'history'. They are figurations of a 'pastness' accessible 'at a glance', abstracted from the inconvenient presence of the historical present:[15]

> In order to become spectacular – something separate with which the public can commune in regular acts of appreciation – history must in one sense be something that is over and done with [...] history becomes 'timeless' when it has been frozen solid, closed down and limited to what can be exhibited as a fully accomplished 'historical past'.[16]

To place the Ripper within such a heritage, as that which demands 'acts of appreciation', may sound peculiar. Even given contemporary 'true-crime' narrative's degraded repetition of De Quincey's appreciation for the 'art' of murder, the Whitechapel murders do not seem to sit comfortably within the same cultural space of 'pastness' inhabited by Wright's favoured examples: Tudor manor houses, the *Mary Rose*, Betjeman's English churches, the Globe Theatre – that construction of Heritage which is one of the cultural legacies of Thatcherism. Yet their 'spectacularization' takes the same essential form: 'Where there was active historicity there is now decoration and display; in the place of memory,

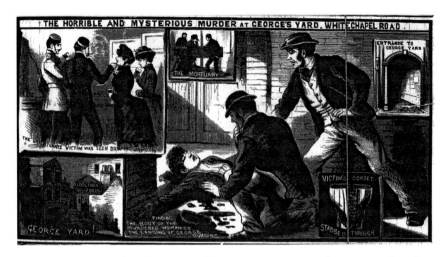

10 The *Illustrated Police News* of 18 August 1888 reveals to its readers the site of one of the early Whitechapel murders.

amnesia swaggers out in historical fancy dress'.[17] As heritage – however gothicized and apparently 'gritty' – the murders are necessarily tensed in the 'past pluperfect', frozen solid in their 'Victorianness'.[18] Hence, no doubt, in more middle-brow 'literary' accounts, the interminable repetition also of a rhetoric of 'timelessness' – an auratic 'beyond history' within which, Ackroyd and others insist, the self-consciously mythicized murders are said to attain their cultural power. Historiography, as one critic puts it, is here effaced by romanticized, Eliotesque 'patterns of disappearance and return that crumple linear time into repeating cycles or unpredictable arabesques'.[19] Removed from the critical conditions of 'active historicity', dissolved into the ever-always-the-same of mythic return, the slaughter of women can indeed become an object of aestheticized appreciation – a form of forgetting, not of memoration.

In the opening pages of the most powerful chapter of her extraordinary book *Misogynies*, Joan Smith writes:

> The difference between Peter Sutcliffe and Jack the Ripper is the difference between fact and fiction. Unlike Sutcliffe, Jack the Ripper is not a name but a *label* connecting a set of related acts; he has no proper name, no address, no biographical details ... And yet, and yet. In the late 1970s, faced with a mass murderer whose death-toll quickly overtook that of the Victorian killer, police in the North of England embarked on a wild goose chase for a man they visualised as Jack the Ripper [...] this is the real reason why Peter William Sutcliffe was able to roam with impunity through the towns and cities of northern England for more than five years, restlessly searching out his victims: if you devote your resources to tracking down a figure from

myth, if you waste your time starting at shadows, you are not likely to come up with a lorry driver from Bradford.[20]

What does it mean to say that Jack the Ripper is *myth*, even *fiction*? Clearly not that the Whitechapel murders did not happen (not even, quite, in some quasi-Baudrillardian sense); nor, as seems most likely, that the perpetrator of these crimes was not himself something like a nineteenth-century, London equivalent of a Bradford lorry driver. Rather it means that the designations of 'the Whitechapel murderer' and 'Jack the Ripper' – a name which came from a probable hoax letter – *are not the same*. If the former, unknown and now unknowable, committed the real, awful murders of working-class women in 1888, the latter has become something quite other. This other is indeed a figure of 'fiction', a Gothic image, constructed almost immediately after the murders themselves, who belongs within a larger cast of such late nineteenth-century characters, including Sherlock Holmes, Jekyll and Hyde, Dracula and Dorian Gray, populating an imaginary fog-engulfed city. The figure of the Ripper, as putative 'origin' of a whole future genus, becomes, equally, both a metonymy of metropolitan alienation and nihilism – the product and expression of a historically specific social form – *and*, as Jane Caputi writes of 'sex crime' more generally, an essentially transhistorical 'force of nature [...] a supernatural evil, a monstrous aberration'.[21] 'Something wicked this way comes', as the Ripper Walk's blurb has it. Moreover, neither of these, ultimately inseparable, figurations is a mere backward formation from a more modern historical culture. They are there in 1888 and constitute the grounds of more apparently contemporary ideas (not least concerning the 'serial killer' *per se*).

Most importantly, as aesthetic object, *misogyny* can never be enough to 'explain' the murders: they must be Masonic ritual, supernatural event, *design*. It is this that ties them into a network of figures that make up a particular urban–Gothic strain of heritage's contemporary formation, most often 'centred' around the late nineteenth century. 'Abstracted and redeployed', each becomes, as Wright says (thinking of the famous analyses by both Walter Benjamin and the Situationists), a unifying mediation of social relations 'purged of political tension'.[22] Stemming from the social synthesis effected by the essential abstracting force of the (exchange) value form, this process would seem to know no natural limit. Indeed the apparently irreducibly 'political' can itself be re-formed as just another element within a heritage picaresque of Victorianness. The matchgirls' strike of 1888, the same year as the Ripper murders, provides an ideal backdrop for the authentic grit of the Bryant & May factory's redevelopment as a gated community of 'stunning loft apartments'.

Monopoly rent and the new heritage

Among other things, the above raises some serious questions for what has, in recent times, presented itself as a certain generalized – post-Benjamin, post-Situationist, post-de Certeau – 'aesthetic of resistance', uniting a range of cultural phenomena, formed around the specificities of *place*; questions which I have sought to elaborate at some length elsewhere.[23] More often than not, such an aesthetic invokes a specifically urban *uncanny*, a traumatic and subversive return of repressed 'Gothic fragments' in contemporary metropolitan experience. It is clearly as such that the Ripper *myth* has proved enticing for various cultural practitioners, from Sinclair and Ackroyd to Moore.

'Preoccupied by traces and residues', this kind of 'aesthetic of resistance' seeks, more generally, to 'chart the underground reverberations of the city' – ones which, in the aesthetic appropriation of an East London history, join together, as so many geological layers of a mythical time, the distant pathos of Jewish immigration and anarchist cells with, for example, post-war gangster chic and both the Ratcliff Highway and Ripper murders.[24] (It is noticeable that the prostitute herself continues, in deeply problematic fashion, to be a privileged 'figure' of much contemporary urban writing in this vein also, subject of a romanticization of an 'authentic' street life now eroded by a 'cleansing' carried out according to the imperatives of bourgeois corporate consumerism. The reality of the sex industry tends as a result, more or less subtly, to be effaced.[25]) A frequently quasi-mystical attuning to the *genius loci* is thus conceived of as an implicitly politicized redemptive project: the revivification of modern experience itself through the juxtaposition of the present with particular pasts that interrupt its smoothed-out surfaces. Such a 'strategy' is characteristically described by John Crary as one of *detourning* 'the spectacle of the city through counter-memory and counter-itineraries': a 'reclaiming' of 'fragments of a demolished past', of 'derelict spaces off its main routes of circulation', that would incarnate 'a refusal of the imposed present' of consumer culture.[26] It is as such that a certain reactivation of a 'placed' history is understood to disrupt the reterritorialization of urban space as what Marc Augé calls a form of 'non–place' determined by the abstractions of commodity exchange.[27]

All this is familiar, now over-familiar perhaps. Yet its tendentious assumption of an automatic criticality inherent in 'history' itself is not without its problems today. If 'places' are, anthropologically or sociologically, defined by the 'minimal stability' of 'identity, of relations, and of history', capitalist modernity's negation of the 'specific values' of

place – what is effectively designated by that tricky concept, 'globalization' – does not efface 'history' altogether.[28] Rather history is represented as 'curiosity', a 'public claim to history' which has the function
of a sort of 'business card' (as Augé puts it in similar terms to Wright's
analysis of the heritage industry). This is partly to do with an intensifi-
cation of the economic compulsion to 'attract and hold the attention of
the passer–by, the tourist', in a context of global urban 'competition' – a
phenomenon exemplified by the Ripper tours just as much as by the
London Dungeon or Madame Tussaud's . However, as Augé implies, it
also signifies something more pervasive: the 'relationship with history
that haunts our landscapes is being aestheticised, and at the same time
desocialised and artificialised'.[29] The problem here, for a would-be 'aesthetic of resistance', is that it is hard not to suspect that the *ideological*
function of much 'preoccupation' with the 'traces and residues' of a gothicized 'past' is, in light of a historical negation of distinctions of place, to
re–present such distinctions in an 'aesthetic' realm, so as to elide and
compensate for their effective effacement. Far from resisting the imperatives of contemporary capitalist development, this can, at another level,
very often amount to a (more or less unknowing) complicity with them.
For, as Hal Foster writes, if 'the local and the everyday are thought to
resist economic development, they can *also* attract it, [insofar as] such
development needs the local and the everyday even as it erodes these
qualities, renders them siteless'.[30]

In this sense, a politicized poetics of place may find itself in a double
bind – compelled to resist this progressive 'sitelessness' by insisting on
the 'active' historicity that it effaces, yet, by doing so, risking simply
feeding its concomitant aestheticization of the 'historical' itself. One of
the first (and best) contemporary writers to draw on the Gothic fragments of the Ripper myth, in the novel *White Chappell, Scarlet Tracings*
(1987) – as a part of his own poetics of place developed from the
early 1970s onwards – Sinclair is almost unique in incorporating an
ironic recognition of such a double bind into his expanding oeuvre.
Commenting on his own contribution (along with Patrick Wright) to the
unearthing of the 'occluded' figure of David Rodinsky, who 'disappeared' from his room in the Princelet Street synagogue, leaving behind
a supposed treasure trove of Gothic ephemera, Sinclair writes:

> The disappearance of the synagogue caretaker, with his presumed cabbal-
> istic practices, was a story fitted to its time. Those with a vested interest in
> defining Spitalfields as a zone of peculiar and privileged resonance needed
> a mythology to underwrite the property values … I'd heard no mention of
> the tale in the Seventies – because it hadn't been formulated. Spitalfields was
> still an antiquarian conceit.[31]

As Sinclair also observes elsewhere of the 'effects' of Ackroyd's fictions: 'As with *Hawksmoor* and Spitalfields, his gesture[s] proved to have a prophetic influence on estate agents'.[32] If Sinclair's, Ackroyd's and Wright's poetics of place are all, in different ways, evidently aimed against the heritage industry's 'restaging' of history, and the economic as well as strictly 'cultural' or 'political' motivations which underlie it, Sinclair's self-reflexive recognition here is that this can itself ultimately amount, not to a critical negation, but to a reformulation and *expansion* of heritage's hold.

The National Heritage Act (1980), passed in the first years of Thatcher's government, defined and 'sited' heritage in some fairly specific ways. Heritage was understood primarily as a populist elaboration of the 'antiquarian conceit' – a post-Betjeman litany of country houses, churches and explicitly 'national' monuments in need of 'preservation'. Early examples of conservation in Spitalfields, exemplified by the 'Spitalfields Historic Buildings Trust', in which Betjeman played a key role, and centred around the bourgeois Georgian architecture bequeathed by Huguenot settlers, evidently belong within such a formation. Something of the flavour of this can be found in Alexandra Artley and John Martin Robinson's 1985 book, the *New Georgian Handbook*, published by Harpers and Queen. Yet the scope of such conservationism, and its commercial potentialities, were always limited. Increasingly it would seem to be displaced by a *new* and far more expansive heritage, one which does not elide a more Gothic or 'marginalized' history, thought to work against a 'cleaned-up' and 're-ancestralized' aestheticization, but positively *incorporates* it as so much 'mythology to underwrite the property values'.[33] While remarking the 'eastward spread of the City [the financial district]', in 1990 Robert Hewison could still write that, by comparison to London's redeveloped Docklands, Spitalfields incarnated an urban 'reality' which, with its 'unpleasant as well as appealing aspects', remained irreducible to 'developers' site values': the location of an ongoing 'struggle for space'.[34] If this now seems naive, it is perhaps because it imagines that the 'site values' of developers might not find a way to absorb those other 'values' that apparently oppose them. In its own Gothic form, capital feasts vampirically off the 'negative', recuperating and reforming it to its own purposes.

This is, then, as Sinclair suggests, not only about tourists 'passing through' – 'inhabitants' of a traveller's space which is the archetype of 'non-place' more generally – but also about the ultimately more lucrative possibilities of land or real estate speculation which, in fact, *rely* upon a certain irreducible 'value' of place: what the architect Peter Eisenman calls 'the capital of location'.[35] Traditionally such 'capital' has been theorized in terms of the 'concrete' economic benefits accrued from, for example, proximity to transport links or other key services. Yet, increasingly, it overlaps with, and is overdetermined by, a more 'abstract' value of location that finds its basis in so-called *symbolic* capital. What is at stake in this can, I think, be approached through the economic category of *monopoly rent*.

As explicated by David Harvey, monopoly rent arises from 'exclusive control over some directly or indirectly tradeable item which is in some respects unique and non-replicable'.[36] It is not hard to see how this relates to Eisenman's capital of location, and it is not of course a new phenomenon. Yet, as Harvey argues, it takes on a particular new significance in our present context, which would seem to be dominated by a spatial logic that *negates* the kinds of monopoly value traditionally associated with place:

> The recent bout of globalisation has significantly diminished the monopoly protections given by high transport and communications costs ... But capitalism cannot do without monopoly powers and craves means to assemble them. So the question upon the agenda is how to assemble monopoly powers in a situation where the protections afforded by the so-called 'natural monopolies' of space and location and the political protections of natural boundaries have been seriously diminished if not eliminated.[37]

Harvey rightly locates part of the answer to this question in a massive new significance accorded precisely to 'collective symbolic capital', the 'struggle' for which becomes more important given the 'general loss of other monopoly powers', and which has a particular investment in the 'aura' provided by the apparent 'uniqueness' of place.[38] The contemporary so-called 'regeneration' of London's East End might well be understood in these terms. In this process, what matters is not so much the presence of a specific kind of heritage, such as was defined by the terms of the 1980 National Heritage Act, as the available resource of *any* kind of 'heritage' which might be mobilized in the production of a spectacularized uniqueness. Indeed, a 'difference' from traditionally defined heritage forms can, in such a situation, prove to be a distinct advantage as regards the realization of monopoly rent. Insofar as nowhere else 'contains' the 'real' history of the Ripper or the Krays or David Rodinsky, the mythologization of each becomes valuable capital.

Nonetheless, as Harvey also observes, this opens up considerable tensions between different aspects of the reconstruction of urban landscape by the imperatives of capital accumulation. For as 'opportunities to pocket monopoly rents galore present themselves', so too 'their irresistible lure draws more and more homogenising commodification in its wake'. The 'later phases' of development often 'look exactly like every other in the western world'.[39] Such is the politics not only of contemporary Spitalfields but of globalization in general. As Julian Stallabrass notes, *a propos* the so-called Young British Artists, many of whom took up residence in the East End during the 1990s (including, like Tracy Emin, in the Georgian houses of Fournier Street), one of the cultural correlatives of this is that:

> There is a dialectic between the homogenising forces of globalisation, and the reaction to create a specifically British [or, more particularly, London] subject matter, the latter being a product of the former, not just a reaction against it, but a way of handling it, of making a distinct product that can appeal to segments of the global market.[40]

This is also apparent in both state and corporate drives to *brand* localities so as to realize monopoly rent. Led by the Corporation of London, the City Fringe Partnership, set up in 1996, for example, explicitly sought to develop a so-called 'cultural quarters' programme centred on the East End. Highlighting 'the pivotal role that interpretation of heritage and the arts is now expected to play in the process of regeneration', this identified areas that could be targeted at 'domestic and international tourists seeking a satisfying alternative to the mainstream attractions of central London'.[41] It is, of course, above all, the Ripper tours that have led the way in such a process of 'place-marketing'.

At the same time, such 'marketing' would now seem to converge with a whole cultural industry surrounding the area, into which the Ripper myth is centrally incorporated. As a recent book blurb has it, listing the Ripper (its 'most notorious criminal') alongside 'mystics and mythmakers', 'political activists and philanthropists', 'the East End has always been London's mysterious alter-ego, with *an identity unlike anywhere else*'.[42] Yet, at a certain point, the impetus behind all this would seem to shift from regeneration via tourism to a more direct promotion of the area as desirable real estate – both a place to live and work, and, more generally, a nodal point for the attraction of flows of capital – at which point the old–style tourist actually becomes more of a mixed blessing. As I said earlier, the Ten Bells pub, which once relied on them, now discourages tourists as markers of an inauthenticity detracting from the contemporary 'reality' it sells.

Ironically, then, what myth has come to stand for is a notion of authenticity, a 'real' experience of metropolitan life, as opposed to the chain-store coffee-shop version of urban culture derided as the shallow product of global commodity culture. In London, the centre of the cultural mainstream comes to be literalized as the West End, with the 'marginalized' East End revalorized as a result. The latter is branded as the unique site of a certain 'unbroken' history, of a collective symbolic capital, beyond the reach of hegemonic consumerism. Ed Glinert, writing of Brick Lane – 'now the most celebrated road in Britain' – terms this a 'chic, urban edginess'. This 'authentic' city life is an apparently gritty realist one of crime, deprivation, immigration, mystical outsiders, haunted by 'the ever-present ghosts of Jack the Ripper, Jack London, Bud Flanagan, the Kray Twins' which together make up part of a more general 'historicized' spectacle of an 'other' existence.[43]

However, precisely as such, Glinert's realism is not a realism of the present. The 'real' city has effectively become identified with Wright's auratic, frozen 'past' rather than with an active history which would invite reflection on the present. A certain gothicized heritage would seem to play a particularly key role here, in the instance of East London, by performing a mythologizing action that asserts the continuity of the past into the present while simultaneously denying it. The flats and houses, as well as the shop spaces, that command the highest prices are not those that overlook the sites where prostitutes still ply their trade, nor are they within the post-war blocks that are the homes of poor Bangladeshi families. They are in the Georgian and Victorian buildings where the Ripper's victims lived, worked and died, and which the now romanticized (because usefully vanished) Jewish community once inhabited. It is not the contemporary prostitutes but the ghosts of their murdered forebears who today open up the 'whole network' of Whitechapel's streets for both the contemporary flâneur and the sedentary 'loft-dweller'. The now safely 'timeless' figures of the past are summoned to displace the inconvenient living bodies of the present in the extraction of monopoly rent. Such is our new heritage.

Notes

My thanks to Alex Warwick for her many comments throughout the writing of this essay.

1 From *Jack the Ripper Haunts*, London Walks brochure, 2004; all emphases in the original.
2 Elizabeth Diller and Ricardo Scofidio, 'Tourisms: Suitcase Studies', in Cynthia C. Davidson (ed.), *Anywhere* (New York: Rizzoli, 1992), p. 84.
3 Peter Ackroyd, *London: A Biography* (London: Chatto and Windus, 2000), p. 273.
4 Walter Benjamin, *Charles Baudelaire: A Lyric Poet in the Era of High Capitalism*, trans. Harry Zohn (London: New Left Books, 1973), p. 69.
5 John Rignall, 'Benjamin's *Flâneur* and the Problem of Realism', in Andrew Benjamin (ed.), *The Problems of Modernity: Adorno and Benjamin* (London and New York: Routledge, 1989), p. 112.

6 Walter Benjamin, 'Berlin Childhood', in *One-Way Street and Other Writings*, trans. Edmund Jephcott and Kingsley Shorter (London: New Left Books, 1979), p. 301.
7 Janet Wolff, 'The Invisible *Flâneuse*: Women and the Literature of Modernity', in Benjamin (ed.), *Problems of Modernity*, p. 149. The notion of 'botanising' derives from Benjamin's description of the flâneur as *he* who 'goes botanising on the asphalt'. See Benjamin, *Charles Baudelaire*, p. 36.
8 Walter Benjamin, *The Arcades Project*, trans. Howard Eiland and Kevin McLaughlin (Cambridge, MA: Harvard University Press, 1999), p. 519.
9 Benjamin cites Eduard Fuchs as mentioning a mid-nineteenth-century 'illustrated catalogue of prostitutes' in which each 'erotic lithograph' has 'printed at the bottom the address of a prostitute'. Benjamin, *Arcades Project*, p. 507.
10 Cited in Ed Glinert, *East End Chronicles* (London: Penguin, 2005), p. 163.
11 Judith Walkowitz, *City of Dreadful Night: Narratives of Sexual Danger in Late Victorian London* (London: Virago, 1992), p. 218.
12 See Franco Moretti, *Atlas of the European Novel 1800–1900* (London and New York: Verso, 1998), pp. 86, 130.
13 In his novel *White Chappell, Scarlet Tracings*, which is in large part constructed around the Ripper myth, Iain Sinclair explicitly presents William Gull – his candidate for the murders borrowed from Stephen Knight's book – as a kind of flâneur. So, too, does Alan Moore in *From Hell*. See Chapter 5 above.
14 The other Gothic figure (more explicitly) engaged here is the detective, to whom indeed Benjamin compares the flâneur. The detective also has the particular power of crossing the social and spatial thresholds of class division. It is appropriate, then, that one of the boasts of the Ripper tour is that its participants will be able to 'get to grips, so to speak, with the main suspects'.
15 Patrick Wright, *On Living in an Old Country* (London and New York: Verso, 1985), p. 69.
16 Wright, *On Living*, p. 78.
17 Wright, *On Living*, p. 78.
18 I take the notion of the heritage industry as that which is tensed in the past pluperfect from Robert Hewison. See *The Heritage Industry* (London: Methuen, 1987) and *Future Tense: A New Art for the Nineties* (London: Methuen, 1990).
19 Roger Luckhurst, 'The Contemporary London Gothic and the Limits of the "Spectral Turn"', *Textual Practice*, 16:3 (2002), p. 531.
20 Joan Smith, 'There's Only One Yorkshire Ripper', in *Misogynies* (London: Faber & Faber, 1989), pp. 117–18.
21 Jane Caputi, *The Age of Sex Crime* (London: The Women's Press, 1988), p. 30.
22 Wright, *On Living in an Old Country*, p. 69.
23 See David Cunningham, 'Re-Placing the Novel: Sinclair, Ballard and the Spaces of Literature', in Jenny Bavidge and Robert Bond (eds), *City Visions: The Work of Iain Sinclair* (Newcastle: Cambridge Scholars Press, 2007). The phrase 'aesthetic of resistance' is taken from Luckhurst, 'The Contemporary London Gothic', p. 533.

24 Anthony Vidler, *The Architectural Uncanny: Essays in the Modern Unhomely* (Cambridge, MA: MIT Press, 1992), p. xiii.

25 See Carina Listerborn, 'Prostitution as "Urban Radical Chic": The Silent Acceptance of Female Exploitation', *City*, 7:2 (2003), pp. 237–45.

26 John Crary, 'Spectacle, Attention, Counter-Memory', in Tom McDonough (ed.), *Guy Debord and the Situationist International* (Cambridge, MA: MIT Press, 2002), p. 464.

27 Marc Augé, *Non-Places: Introduction to an Anthropology of Supermodernity*, trans. John Howe (London and New York: Verso, 1995).

28 The notion of the 'specific values' of place is taken here from Georg Simmel's classic analysis of the modern metropolis. See David Cunningham, 'The Concept of Metropolis: Philosophy and Urban Form', *Radical Philosophy*, 133 (September/October 2005), pp. 13–25.

29 Augé, *Non-Places*, pp. 52, 68, 73.

30 Hal Foster, 'Artist as Ethnographer', in *The Return of the Real* (Cambridge, MA: MIT Press, 1996), p. 197.

31 Rachel Lichtenstein and Iain Sinclair, *Rodinsky's Room* (London: Granta, 1999), pp. 66–7.

32 Marc Atkins and Iain Sinclair, *Liquid City* (London: Reaktion, 2000), p. 84.

33 See Patrick Wright, *Journey Through the Ruins* (London: Flamingo, 1993), p. 150.

34 Hewison, *Future Tense*, pp. 93, 15.

35 Peter Eisenman, 'Critical Architecture in a Geopolitical world', *D: Columbia Documents of Architecture and Theory*, 6 (1997), p. 108.

36 David Harvey, 'The Art of Rent', in *Spaces of Capital: Towards a Critical Geography* (Edinburgh: Edinburgh University Press, 2001), p. 395.

37 Harvey, 'Art of Rent', pp. 398–9.

38 My use of the term 'aura' here relates to its famous definition in Benjamin's work as precisely referring to a quality of non-reproducible uniqueness and 'authenticity'. See 'The Work of Art in the Age of Mechanical Reproduction' in *Illuminations*, trans. Harry Zohn (London: Fontana, 1973).

39 Harvey, 'Art of Rent', p. 406.

40 Julian Stallabrass, *High Art Lite* (London and New York: Verso, 1999), p. 234.

41 Stephen J. Shaw, 'Multicultural Heritage and Urban Regeneration in London's City Fringe', paper delivered at 5th European Commission Conference on Research for Protection, Conservation and Enhancement of Cultural Heritage, 16–18 May 2002, Cracow, Poland, p. 148. http://heritage.xtd.pl/pdf/full-shaw.pdf

42 Inside cover of Glinert, *East End Chronicles*, my emphasis.

43 Glinert, *East End Chronicles*, p. 295.

Part III

History

11

Narratives of sexual danger

Judith Walkowitz

Although coroners and expert witnesses in the Whitechapel murders established an interpretive authority over inquest proceedings, the poor also took the occasion to produce their own truths and fictions about the murdered women. Neighbours and friends gave detailed accounts of the victims' lives and of the circumstances surrounding the crimes. Their reaction to the murders sharply diverged from those of the organized working class and middle-class philanthropists. To the Whitechapel poor, Annie Chapman and Mary Jane Kelly were not degraded outcasts but members of their own community. Mary Jane Kelly seems to have remained on good terms with a number of her regular customers. On the night of her death, she encountered George Hutchinson, who deposed that he had occasionally given her a few shillings in the past. Kelly had asked him if he had any money to give her. Most of the other murdered women had lovers with whom they lived and pooled their resources. These were practical relationships, but they often entailed strong emotional bonds. John Kelly explained how he and Catherine Eddowes paired off in the following way: 'We got throwed together a good bit here in the lodging house,' recounted Kelly, 'and the result was we made a regular bargain'.[1]

The murdered women were also part of an intense female network. Prostitutes as well as non-prostitutes inhabited a distinct female world where they gossiped, entertained each other and participated in an intricate system of borrowing and lending. This female network supplemented women's heterosexual ties, but it occasionally challenged those male-female allegiances. When Catherine Picket, a flower seller and neighbour of Mary Jane Kelly, was attracted to Kelly's singing on the night of her murder, she arose from bed to go out and join her; at which point she was reprimanded by her husband, 'You just leave the woman alone', and crawled back to bed. Kelly herself was not as deferential to male authority; according to Joseph Barnett, her lover, she had just separated from Barnett after the two had quarrelled over her taking in another 'unfortunate' named Harvey 'out of compassion'.[2]

Clearly the murdered women were well known in the neighbourhood and many were well liked. Most popular of all was the last victim, Mary Jane Kelly. When local men were asked if they knew Kelly, they responded, 'Did anyone not know her?' Kelly was respected in the neighbourhood for being generous and gay-hearted, and 'frequent in street brawls, sudden and quick in quarrels and – for a woman – handy with her fists'. During Kelly's funeral procession, the coffin was covered with wreaths from friends 'using certain public houses in common with the murdered woman'. As the coffin passed, 'ragged caps were doffed and slatternly looking women shed tears'. Dense crowds also lined the streets for the funeral cortège of Catherine Eddowes: 'Manifestations of sympathy were everywhere visible', reported the *East London Observer*, 'many among the crowd uncovering their heads as the hearse passed'.[3]

In general, press commentary emphasized the 'ghastly sameness' of the naturalistic stories emerging from the inquests and stressed that the 'element of romance' was 'altogether lacking in [the victim's] history'.[4] The matter-of-fact manner in which poor neighbours seemed to recount the dead women's stories, with no moral gloss or condemnation, shocked respectable commentators, as did the tendency of the Whitechapel poor to treat screams of murder or the spectacle of bodies crumpled in a heap on a Whitechapel street as unremarkable and commonplace.

Yet the 'element of romance' was not missing in the histories produced by the poor. Many of the witnesses consciously dissimulated, refusing to acknowledge that the victims drank or were streetwalkers. Sometimes they struck melodramatic poses and even resorted to exaggerated gestures to re-enact their part 'when called to the scene of the crime'. Legal decorum did not inhibit one witness at Annie Chapman's inquest from performing an elaborate pantomime about his discovery of the body: 'When he had arrived [in his performance] at the discovery of the body ... the hands of the witness were kept in constant motion – describing alternatively, in pantomime show, how the intestines of the woman were thrown slightly over the left shoulder, and what position the body precisely occupied in the yard'.[5]

The murdered women were objects of fantasy for residents of Whitechapel as well as for the educated reading public. Fictions of kinship surfaced at the inquest of Elizabeth Stride, the 'Berner street victim', who was 'strangely identified as two persons'. At Stride's inquest, Mary Malcolm came forward and insisted that 'the woman who had been murdered was her sister because when she was in bed, the poor creature came and kissed her hand'. Malcolm's testimony excited considerable attention, inspiring many newspaper readers to call for the 'aid of spiritualism and other more or less occult agencies'; it was entirely discredited when her sister turned up alive and well and full of outrage. Michael Kidney also positively identified the body as that of Elizabeth Stride, whom he had known for nearly three years. Stride had told Kidney that her husband and children had died on the *Princess Alice* (a shipping disaster), but even this proved to be a fiction on Stride's part to conceal marital estrangement. After Stride's nephew recognized her photograph, he came forward to identify her as the widow of John Thomas Stride, a carpenter, who had died in a workhouse in 1884.[6]

The thickest layer of fantasy settled around the life and death of Mary Kelly, the last and youngest Ripper victim, who had been brutally disembowelled and mutilated in her room in Dorset Street. Newspapers and memoirs from the period set Kelly apart as the least 'impoverished', most attractive Ripper victim – 'an aristocrat among street women' with 'well-to-do' friends.[7] The principal identificatory witness at the inquest was Joseph Barnett, a fish porter, who 'appeared to be in full possession of the facts of the unhappy woman's life'. At the inquest, Barnett identified Kelly by 'the ears and eyes'. His narrative of her life history, based on Kelly's version of her own story, reads like a penny-dreadful rendition of the harlot's progress and the 'Maiden Tribute'. With the vaguest of storyline and detail, Barnett outlined Kelly's career in West End vice. Widowed at twenty, she arrived from Wales and settled in a 'gay house in the West End'. 'There a gentleman came to her and asked her if she would like to go to France, so she described to me.' 'She went to France', he continued, 'as she told me, but did not stop there long, as she did not like the part'. Reporting on the inquest, the *Star* immediately seized the opportunity to elaborate the melodrama of high and low life further: 'It would appear that on her arrival in London she made the acquaintance of a French lady residing in the neighbourhood of Knightsbridge who ... led her into the degraded life which has brought about her untimely end ... while she was with this lady she drove about in a carriage ... and led the life of a lady'.[8]

After Kelly's return to England, Barnett continued, she went to the 'Ratcliffe Highway'. At this point in the narrative, 'hard facts' creep into Barnett's 'disclosures': she lived opposite the gasworks with a man named Morganstone, then went to Pennington Street and lived with James Flemming, a mason's plasterer. Barnett 'picked up with her in Commercial street, one night when we had drunk together'.[9]

This East/West romance set the scene for George Hutchinson's detailed description of the 'gentleman' accompanying Kelly on the night of her death. One day after the inquest, Hutchinson, a labourer, deposed to the police that his 'suspicions were aroused by seeing the man so well-dressed'. He gave a remarkably precise description of the mysterious stranger:

> age about 34 or 35, height 5 ft. 6, complexion pale. Dark eyes and eye lashes. Slight moustache curled up each end and hair dark. Very surly looking. Dress, long dark coat, collar and cuffs trimmed astrakhan and a dark jacket under, light waistcoat, dark trousers, and gaiters with white buttons, wore a very thick gold chain, white linen collar, black tie with horseshoe pin, respectable appearance, walked very sharp, Jewish appearance.

As a number of commentators have noted, this description carefully replicates the costume and stance of the classic stage villain, sinister, black-moustached, bejewelled and arrogant, who manipulated his privilege and wealth to despoil the vulnerable daughters of the people. With Hutchinson's evidence, the 'image of the toff, a man of education, influence, and money was consolidated'. Inquest stories and depositions around Kelly's death provided fodder for the next one hundred years of conspiratorial theories, focused on Kelly as the intended object of the Ripper's revenge, and as the centre of a set of interwoven relationships, linking high and low, East and West in class-divided London.[10]

Response to the Ripper murders, then, reveals significant class divisions and class-based fantasies. It also exposes deep-seated sexual antagonism, most frequently expressed by men towards women. This antagonism was aided and abetted by sensational newspaper coverage that blamed 'women of evil life' for bringing the murders on themselves, though it warned elsewhere that 'no woman is safe while this ghoul's abroad'.[11] The popular press seemed to glory in intensifying terror among 'pure' and 'impure' women by juxtaposing reports on less serious 'attacks on women' with an account of the Whitechapel 'horror'; by featuring an illustration of a 'lady frightened to death' by a Ripper impersonator on the cover of the *Police Illustrated News*; and by proposing that the Ripper might change his venue to more respectable parts as Whitechapel became too dangerous for him. Although the most popular theories and fantasies about the Ripper contained coded discussion of the dangers of unrestrained male sexuality, misogynist fears of female sexuality and female autonomy also surfaced in speculations about a female Ripper. Most of these hostilities focused on prostitutes, who, in the words of one influential commentator, were so 'unsexed' and depraved that they were capable of the most heinous crimes; but suspicion also extended to midwives and medical women inasmuch as the 'knowledge of surgery ... has now been placed within female reach'. However different their social class and occupational mobility, prostitutes, midwives and medical women shared two common characteristics: they possessed dangerous sexual knowledge and they asserted themselves in the public male domain.[12]

Copycat activities mirrored these misogynist attitudes and took a variety of forms, including a conscious imitation and impersonation of the Ripper as well as a more latent identification with the criminal and subtle exploitation of female terror.[13] In Whitechapel, it seems, gentlemen of all sorts were walking about in the evenings looking for women to frighten. Here is a case in point: 'On November 11, a woman named Humphries was passing George Yard and she met a man in the darkness. Trembling with agitation she asked him what he wanted. The man made no answer but laughed. He then made a hasty retreat. The woman yelled "murder".'[14] She attracted the police, who caught up with him, but 'he referred the police to a well-known gentleman at the London Hospital and as a result he was set at liberty'. Similar incidents occurred in the West End, involving respectable women; as soon as the assaulting gentleman could produce his business card and show a respectable address, both the lady and the police dropped the case. Labouring men were not immune from acting out the Ripper role themselves. In pubs across London, drunks bragged of their exploits as Jack the Ripper. Some Ripper impersonators harassed prostitutes and tried to extort money from them. James Henderson, a tailor, was brought before the Dalston magistrates for threatening Rosa Goldstein, an 'unfortunate,' with 'ripping' her up if she did not go with him and for striking her several hard blows with his cane. Henderson was let off with a fine of forty shillings, on the grounds that he had been drunk – this, despite the fact that the severely injured Goldstein appeared in court 'with surgical bandages about her head' and 'weak from loss of blood'.[15]

Besides these public acts of intimidation, there was also a domestic re-enactment of the Ripper drama between husbands and wives in various working-class districts. (I have no evidence of middle-class cases.[16]) In Lambeth, for example, right after the 'double event', magistrates received many applications 'with regard to threats used by husbands against their wives, such as "I'll Whitechapel You" and "Look out for Leather Apron"'. The *Daily News* reported the case of a man who actually offered ten shillings for anyone who would rid him of his wife by the 'Whitechapel process'.[17]

One case that reached the Old Bailey may provide some insight into the circumstances that led up to the threat.[18] Sarah Brett of Peckham was living out of wedlock with Thomas Onley. On 3 October 1888, three days after the 'double event', her son arrived home from sea with a friend. Brett permitted the friend, Frank Hall, to board with them. On

15 October, the common-law husband and the visitor went out and got drunk; when they returned, both abused and swore at her. Brett told the visitor not to interfere; he smacked her and she returned the blow, knocking him off his chair and ordering him to leave. This angered her man, who then declared they were not even married and threatened to do 'a Whitechapel murder upon you'. He was clearly too drunk to carry out this undertaking and so retired upstairs to bed, leaving her with the visitor, who then stabbed her, wounding her severely.

What sense can we make out of this event? Typically, alcohol consumption helped to precipitate the conflict. Sarah Brett's role was defensive but firm; she did not challenge the boundaries of her 'sphere', but she did exercise her prerogatives as manager of household resources and amply demonstrated her own capacity to defend herself. Although her common-law husband abused her first, she only reprimanded the visitor: 'It is quite sufficient for Mr Onley to commence upon me without you interfering.' By ordering the visitor out of the house, she nonetheless shamed Onley. She threatened his masculinity; he responded by denying the legitimacy of their relations – in sum, calling her a whore. He then invoked the example of that most masterly of men, the Whitechapel killer, leaving her with the young visitor, who had the strength to carry out the husband's threat.

I am not trying to argue that the Ripper episode directly increased sexual violence; rather it established a common vocabulary and iconography for the forms of male violence that permeated the whole society, obscuring the different material conditions that provoked sexual antagonism in different classes.[19] The Ripper drama invested male domination with a powerful mystique; it encouraged little boys in working-class Poplar and suburban Tunbridge Wells to intimidate and torment girls by playing at Jack the Ripper: 'There's a man in a leather apron coming soon, to kill all the little girls in Tunbridge Wells. It's in the paper.' 'Look out, here comes Jack the Ripper', was enough to send girls running from the street or from their own back yards into the safety of their homes.[20] Whatever their conscious ethos, male night-patrols in Whitechapel had the same structural effect of enforcing the segregation of social space: women were relegated to the interior of a prayer meeting or their homes, behind locked doors; men were left to patrol the public spaces and the street. Male vigilantes also terrified women of the locale, who could not easily distinguish their molesters from their disguised protectors: 'If the murderer be possessed ... with the usual cunning of lunacy', one correspondent suggested in the *Saint James Gazette*, 'I should think it probable that he was one of the first to enrol himself among the amateur detectives'.[21]

Although the Ripper murders reinforced the spatial polarities of gender and class, they also stimulated male fantasies of vulnerability and identification with the female victims. Men fantasized about the female experience of terror; amateur detectives donned female garb to attract the murderer's attention. Although some boys played at being 'Leather Apron', others found the Ripper episode to be personally threatening and terrifying. At three and a half, Leonard Ellisden believed the Ripper to be a particular 'evil-looking man with a beard who used to eat fire at Margate sands'. When this 'worthy gentleman' entered his parents' tobacconist shop, Ellisden 'drove the ladies of the family nearly round the bend by rushing in shrieking in terror "Jack the Ripper's in the shop" '. Middle-class boys as well as girls identified the Ripper with the dangers of the street – dangers that seemed to penetrate the sanctity of the home, thanks to the cries of the newspaper boys hawking news of the latest Whitechapel horror and the avid interest of maidservants and nannies, who spread copies of illustrated Sunday papers across the nursery table. The nightly 'fears and fantasies' of Jack the Ripper made the prospect of 'going to bed almost unendurable', Compton Mackenzie recalled:

> Whitechapel became a word of dread, and I can recall the horror of reading 'Whitechapel' at the bottom of the list of fares at the far end inside an omnibus. Suppose the omnibus should refuse to stop at Kensington High Street and go on with its passengers to Whitechapel? What could that Eminent QC in his wig ... do to save everybody inside that omnibus from being cut up by the knife of Jack the Ripper?[22]

Women's reaction to the events surrounding the Ripper murders were as diverse as men's, yet even more heavily overlaid by feelings of personal vulnerability. Women in Whitechapel were both fascinated and terrified by the murders: like their male counterparts, they bought up the latest editions of the halfpenny evening newspapers; they gossiped about the gruesome details of the murders; and they crowded into the waxwork exhibits and peep shows where representations of the murdered victims were on display. As we have seen, many also sympathized with the victims and came to the aid of prostitutes in their time of crisis. As one clergyman from Spitalfields remarked of the 'fallen sisterhood': 'these women are very good natured to each other. They are drawn together by a common danger and they will help each other all they can'. Because the woman clubbed together, and because keepers of common lodging houses were generally 'lenient' to regular customers, distress among prostitutes during the month of October was 'not as great as one might expect', reported the *Daily News*.[23]

11 An optimistic view of the power held by East End women.

On the whole, respectable working women offered little collective resistance to public male intimidation. I found accounts of two exceptions among matchgirls and marketwomen who were part of an autonomous female work culture. On their own territory, marketwomen could organize *en masse*: a number of women calling out 'Leather Apron', for instance, chased Henry Taylor when he threatened Mary Ann Perry with 'ripping her up' in Clare market; and similar incidents occurred in Spitalfields market, nearby the Ripper murders. Marketwomen enjoyed an *esprit de corps* akin to that of the feisty, street-fighting matchmakers, who had just won a successful strike from the Bryant and May match factory, and who, according to one anonymous letter purporting to come from Jack the Ripper, openly bragged about catching him.[24]

Those women who could, stayed inside at night behind locked doors, but women who earned a living on the streets at night – prostitutes – did not have that luxury. Some left Whitechapel, even the East End, for good. Others applied to the casual wards of the workhouse. Some slowly went back to the streets, first in groups of two or three, then occasionally alone. They armed themselves, and although they 'joked' about encountering Jack – 'I am the next for Jack', quipped one woman – they were obviously terrified at the prospect. Some even went to prayer meetings to avoid remaining home alone at night: 'Of course we are taking advantage of the terror', explained one Salvation Army lass.[25]

Another woman who took advantage of the terror was Henrietta Barnett, wife of Samuel Barnett of Toynbee Hall. Distressed at hearing women gossiping about the murders, she got up a petition to the Queen and, with the aid of board (state) schoolteachers and mission workers, obtained four thousand signatures from the 'Women of Whitechapel'. The petition begged the Queen to call upon 'your servants in authority' to close down the lodging houses where the murder victims resided.[26] Although not entirely absent from the Ripper mobilization, female moral reformers like Barnett occupied a subordinate role within it; they remained physically constrained within the female sphere and bent on keeping neighbourhood women there as well, moving them inside into prayer meetings, out of earshot of salacious discussions of sex and violence, relinquishing public spaces and sexual knowledge to men.

It is difficult to determine how much Barnett's petition truly represented the opinion of Whitechapel women. Jewish artisan wives regarded the women of the lodging houses as 'nogoodnicks, prostitutes, old bags and drunks', but they still employed Catherine Eddowes and others like her to char and wash for them, to light their sabbath fires, sometimes even to mind their children.[27] There was a tense and fragile social ecology between rough and respectable elements in Whitechapel, one that could be easily upset by outside intervention. The murders threatened the safety of respectable women; they undoubtedly strained class relations in the neighbourhood and intensified gender divisions. They temporarily placed respectable women under 'house arrest' and made them dependent on male protection.

Local folklore, however, tested the spatial boundaries of gender erected by the Ripper danger. Family stories, passed down among Jewish and Irish cockney residents in the Whitechapel area over three generations, accorded working-class women a more active role in the Ripper episode than did the night patrols of Whitechapel. These tales recount how 'mother', forced to go out late one 'wintery' night either to obtain medicine for a sick child or to visit an ailing husband in the London Hospital, was accosted by a 'stranger' in the darkness. After interrogating her about the nature of the medical emergency propelling her out of her home (or examining the visitor's card to the hospital), the mystery man realized she was 'poor' but 'honest' and let her go. The next morning, two hundred yards down the road, the 'mutilated' body of a prostitute was found.[28]

'Mother Meets Jack the Ripper' vividly illustrates how working-class women organized their own identity around the figure of the prostitute, who served as a central spectacle in a set of urban encounters and fantasies. In public, a poor woman continually risked the danger of being mistaken for a prostitute; she had to demonstrate unceasingly in her dress, gestures and movements that she was not a 'low' woman. Like her middle-class counterpart, a working-class woman established her respectability through visual self-presentation and through her status as wife and mother.[29]

As a wife and mother, the female protagonist in 'mother's' story claims immunity from the Ripper's knife. Although the tale vindicates female virtue over female vice, it also establishes a certain identification with the plight of fallen women. Unlike the men in their civic tales of hunting down Jack the Ripper, 'mother' could insert herself into the drama only by impersonating a potential victim, who is resourceful enough to talk her way out of a difficult situation.[30] 'Mother's' story also draws on media fantasies of the Ripper as a dark representation of conflicted masculinity: the 'midnight murderer' appears as a compelling but dangerous stranger, a savage/savant, knowledgeable about medical matters, able to interrogate and discern female virtue, yet capable of maniacal violence towards women of 'evil life'.

Women outside of Whitechapel also took a keen interest in the murders. Queen Victoria repeatedly wrote to the Home Office and Scotland Yard with her pet theories, and actually forced Lord Salisbury to hold a cabinet meeting on a Saturday to consider the question of a reward. All across London, female mediums tried their hands at armchair detection by calling up the spirits of the murdered women: at a private seance held in West Kilburn on 16 October, the spirit of Annie Chapman directed the group to look to the 'military medicals' who 'want our bodies for a particular reason', 'they want to find something'. Female spiritualists restricted their sleuthing to the seance circle, unlike the clairvoyant R. J. Lees, who claimed to have used his powers to track down the 'mad doctor' at his West End mansion.[31]

At least one woman emulated the copycat activities of men and gained some notoriety from the case: at Bradford Police Court on 10 October 1888, a 'respectable young woman, named Maria Coroner, aged twenty-one, was charged with having certain letters tending to cause a breach of the peace; they were signed "Jack the Ripper" '. Like the Whitechapel mothers who encountered Jack the Ripper in the dead of night, one female correspondent believed that 'respectable women like herself had nothing to fear from the Whitechapel murderer', as she thought it was true that he 'respects and protects respectable females'. This was, of course, the line taken by police officials, who expressed amazement at what they regarded as the widespread female hysteria over the murders, since they were perpetrated only on prostitutes.[32]

For many women, this was small comfort. While many middle-class women were determined to resist the panic and to assert their right to traverse public places, female vulnerability extended well beyond the boundaries of Whitechapel. Mary Hughes, a secondary-school teacher who lived in the West End in 1888, recalled

> how terrified and unbalanced we all were by the murders. It seemed to be round the corner, although it all happened in the East End, and we were in the West; but even so, I was afraid to go out after dark, if only to post a letter. Just as dusk came on we used to hear down our quiet and ultra-respectable Edith Road the cries of newspaper boys in tones made as alarming as they could: 'Another 'orrible murder ... Whitechapel! Disgustin' details ... Murder!'[33]

What about the politicized edge of middle-class womanhood, the feminists? Did they mount any counter-attack? Josephine Butler and others expressed concern that the uproar over the murders would lead to the repression of brothels and subsequent homelessness of women. In so doing, they broke with more repressive purity advocates who were totally indifferent to the fate of the victims and to the rights of prostitutes. In the end, only the strict libertarians, female and male, came forward to defend prostitutes as human beings, with personal rights and liberties: 'Not till the personal rights of the poor pariahs are counted as worthy of recognition and defence as, let us say, those of their patrons, will mankind [be on] the road towards the extinction of this evil', declared the *Personal Rights Journal*.[34]

Some female publicists also used the occasion to air feminist critiques of male violence in regard to medical sadism and wife-beating. Frances Power Cobbe enthusiastically entered into the fray; speculating that the murderer was a 'physiologist delirious with cruelty', she called for the use of female detectives whose 'mother wit' would guide them to the murderer. The only piece of feminist anger against male violence to receive extensive coverage appeared in the pages of the Liberal *Daily News*. The Whitechapel murders were not just homicides but 'womenkilling', declared Florence Fenwick Miller, London journalist and 'platform woman', in her letter to the editor. Researching the police columns, she concluded that attacks on prostitutes were not different from other violent assaults on women by men. They were not isolated events but a part of a 'constant but ever increasing series of cruelties' perpetrated against women and treated leniently by judges.[35]

Miller's letter generated a small flurry of responses supportive of her position and calling for women's economic and political emancipation. Kate Mitchell, a physician and feminist, applauded Miller's letter and cited the case of James Henderson, who was let off with a fine of forty shillings after severely beating a prostitute. Unless women were publicly emancipated, argued Mitchell, they would remain 'ciphers' in the land and subject to male physical abuse. The letters made an important association between public and domestic violence against women, but it would be a mistake to exaggerate their political impact. They remained isolated interventions in an overwhelmingly male-dominated debate; they were discounted or ignored by other dailies and failed to mobilize women over the issues.[36]

The Radical *Star,* whose pages were open to socialists, disagreed with Miller: 'It is the class question rather than the sex question that is the issue in this matter.' The *Star*'s opposition of class and sex signalled a tendency among Victorians to conceptualize social problems and identities as stark dichotomies, rather than as multiple and intersecting determinants. Commenting on the Whitechapel murders in their own journals, prominent socialists like William Morris and H. M. Hyndman also refused to address the issue of sex antagonism; they tended to see gender oppression as a result of capitalist productive relations alone. For all their contempt for the proprietary press, the socialists' assessment of the murdered prostitutes as 'unsexed', dehumanized 'creatures' who had 'violated their womanhood for the price of a night's lodging' was remarkably similar to that of the conservative and misogynist *Morning Post* and *The Times*. To distinguish themselves from the bourgeois press, socialists would have had to overcome their ambivalence towards prostitutes and the unrespectable poor of Whitechapel and address the subject of male dominance.[37]

The Whitechapel horrors provoked multiple and contradictory responses, expressive of important cultural and social divisions within Victorian society. Nonetheless, the alternative perspectives – of feminists and libertarians, of the Whitechapel poor themselves – were ultimately subordinated to a dominant discussion in the media, one that was shaped and articulated by those people in positions of power, namely, male professional experts. Within this dominant discourse, the discussion of class, particularly of a dangerous class marked off from respectable citizens and the 'people' of London, was more explicit and self-conscious than that of gender. In part, this fact relates to the precise moment of class anxiety when Jack the Ripper stalked the streets of London. The events in Whitechapel could be easily slotted into the 'Outcast London' theme. They reinforced prevailing prejudices about the East End as a strange territory of savages, a social abyss, an inferno. *The Times* might well wring its hands about the responsibility of 'our social organisation' for spawning the crimes, but this momentary soul-searching was readily domesticated into an attack on the symptoms, rather than on the causes, of urban poverty.[38]

Throughout the 'autumn of terror', one theme overshadowed all the other proposals to cure the social ills of Whitechapel: the necessity of slum clearance and the need to purge the lawless population of the common lodging houses from the neighbourhood.[39] 'Those of us who know Whitechapel know that the impulse that makes for murder is abroad in our streets every night', declared two Toynbee Hall residents.[40] The 'disorderly and depraved lives of the women', observed Canon Barnett, were more 'appalling' than the actual murders.[41] Men like Barnett finally dominated public opinion and consolidated it behind razing the common lodging houses of the Flower and Dean Street area. The notoriety of the street impelled the respectable owners – the Henderson family – to sell their property as soon as the leases were up. The Rothschild Buildings (1892), for respectable Jewish artisans and their families, appeared over the site of the lodging houses where Catherine Eddowes and Elizabeth Stride once lived. Prostitutes and their fellow lodgers were thus rendered homeless and forced to migrate to the few remaining rough streets in the neighbourhood. Through the surveillance of the vigilance committees and through this 'urban renewal', the murders helped to intensify repressive activity already underway in the Whitechapel area.[42]

Such reform-minded responses coincided with a general dissipation of middle-class fears of 'Outcast London'. The disciplined and orderly 1889 dock strike persuaded many respectable observers that the East End poor were indeed salvageable because they could be organized into unions. Meanwhile, Charles Booth's massive survey of East London, also published in 1889, graphically demonstrated how small and unrepresentative the 'criminal' population of the Flower and Dean Street rookery actually was. When another Ripper-like murder occurred in July 1889 in Whitechapel, newspaper coverage was far less sensational and relentless. In class terms, the immediate crisis had passed.[43]

Sexual fears and hostilities, on the other hand, were less satisfactorily allayed. After Mary Kelly's death, the police, finding themselves completely at sea, dropped the whole matter in the lap of Dr Thomas Bond, syphilologist and expert in forensic medicine, asking him to provide them with a psychological profile of the murderer. In his letter to Scotland Yard, Bond pronounced the series of 'five murders', beginning with Polly Nichols and ending with Mary Kelly, to be the 'work of one hand'. Bond discounted the possibility that the culprit was a revengeful religious fanatic or that the mutilations demonstrated 'scientific or anatomical knowledge'. The murderer, Bond explained, was suffering from 'satyriasis' (i.e. he was oversexed and resorted to violence to satisfy his excessive sexual cravings). In external appearance, he might well be a 'quiet, inoffensive man probably middle-aged, and neatly and respectably dressed ... he would be solitary and eccentric in his habits, since he is most likely to be a man without regular occupation, but with some small income or pension'.[44]

To construct this profile, Bond relied on newspaper theories of an erotic maniac leading a 'Jekyll and Hyde' double life, as well as on emerging typologies of sex crime formulated by continental sexologists like Krafft-Ebing. Newspaper coverage of the Ripper murders not only helped to popularize expert medical opinion on sexual pathology; it also provided narrative materials that sexologists would process into the most notorious case history of sex crime to date. Contemporaneous with Bond's report there began a public recycling of Jack the Ripper as a medical specimen. In November and December 1888, two articles appeared in American medical journals, 'Sexual Perversion and the Whitechapel Murders', by Dr James Kiernan, and 'The Whitechapel Murders: Their Medico-Legal and Historical Aspects', by Dr E. C. Spitzka. Both articles catalogued prior case histories of 'lust murder' to counter the impression that the murders were unprecedented in the annals of crime; and both located the Ripper along a spectrum of contemporary perverts, from female masturbators and 'urnings' of both sexes, to the exclusively male perpetrators of 'lust murder' and sexual sadism (including reference to the 'Minotaur' of the 'Maiden Tribute'). Both relied on newspaper accounts of post-mortem reports of the mutilations and murders to diagnose the criminal; both remained undecided as to 'his' legal responsibility, whether his actions were the result of congenital disease or acquired vice. In the published Jack the Ripper letters that forecast more murders to follow, Spitzka found 'the genuine expression of intention' to be at variance with any diagnosis of 'impulsive', 'periodical' or 'epileptic insanity'. Spitzka was quite taken with the discursive propensities of the murderer, a 'speaking pervert' who communicated his 'truth' to the reading public: 'It would not be the first time that a subject of sexual perversion had entered the lists as a writer', he insisted, 'no artifice ... would be too cunning for one of this class'. Drawing on the writings of Spitzka and Kiernan, Krafft-Ebing included the Ripper in his next edition of *Psychopathia Sexualis*, as a clinical specimen – the most famous clinical specimen – of lust murder. From newspaper accounts that linked a monstrous crime and a monstrous individual to a monstrous social environment, the Ripper story was reduced to a notorious case history of an individual erotic maniac, whose activities were seemingly unconnected to normal interactions of men and women.[45]

The social contexts of the Ripper's exploits, however, have not disappeared from twenty-first-century representation, although they too have undergone a mythic revision. The Whitechapel murders have continued to provide a common vocabulary of male violence against women, a vocabulary now more than one hundred years old. Its persistence owes much to the mass media's exploitation of Ripper iconography. Depictions of female mutilation in mainstream cinema, celebrations of the Ripper as a 'hero' of crime, intensify fears of male violence and convince women that they are helpless victims. Changing historical circumstances, however, can provoke and enable a different response to these media productions. The case of the Yorkshire Ripper constitutes a late twentieth-century 'replay' of the Ripper episode that engendered a different political reaction from contemporary British feminists, who took to the streets to protest the crimes and the media amplification of the terror.

Notes

1 John Kelly, testimony at Catherine Eddowes's inquest, Elwyn Jones (ed.), *Ripper File* (London: Barker, 1975), p. 51.

2 *Daily Chronicle*, 10 November 1888; *Daily Telegraph*, 10 November 1888.

3 'The Terrible Crime', *Echo*, 10 November 1888; *Daily Chronicle*, 10 November 1888; 'The Whitechapel Horrors', *East London Observer*, 13 October 1888.

4 Quoted in Martin Howells and Keith Skinner, *The Ripper Legacy: The Life and Death of Jack the Ripper* (London: Sidgwick and Jackson, 1987), p. 112.

5 'Reign of Terror in the East End', *East London Observer*, 15 September 1888.

6 'East End Horrors', *Lloyd's Weekly Newspaper*, 7 October 1888; *Daily Telegraph*, 4 October 1888; Melvin Harris, *Jack the Ripper: The Bloody Truth* (London: Columbus Books, 1987), pp. 23, 24; Donald Rumbelow, *The Complete Jack the Ripper* (London: W. H. Allen, 1987), pp. 74, 75.

7 Leonard W. Matters, *The Mystery of Jack the Ripper* (London: Hutchinson, 1929), p. 243. 'I knew Marie quite well by sight', declared Walter Dew, who had been a constable in Whitechapel in 1888: 'Often I had seen her parading along Commercial Street ... in the company of two others of her kind, fairly neatly dressed and invariably wearing a clean white apron, but no hat'. Walter Dew, *I Caught Crippen* (London: Blackie and Son, 1938).

8 'Whitechapel: Important Evidence at the Inquest Today', *Star*, 12 November 1888.

9 Rumbelow, *Complete Jack the Ripper*, pp. 88, 89. The transition to the East End proved a difficult narrative move: 'By some means, however, at present not exactly clear, she suddenly drifted into the East End'. 'Whitechapel', *Star*, 12 November 1888.

10 George Hutchinson, deposition, reproduced in Colin Wilson and Robin Odell, *Jack the Ripper: Summing Up the Verdict* (London: Bantam, 1987),

p. 63; Martin Fido, *The Crimes, Detection and Death of Jack the Ripper* (London: Weidenfeld and Nicolson, 1987), p. 178.

11 *Star*, 8 September 1888.

12 *Evening Standard*, 9 November 1888; *Daily Chronicle*, 18 September 1888; *Police Illustrated News*, 3 November, 1 December 1888; *Woman's Penny Paper*, 6 November 1888; 'G.S.O.' to the Editor, *The Times*, 22 September 1888; letters to the Editor, *Saint James Gazette*, 12 November 1888.

13 It should be noted that male libertarians came to the defence of prostitutes in the pages of the *Personal Rights Journal*, November 1888, pp. 69, 76, 84.

14 *The Times*, 12 November 1888.

15 Tom Cullen, *Autumn of Terror: Jack the Ripper, the Crimes and Times* (London: Fontana, 1973), p. 78; *Echo*, 1, 2, 3 October 1888; *East London Observer*, 6 October 1888; *Morning Post*, 4 October 1888.

16 On marital cruelty in middle-class households, see James A. Hammerton, 'Victorian Marriage and the Law of Matrimonial Cruelty', *Victorian Studies*, 33:2 (Winter 1990), pp. 269–92.

17 *The Times*, 1 October 1888; Cullen, *Autumn of Terror*, p. 79; *Echo*, 3 October 1888.

18 Criminal Court, *Sessions Papers*, London, 109 (1888–9), pp. 76–8. Thanks to Ellen Ross for this citation.

19 Ellen Ross, ' " Fierce Questions and Taunts": Married Life in Working-Class London, 1870–1914', *Feminist Studies*, 8:3 (Fall 1982), pp. 575–602.

20 Helen Corke, *In Our Infancy: An Autobiography, Part 1, 1882–1912* (Cambridge: Cambridge University Press, 1975), p. 25 (thanks to Dina Copelman for this citation); Mrs Bartholmew, interview (thanks to Anna Davin for the transcript).

21 Letter to the Editor, *Saint James Gazette*, 16 November 1888.

22 Leonard Ellison, 'Starting from Victoria', 229, Burnett Collection, Brunel University; Leonard Woolf, *Sowing: An Autobiography of the Years 1880 to 1904* (New York: Harcourt Brace, 1960), pp. 60–2; Sylvia Pankhurst, *The Suffragette Movement* (London: Longman, 1931), pp. 110, 111; Compton Mackenzie, *My Life and Times: Octave One 1883–1891* (London: Chatto and Windus, 1963), pp. 164, 165.

23 Montagu Williams, *Round London: Down East and Up West* (London: Macmillan, 1892), p. 12; *Pall Mall Gazette*, 18 October 1888; *Daily News*, 4 October 1888.

24 *Daily Telegraph*, 4 October, 10 September 1888; *Reynolds Newspaper*, 9 September 1888; Mepo 3/142, 5 October 1888.

25 Dew, *I Caught Crippen*, p. 95. 'Ready for the Whitechapel Fiend: Women Secretly Armed', *Police Illustrated News*, 22 September 1888; *Daily Telegraph*, 2 October 1888; *War Cry*, 1 December 1888.

26 *War Cry*, 1 December 1888; Mrs H. O. R. Barnett, *Canon Barnett: His Life, Work and Friends by his Wife* (London: Murray, 1921), p. 306.

27 Quoted in Jerry White, *The Rothschild Buildings: Life in a Tenement Block, 1887–1920* (London: Routledge & Kegan Paul, 1980), p. 125.

28 In interviews conducted in East London in July 1983, four informants, three women and one man, told this story as their family history. As far as I can discern, this story has not entered print culture.

29 Lynda Nead, *Myths of Sexuality: Representations of Women in Victorian Britain* (Oxford: Blackwell, 1988), pp. 176–80; Ellen Ross ' " Not the Sort that Would Sit on the Doorstep": Respectability in Pre-World War I London Neighbourhoods', *International and Working Class History*, 27 (Spring 1985), pp. 39–59.

30 In 1966, a woman who, as a young woman, had lived in Jubilee Road, 'in the heart of the area terrorised by Jack the Ripper', remembered her father taking part in nightly patrols to protect the women. She herself came close to stumbling on the murderer as she walked along Hanbury Street one night at dark. When, the next morning, she found out a '42-year old widow' (Annie Chapman) had been murdered, 'I was terrified to put my head outside the house for days'. 'R. J. Lees – the Jack the Ripper Case', Society for Psychical Research Archives, London.

31 Rumbelow, *Complete Jack the Ripper*, p. 86; 'The Whitechapel Murders', *Medium and Daybreak* (London), 2 November 1888. On R. J. Lees, see the reprint of an article in the *Chicago Sunday Times-Herald* of 1895, in Jones, *Ripper File*, p. 166; Nandor Fodor, *Encyclopaedia of Psychic Science* ([1933] New Jersey: Citadel Press, 1974), p. 193; 'R. J. Lees – the Ripper Case'; Harris, *Jack the Ripper*, chs 18, 19.

32 Quoted in Donald McCormick, *The Identity of Jack the Ripper* (London: Arrow Books, 1970), p. 81; quoted in Rumbelow, *Complete Jack the Ripper*, p. 101.

33 On women who resisted the terror, see Margot Asquith, *The Autobiography of Margot Asquith*, ed. Mark Bonham Carter ([1962] London: Methuen, 1985), pp. 43, 44; Margaret Nevinson, *Life's Fitful Fever: A Volume of Memories* (London: A & C Black, 1926), p. 106. On the effects of the terror, see M. V. Hughes, *A London Girl of the 1880s* (Oxford: Oxford University Press, 1978), p. 218.

34 *Personal Rights Journal*, November 1888, pp. 69, 76, 84; *Dawn*, 1 November 1888; *Sentinel*, December 1888, p. 145.

35 Jan Lambertz, 'Feminists and the Politics of Wife-Beating', in Harold L. Smith (ed.), *British Feminism in the Twentieth Century* (Amherst: University of Massachusetts Press, 1990), pp. 25–46; Frances Power Cobbe to the Editor, *The Times*, 11 October 1888; *Daily News*, 2 October 1888.

36 *Daily News*, 4, 6, 9, 11 October 1888.

37 *Star*, 4 October 1888. On other responses of Radicals and socialists, see *Justice*, 6 October 1888 and 17 November 1888; *Star*, 1 October 1888; Ben Tillett, quoted in William J. Fishman, *East End Jewish Radicals 1875–1914* (London: Duckworth, 1975), p. 236.

38 Peter Keating, 'Fact and Fiction in the East End', in H. J. Dyos and M. Wolff (eds), *The Victorian City: Images and Realities*, 2 vols (London: Routledge

& Kegan Paul, 1973), vol. 1, pp. 585–603; *The Times* leader, quoted in 'Murder as an Advertisement', *Pall Mall Gazette*, 19 September 1888.

39 White, *Rothschild Buildings*, ch. 1. See, for example, *The Times*, 22 September, 2, 11, 18, 26, 29, 30 October, 6, 16, November 1888. See the series of letters in the *Daily Telegraph* on the 'Safe Four Per cent', 21, 24, 26 September 1888.

40 Thomas Hancock Nunn and Thomas Gardner to the Editor, *The Times*, 6 October 1888. Both Nunn and Gardner were members of the National Vigilance Association.

41 *The Times*, 16 November 1888.

42 White, *Rothschild Buildings*, ch. 1.

43 Gareth Stedman Jones, *Outcast London: A Study of the Relationship Between Classes in Victorian Society* (Oxford: Clarendon, 1971), ch. 17; Keating, 'Fact and Fiction', pp. 595, 596; *Star*, 20 July 1889.

44 Dr Thomas Bond, to the Commissioner of the Metropolitan Police, 10 November 1888, Mepo 3/141. See the letter from Arthur MacDonald, requesting the 'medical reports on the bodies of the victims' for publication in 'American Blue Books' and in a French publication. 15 October 1892, H.O. 144/A49301/219. See a similar request from Dr Gustave Ollive of Nantes, requesting a copy of Dr Bond's report. 8 November 1894, H.O. 144/A49301/C/36.

45 James G. Kiernan, 'Sexual Perversion and the Whitechapel Murders', *Medical Standard*, 4:5 (November 1888), pp. 129–30; 4:6 (December 1888), pp. 170–1; E. C. Spitzka, 'The Whitechapel Murders: Their Medico-Legal and Historical Aspects', *Journal of Nervous and Mental Diseases*, 13:12 (December 1888), pp. 765–78. On Jack the Ripper as a medical case, see also 'The Whitechapel Murders' appearing contemporaneously in the *British Medical Journal* (8 December 1888), p. 1302, as well as a letter to the Editor from 'A Medical Man', 'A Theory of the Whitechapel Murders' in the *Evening News*, 15 October 1888. 'The mere existence of anthropophagy, necrophilism, or sexual perversion when unaccompanied by other evidences of nervous or mental disease, is not sufficient proof of insanity', declared Spitzka ('The Whitechapel Murders', p. 775).

12

Jack the Ripper as the threat of outcast London

Robert F. Haggard

During the autumn of 1888, a killer terrorized London. He chose as his victims mostly older, decrepit, drink-ridden prostitutes from the East End district of Whitechapel. The name 'Jack the Ripper' appeared on a number of letters mailed to the police and to various news agencies. The publication of several of these letters, in the hope that someone would recognize the handwriting, vastly increased the killer's fame. It has never been established that the murderer wrote any of the letters. Nevertheless, without them, the memorable appellation would never have been attached to the killer, and the murders themselves would probably now be long forgotten. The question of who performed the brutal killings and sexual mutilations has baffled later writers as much as it did the London Metropolitan Police in 1888. Many authors have posited theories, but no one hypothesis has been proven conclusively.

Unlike most papers on this subject, I intend to avoid the issue of who committed these horrible crimes, but instead to examine the reactions of London, both West and East Ends, to the killings. Jack the Ripper should be studied within the context of the 1880s, a period of economic uncertainty and heightened class tensions. The Whitechapel murders provide a case study of sorts. The reactions of the West End mirrored the debate over 'outcast London' and the fear of social revolution on the part of the poor of the East End. The reactions of the East End reflected ingrained prejudices against foreigners, Jews, the police and upper-class society. By examining the social conditions in East London, particularly Whitechapel, where the killer operated most often, I hope to show why the East End was viewed with such concern and distrust even before the autumn of 1888. By discussing social unrest in East London and the fear of revolution among many in the West End in the 1880s, I plan to show how the Jack the Ripper murders reinforced a whole series of larger long-standing concerns and preconceived notions. Finally, by looking at the types of individuals who were suspected of being involved in these hideous events, I will reveal how the more affluent Victorians' reaction to Jack the Ripper exhibited deep-seated prejudices against certain social classes and elements of the population.

By the mid-1880s, 'the East End had become as potent a symbol of urban poverty ... as Manchester had been of industrial conditions in the 1840s'.[1] Many in the West End viewed the East as a place where the 'vilest practices are looked upon with the most matter-of-fact indifference ... [and where] the filthy and abominable from all parts of the country seem to flow. Entire courts are filled with thieves, prostitutes, and liberated convicts.'[2] A number of journalists and social commentators, such as Walter Besant, Jane Stuart-Wortley and Samuel Barnett, tried to alter West End perceptions and prejudices. Yet, East London was too firmly fixed in most people's minds as a symbol of decadence, immorality, criminality and poverty to be replaced easily. Such negative perceptions, in fact, migrated from West to East; Dr Curshan Corner noted that people in the East were 'coming to think that any discomforts or annoyances, any offensive innovations or dangerous nuisances ... must be resignedly tolerated because it is East London'.[3]

There is no doubt that life in East London was difficult for many of its 900,000 inhabitants. Whitechapel, with a population of 76,000, had 39.2 per cent of its citizens on or below the poverty line.[4] Many workers could only find intermittent employment, and those who had regular employment often did not fare better. The sweating system, characterized by overcrowded, unsanitary workshops, long hours and low wages, was widely utilized. Many were forced to toil for fifteen to eighteen hours a day in the numerous tailoring, boot-making and cabinet-making shops of the East End.[5]

Poverty was not the only problem leading to social unrest in London. The influx of foreigners, many of them Russian or German Jews fleeing persecution or economic hardship on the continent, caused concern that 'English' jobs were being lost to the flood of newcomers. The belief that a rising tide of Jewish immigration was reducing native Englishmen to destitution led to an increase in popular anti-Semitism. The comment that 'the foreign Jews are filthy in their lives, and present a substantial similarity to the Mongolian type of character' did not seem out of the ordinary during periods of economic distress.[6] Contemporary social thinkers Charles Booth and Stephen Fox attempted to alter this impression by stating that Jews were hard working and law abiding, and, most importantly, were not immigrating in unprecedented numbers.[7] However, negative perceptions of Jews, like ones of East London generally, were extremely difficult to combat.

The fact remained that most foreign Jews immigrating to England took up residence in London. The Jewish community in Whitechapel was particularly compact. Of the 60–70,000 Jews in London, 90 per cent lived in the East End. Only one-half were born in England. Whitechapel alone had a Jewish population of 30–40,000.[8] Like their forebears, most Jewish refugees made good on the few opportunities presented to them. As Charles Booth noted:

> They are set down on an already over-stocked and demoralized labour market. They are surrounded by the drunkenness, immorality and gambling of the East-End streets ... in the midst of the very refuse of our civilization, and yet ... whether they become bootmakers, tailors, cabinet-makers, glaziers, or dealers, the Jewish inhabitants of the East End rise in the social scale.[9]

The Jews' success created some animosity with the Irish community. It may have troubled some Irishmen to see that long hours, periods of unemployment, bad food, overcrowding, in fact, 'all the conditions which ruin the Anglo-Saxon or Irish inhabitant of the East End seem to leave unhurt the moral and physical fibre of the Jew'.[10]

In addition to the supposed dislocation caused by the influx of foreigners into East London, social commentators recognized a large number of long-standing problems which needed to be solved: overcrowding, poor sanitation, excessive drinking, immorality and poverty. All of these concerns were intimately connected. Victorian social legislators had long adhered to the notion that improved living conditions in the East would lead to a decrease in the amount of vice and crime. There would be little change as long as there were 'reeking courts, crowded public-houses, low lodging houses, and numerous brothels ... poverty, rags, and dirt everywhere'.[11]

Overcrowding was a huge problem in East London. In 1891, 55.5 per cent of the people in Whitechapel lived with more than two persons per room in apartments with fewer than five rooms. Two districts of East London had even higher rates. Such living conditions were due in part to the large rent increases in the East over the previous quarter century. Although rents in the West only rose by 11 per cent between 1880 and 1900, those in the East End jumped by 25 per cent.[12] Overcrowding led to the association of the honest poor with criminal elements, and produced 'incest, illegitimacy, juvenile prostitution, drunkenness, dirt, idleness, [and] disease'.[13]

It also prompted people to spend as much of their time as possible away from home; although many joined social, religious or philanthropic clubs, a larger number spent much of their spare time in the local public houses. Drunkenness led to disease, the loss of jobs and, often, violence.[14] Poor sanitation, another problem intimately linked with overcrowding, caused a high rate of child mortality. According to the *Lancet*, the prestigious medical journal, reform on this front would not only be useful 'in saving human life and health, but also in reducing the prevalence of crime'.[15] An inadequate water supply made personal cleanliness impossible. The lack of mortuaries forced some poor families to keep the corpses of their loved ones in their own living room until the day of the funeral.[16]

Part of the problem of overcrowding was due to the policies of the government and to middle-class reformers. The demolition of unsanitary buildings, under the provisions of the 1875 Artisans and Labourers Dwelling Act, led to some rebuilding, but often the new apartments were too expensive for the earlier tenants to rent. This led to more crowding in the slums adjacent to the 'improved' areas.[17] Some commentators were outraged by the government's lack of foresight; the journalist George Sims revealed that 'in scores of instances the work of improvement has stopped with the pulling down' and argued that instead of 'civilizing the Zulu and improving the condition of the Egyptian fellah the Government should turn its attention to the poor of London'.[18] Other writers noted that rising rents defeated the purpose of the housing legislation. The philanthropist Octavia Hill commented that the government should 'be thankful if [it] can secure for the same rent even one room in a new, clean, pure house'.[19]

For many of the poor, common lodging houses provided the only escape from spending the night on the streets. These houses were as profitable to their owners as they were wretched and degrading for their boarders. In such houses, it was often difficult to distinguish between the honest and the criminal poor. Indeed, the police frequently did not make any distinction between the two at all. The common lodging house system did allow the police a larger measure of social control. The owners of the houses were often prepared 'to assist the police with information, and the inmates [were] under police supervision to a greater extent than they would be if they were driven to live elsewhere'.[20]

There was a strong perception among middle-class reformers that there was a close connection between the common lodging houses and prostitution in London. One writer expressed it this way: 'want first, exigency next, bad companions in low lodging-houses next, and the fatal step – the last [prostitution]'.[21] Both prostitution and lodging houses flourished in the East End. Whitechapel contained 63 brothels, 1,200 known prostitutes (a conservative estimate) and 233 common lodging houses capable of holding 8,500 people. In addition to those who chose prostitution as a full-time profession, many women engaged in certain low-paying trades (specifically needlewomen, slopworkers, actresses, seamstresses and lacemakers) resorted to 'casual prostitution' in times of economic hardship. Such activity was often the only way these women could make ends meet; their neighbours, families and friends usually understood the pressures of economic necessity and did not shun them.[22]

London was an extremely hospitable environment for the practice of prostitution. Its size provided anonymity, protection from police harassment and a constant supply of customers. The police were generally more concerned with prostitution in the West End, since 'it was [there] more likely to come to the notice of respectable persons, press reporters, and foreigners'.[23] For most of the 1880s, East End prostitutes were left to ply their trade in relative peace. Prostitution was not actually a crime in Victorian England; the police could only take action if the prostitutes' solicitation created a public disturbance.[24]

In the mid-1860s, the government passed a series of laws in an attempt to control the spread of contagious diseases in the armed forces through the incarceration of infected prostitutes. Although these acts were removed from the statute books in 1886, opposition to the state-regulated prostitution of the Contagious Diseases Acts spawned a social purity movement. Moralist activity turned from the protection of working-class women from police harassment to the repression of prostitution.[25] Recognizing that the 'attitude of the average working girl towards ... her sexuality, and the sexual act itself was so foreign, and so inimical to prevailing middle class conventions',[26] the social purity movement wished to root out 'the traditional social and sexual habits of the poor'.[27]

Josephine Butler, the leader of the opposition to the Contagious Diseases Acts, disapproved of and spoke out against such attempts to legislate morality. Furthermore, the *Pall Mall Gazette* published a letter arguing that it was 'impossible to do anything furthering morality by the law of the land without also touching the economical relations of society'.[28] No one heeded their pleas. Parliament raised the age of consent from thirteen to sixteen, and attempted to crack down on houses of ill-repute. Between 1885 and 1914, 1,200 brothels were prosecuted annually in England and Wales; between 1875 and 1884, the average had been 86 per year. Even though the head of the Metropolitan Police, Sir Charles Warren, tried to initiate a policy of laissez-faire towards prostitution in the summer of 1887, two hundred brothels in East London were closed in that year as a result of the actions of the government and various purity groups. Coming shortly before the outbreak of the Jack the Ripper murders, these closings rendered 'thousands of women homeless, hence vulnerable to attack, and certainly [made] the lower stratum of prostitution ... even more precarious as a means of subsistence'.[29]

In the best of times, the East End was a brutal environment. The Vicar of St Jude 's Church in Whitechapel, Samuel Barnett, called for the closing of the open slaughter-houses because of 'his concern for the moral consequences, especially for the children of the poor, of this open peep-show of cruelty to animals'.[30] George Sims, in his works *How the Poor Live* and *Horrible London*, related that 'the spirit of murder hovers over this spot [East London], for life is held of little account'.[31] He argued that the constant association of the honest with the criminal poor led to the moral deterioration of the former. Sims stated that the people of the East were so used to the sound of violence, that few would stir to see what was the matter. In fact, Sims found that 'they became hardened and the cruelty at which we shudder is their second nature ... only the ferocious instincts of the brute are fostered'.[32] Drunkenness often led to violence. Assaults of men on women occurred with great frequency. In a scene which certainly harkens to the later Whitechapel slayings, Sims wrote, 'Down from one dark court rings a cry of murder, and a woman, her face hideously gashed, makes across the narrow road, pursued by a howling madman. It is only a drunken husband having a row with his wife.'[33] What made the East End especially disturbing was the fact that the rest of Victorian society was becoming noticeably less violent; crime had been declining in proportion to the population since the middle of the century. Violent crimes were very rare. Trials for homicide declined by 70 per cent between the 1830s and 1914, and 53 per cent fewer homicides were reported between 1870 and the start of the First World War. The East End generally, and Jack the Ripper specifically, served as a reminder of the scope of the problems remaining to be solved.[34]

All of the problems listed above, from crime to prostitution to poverty, were long-standing. For a number of reasons, these issues became much more hotly debated in the 1880s than previously. The writings of Andrew Mearns, Beatrice Potter, Samuel Barnett, Charles Booth, George Sims and others were read and understood in a new way. One wrote that the poor will someday 'burst their barriers at last, and declare open and violent war against law and order and property'.[35] Another stated that 'the life of a sweaters' man is so hopeless and dreary that their feelings against the order of things are not unnaturally bitter and intense'.[36] Governmental procrastination had not made the problems disappear. Now the plight of the East End was seen to inflame class tensions and, perhaps, provoke bloody insurrection.

The reason for this renewed interest in writings on the problems of East London was, simply, the fear among many in the West that the East End's revolutionary tendencies were beginning to bubble to the surface. The 1880s was a period of industrial depression in which 'the dangerous possibility [existed] ... that the respectable working class, under the stress of prolonged unemployment, might throw in its lot with the casual poor'.[37] The casual labouring poor, who were viewed as morally degenerate by many in the West, were often confused with the criminal poor. The threat would come from the casuals of the East End, because 'only there ... could a formidable riot take place, given the combination of 12,000 sailors ... and the 7,000–8,000 dock labourers and lightermen'.[38]

It is clear that it would take more than a new spate of pamphlets on the problems and hypothetical revolutionary tendencies of East London to stir the West out of its comfortable apathy. The spark was provided by the riots and demonstrations centring around Trafalgar Square between early 1886 and November 1887. On 8 February 1886, the Fair Trade League held a meeting in Trafalgar Square to demand protective tariffs and public works to cure unemployment. Roughly 20,000 people, many of them dock and building workers, assembled. When the Social Democratic Federation interrupted the meeting and led part of the crowd in the direction of Hyde Park, a portion of the crowd marched west, bent on mischief. In the looting that followed, roughly £50,000 in damage was done. Over the next two days, a dense fog covered London, increasing the nervousness of West End shop owners. On the advice of the Metropolitan Police, many businessmen closed and barricaded their shops. Public confidence in the police was shaken by the ordeal.[39]

In the summer of 1887, a large number of homeless, unemployed vagrants began to camp in Trafalgar Square. The police weres reluctant to remove them at first. The fact that charitable organizations in the West End provided the squatters with donations of free food made the problem worse. On 8 November, after many heated arguments with the Conservative Home Secretary, Henry Matthews, Sir Charles Warren, the head of the Metropolitan Police, took decisive action to disperse what he called the 'veriest scum of the population';[40] he banned all meetings in and processions to Trafalgar Square. On 'Bloody Sunday', 13 November 1887, the Metropolitan Federation of Radical Clubs organized a series of marches and demonstrations to protest the government's policy of coercion in Ireland. The police violently dispersed the marchers before they reached Trafalgar Square.[41]

The reaction of the West End to 'Bloody Sunday' was, on the whole, positive. *The Times* rejoiced that Warren's decisive action had defeated 'a deliberate attempt ... to terrorize London by placing the control of the streets in the hands of the criminal classes'.[42] Nevertheless, the threat of the East End had been twice demonstrated. The danger was multiplied many times in the minds of many in the West because of their inability to 'adequately distinguish between the ordinary poorer classes and the

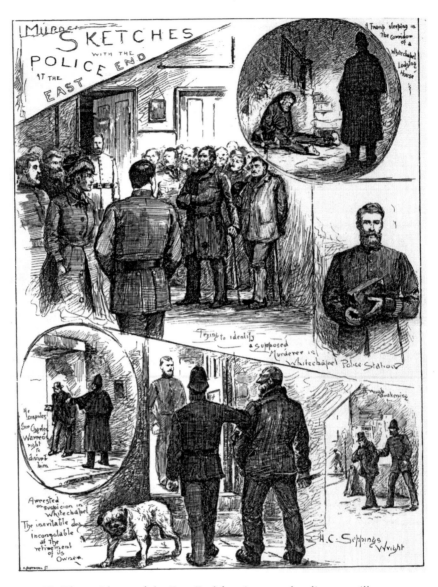

12 The residents of the East End face increased police surveillance.

criminal classes'; thus, 'every large assembly of people assumes to their disordered imagination the aspects of a dangerous and hostile mob'.[43]

This period represented a culmination of tensions between West and East. By the autumn of 1888, 'the respectable classes were obsessed with fears of class conflict and social disintegration[;] coming so fast on the heels of the West End riots, the Jack the Ripper murders fed the flames of class hatred and distrust'.[44] The fact that Whitechapel was situated at the western edge of the East End, next to the important financial district of London, made the killings seem even more ominous. The horrifying crimes of the Whitechapel murderer condensed the vague fears of the West End about the brutality, immorality and destructiveness of the East into one mysterious entity. While many in the West End viewed the crimes as a logical result of conditions in East London, the reaction of the East End was marked by anti-Semitism, xenophobia and hostility towards the police, intensifying social divisions which already existed.

The Metropolitan Police had vast powers available to solve the Whitechapel murders. It could investigate 'every pawnshop, every laundry, every publichouse, and even every lodging-house in the huge area of London in a couple of hours'.[45] Furthermore, there was a great willingness on the part of the people of the East End to aid in the capture of the killer. Thus, a contemporary noted that 'arrests were made by the score, principally of people of a low class who inhabited the locality where the murders were committed'.[46] The scope and lack of focus of police activity can be clearly seen in a report sent to the Home Office on 19 October 1888 by Chief Inspector Swanson. He noted that 80,000 handbills had been distributed, house-to-house searches conducted, 2,000 lodgers questioned, and inquiries made of sailors on the Thames, Asians in London's opium dens, Greek gypsies and cowboys from the American Exhibition. Furthermore, 'three hundred people were questioned as a result of communications from the public ... [including] seventy-six butchers and slaughterers'.[47]

By an examination of the sorts of people who were suspected of committing the Whitechapel murders, one can get a sense of the racial prejudices and class tensions that were very much a part of Victorian life. The police and press exhibited a strong suspicion of foreigners and Jews from the beginning of the investigation. One writer commented in 1891 that Whitechapel 'harboured a cosmopolitan population, chiefly Jews, many of whom were decent hardworking folk though others were the very scum of Europe'.[48] There was a widely held suspicion that Jews were involved in the killings. The coroner, Mr Wynne Baxter, described the killer as using 'Judas-like approaches'[49] and Will Cross, the carter who found the sexually mutilated body of Mary Nichols, supposedly pointed at the nearby Jewish cemetery and said that the murderer was 'probably some sneaking Yid who wouldn't pay for his fun'.[50] On 10 September 1888 the *Manchester Guardian* reported that 'all are united in the belief that [the murderer] is a Jew or of Jewish parentage[,] his face being of a marked Hebrew type'.[51] Sir Robert Anderson, the Head of the Central Intelligence Division, was adamant in his memoirs that the killer was a Polish Jew.[52]

Several other examples can be cited to illustrate London's preoccupation with the Jews. *The Times* published several articles from its Vienna correspondent during the first week of October 1888 on the 1884 trial of a Galician Jew charged with the mutilation of a woman near Cracow. On 2 October another report from Vienna stated that one method for a Jewish man to atone for the sin of sexual relations with a Christian woman was to kill and mutilate her. Hermann Adler, a London Rabbi, responded to these charges by stating that 'in no Jewish book is such a barbarity even hinted at. Nor is there any record ... of a Jew having been convicted of such a terrible atrocity ... [things were bad enough] without the revival of moribund fables and the importation of prejudices'.[53]

On the night of the murder of Catherine Eddowes, 29 September 1888, an officer found a chalk-written message on a wall in Goulston street near the spot where a fragment of the victim's apron had been dropped by the murderer.[54] The message, 'The Juwes are the men who will not be blamed for nothing', was erased on the express orders of Sir Charles Warren. Superintendent Arnold in his report to the Home Office explained that 'a strong feeling existed against the Jews generally ... I was apprehensive that if the writing were left it would be the means of causing a riot.'[55]

Jews were not the only ones to be suspected or arrested. A number of non-Jewish foreigners also fell under suspicion. Some detectives felt that anarchists or nihilists in the East End were behind the killings. On 4 October, an American was taken into custody for threatening to 'rip up' a woman. Another man, with an American accent, was arrested because his features supposedly matched the admittedly vague police description. The police requested information about an Austrian seaman, whose signature supposedly corresponded with the letters signed 'Jack the Ripper' and whose description also 'matched that of the Whitechapel murderer'.[56] Charles Ludwig, a German citizen, was accused of being the killer after his arrest for pulling a penknife during a drunken brawl.[57]

Even more exotic suspects were found in the Malays and Lascars of East London. Chief Inspector Abberline felt that the murders were neither typically British nor Jewish. He believed that '[s]exual maniacs of the type of the "Ripper" were more to be found on the continent of Europe, or in Asia, than in Britain'.[58] In early October, another writer remarked that the Ripper used 'peculiarly Eastern methods' and that the killer acted when he was 'primed with his opium, or bang, or gin, and inspired with his lust for slaughter'.[59] On 6 October *The Times* printed a telegram from an English sailor, then in New York, stating that a Malaysian cook the previous August had told him that 'he had been robbed by a woman of bad character, and that unless he found the woman and recovered his money he would murder and mutilate every Whitechapel woman he met'.[60]

After taking all of the reports regarding the suspicion of foreigners into account, it is difficult to come to any conclusion other than that the police and press were especially eager to believe that an 'outsider' had committed these horrible crimes. Many agreed with *The Times* editorialist who on 4 October stated that 'the celerity with which the crimes were committed is inconsistent with the ordinary English phlegmatic nature'.[61] If the suspicion of foreigners did not lead to the arrest of the perpetrator of the horrors, the police could turn to a number of other 'outcast' groups, which were, for one reason or another, beyond the pale of the respectable.

The mentally ill were naturally suspected. The suspicion of lunatics followed from the common belief that no sane Englishman would commit such brutal crimes. If the murders could not be tied to a foreigner, then the guilty Englishman must be insane. The *East London Advertiser* described the killer as being a 'murderous lunatic, who issues forth like another Hyde'.[62] A number of individuals turned themselves in to the police claiming to be the Whitechapel killer. Those whose stories were due to alcohol were often fined; others with more serious psychological problems were placed under restraint in an asylum. The police rigorously attempted to clear East London of anyone who seemed unbalanced. Some suspects brought in for questioning were determined insane and were also placed into confinement.[63]

Theories that the killer did not come from the poverty-stricken East End were neither common nor popular in the West during the autumn of 1888. The belief that the Ripper belonged to a higher class of society than both his victims and the usual suspects, however, found greater resonance among the less prosperous and educated in the East. The two main theories were that the killer was either a religious fanatic intent on ridding the world of prostitution or a medical doctor. The belief that the killer might be a 'homicidal maniac of religious views' was first postulated by the eccentric Dr L. S. Winslow early in the investigation.[64] Winslow was adamant that the Ripper was 'not of the class of which "Leather Apron" belongs, but is of the upper class of society'.[65] In *The Times* of 1 October, another doctor, Edgar Sheppard, agreed with Winslow's conclusions and added that the murderer 'may be an earnest religionist, believing that he is extirpating vice and sin'.[66]

The theory that the Ripper was a doctor was more widely respected. In essence, the case against the medical profession revolved around the question of whether the killer needed to possess surgical skills and instruments to have performed his grisly dissections. Some believed, as Dr Winslow did, that 'considerable anatomical knowledge was displayed by the murderer, which would seem to indicate that his occupation was that of a butcher or a surgeon'.[67] Some people went even further. At the close of the inquest for Anne Chapman on 26 September, Dr Wynne Baxter concluded that 'no unskilled person could have known where to find [the uterus] or have recognized it when found. For instance, no mere slaughterer of animals could have carried out these operations. It must have been someone accustomed to the post-mortem room.'[68] An editorialist, writing in the *Lancet* on 29 September, expressed his opinion that no one without experience in anatomical or pathological examinations could have performed such skilful mutilations in so rapid a fashion.[69] Other medical experts, perhaps in an attempt to deflect criticism from their profession, disagreed and stated that the killer showed little or no medical knowledge.

Debate also raged about what sort of weapon the Ripper used to kill and mutilate his victims. The discovery or accurate description of this instrument might have given a clue as to the class or profession of the murderer. As early as the second week in September, the coroner stated that a surgical knife might have been used. By mid-October, anyone carrying a small black bag, one of the symbols of the medical profession, in East London was suspected of being the killer.[70] A final reason for suspicion to be tied to the medical profession was the fact that in several of the killings, organs had been removed from the victim's bodies. It was commonly believed that there was a market for such organs. J. R. Bennett, in a letter to *The Times* in late September, exclaimed that such theories were just an attempt to defame the medical profession and should not be believed. To this day, however, many suspect that a doctor was, in fact, involved in the murders.[71]

Members of a number of other occupations were suspected of being involved in the Whitechapel horrors. Men with such diverse livelihoods as bootmakers, cork-cutters, butchers, slaughterers, sailors and servicemen on leave attracted the attention of the police. During the inquest for Catherine Eddowes in mid-October 1888, Drs George Sequeira and William Saunders stated that the killer did not possess medical skills or knowledge of anatomy. At the same time, Drs Frederick Brown and George Phillips argued that though the murderer showed some anatomical knowledge, 'the murder could have been committed by a person who had been a hunter, a butcher, a slaughterman, as well as a student in surgery or a properly qualified surgeon'.[72] A letter sent by Mr R. Hull in early October made the same point; he had been a butcher for fifteen years and remarked that doctors did not understand 'how terribly dexterous a good slaughterman is with his knife. There has been nothing done to these poor women that an expert butcher could not do almost in the dark.'[73] Another concern related to the curious fact that the murders occurred only on weekends; suspicion attached itself to butchers or drovers working on cattle boats bringing live freight from the continent. These individuals had the necessary skill, and their absence from London would explain the intervals between the Ripper's murders.[74]

Since the police had no witnesses to the murders and few leads to follow, they cast a wide dragnet in the hopes that the killer would fortuitously fall into their hands. Whitechapel was densely populated with foreigners, Jews and drifters of one sort or another; thus, these were obvious groups to target. The attaching of suspicion to butchers, slaughterhouse workers and boot-makers, because of their proficiency with knives, also seemed to be reasonable. The attempt to round up all the mentally unbalanced of Whitechapel may well have been a sensible precaution. The suspects taken together, however, produce not a portrait of one killer, but a catalogue of those considered by the West End to be brutal and callous enough to perform such deeds. Much as in the East End, the police and press revealed their xenophobia and anti-Semitism. There is a third element which enters the West End equation: that of class. The brutality exhibited by the Whitechapel murderer was felt to be confined to the lower classes. Few in the West would have argued with the following logic: an Englishman would not be likely to commit such crimes; if the killer were English, then he was probably a member of the refuse of Victorian civilization residing in the East End.

The reactions of London to the murders reveal that Jack the Ripper's activities reinforced earlier notions about the relationships between classes, segments of the population and parts of London. Clearly, the Whitechapel murders were considered by the West End to be part of a larger problem, that of 'outcast London'. It should not be surprising that the cures suggested by the press, social critics and philanthropists were of the most conventional kind. For most middle- and upper-class Victorians, the relationships between poverty, poor sanitation, immorality and crime were too strongly entrenched to be challenged. Examples of this phenomenon are numerous. On 6 October, an article in the *Lancet* proclaimed that 'great poverty, overcrowding, dirt, and bad sanitation ... renders [sic] more probable the conception and the execution of such crimes as those that now absorb the public attention'.[75] There were many calls for reform. Several writers commented in *The Times* that if the government ever roused itself 'to suppress disorderly houses, to cleanse and widen the streets, to pave and light the courts and alleys, the chief external conditions which favour murder will have been removed'.[76]

Some called for additional police protection in the 'criminal quarters'. Others lamented the living conditions of the poor, especially with regard to common lodging houses in East London. If the dwellings were not improved, then 'we shall have still to go on – affecting astonishment that in such a state of things we have outbreaks from time to time of the horrors of the present day'.[77] Finally, there was an attempt to encourage missionary activities in the East End.[78]

The reaction of the East End reflected a different tone entirely. From the first, there seems to have been a genuine desire on the part of the vast majority of those living in the East to aid in the capture of the Ripper. Local tradesmen formed vigilance committees and helped to patrol the streets at night. On a less organized level, 'any passer-by who aroused the suspicion of a street crowd was forcibly seized and hauled into the local police station'.[79] With the ineptitude of the police proven by its inability to bring the killer to justice and public activities failing to achieve results either, a more paranoid attitude took hold in Whitechapel. *The Times* described this feeling by stating that 'it seemed as if every person in the streets were suspicious of everyone else he met ... as if it were a race between them who should first inform against his neighbour'.[80] The Home Secretary refused to offer a reward for the capture of the Whitechapel murderer at least in part because the 'danger of false charge is intensified by the excited state of public feelings [in East London]'.[81]

By early November, the East End was in such a state of exasperation at the police's failure to end the string of murders that each arrest brought crowds into the streets; on several occasions, innocent men were very nearly lynched. On 15 November, there were two such instances. In the first, a plainclothes policeman was chased through the streets with an East End crowd in pursuit. Secondly, after a man was arrested for staring at a woman in a supposedly threatening manner, the police were 'followed by an enormous mob of men and women, shouting and screaming at him in a most extraordinary manner'.[82] In one of the worst cases of this kind, a crowd watching an officer chase a man wanted for throwing bricks at policemen jumped to the conclusion that Jack the Ripper was about to be arrested. A large police escort brought the man in to the local station. The East End crowd, however, had their own ideas about how the suspect should be dealt with, and stormed the building several times. It took a couple of hours for the crowd to be dispersed and peace to be restored.[83]

The Jack the Ripper murders have been studied on numerous occasions over the past one hundred years. Most writers are primarily interested in determining the identity of the killer. Some have examined the social conditions that made East London a blemish on the landscape long before the autumn of 1888. Very little has been done to synthesize Jack the Ripper's story with the crisis of the 1880s. It is important to do this. In the 1880s, many eyes in the West End were reopened to problems which had been ignored for some time; poverty, overcrowding, poor sanitation, immorality and criminal behaviour had not disappeared in the interval. The riots and demonstrations of 1886 and 1887 revealed to the West End residents that, whatever their contempt for the East End, complacency could be dangerous. It was at that moment, a time when the West was most concerned about the threat from the East, that Jack the Ripper stepped onto centre stage. The Whitechapel murderer represented the callousness, brutality, destructiveness and malicious cruelty that the West had most reason to fear. The killings, in a more efficient fashion than any parliamentary bluebook or social commentator's pamphlet, revealed the extent of the rot in the East End. Only there, many in the West End preferred to believe, could such a creature have evolved and prospered. The types of people who were suspected by the police and the press accurately reflected many of the tensions and prejudices of Victorian London. Anti-Semitism, xenophobia and distrust of the poorer classes all made an appearance. The East End, although harbouring all of these prejudices, remained suspicious of the intentions of the more prosperous West and of the ability of the police to protect the residents of East London. Taken together, the reactions of London to the Whitechapel murders present a snapshot of social tensions only a short time before the bloodless dock workers' strike of 1889 relieved the West End of many of their fears concerning East London.[84]

Notes

1 P. J. Keating, 'Fact and Fiction in the East End', in Harold Dyos and Michael Wolff (eds), *The Victorian City* (London: Routledge & Kegan Paul, 1973), vol. 2, p. 585.

2 Andrew Mearns, *The Bitter Cry of Outcast London* (London: James Clarke & Co., 1883), p. 61.

3 Jane Stuart-Wortley, 'The East End as Represented by Mr. Besant', *Nineteenth Century* (September 1887), p. 362.

4 Charles Booth, *Life and Labour of the People of London*, 17 vols (London: Macmillan, 1902), vol. 1, p. 32.

5 Booth, *Life and Labour*, vol. 4, p. 117, and Beatrice Potter, 'East End Labour', *Nineteenth Century* (August 1888), p. 181.

6 Stephen Fox, 'The Invasion of the Pauper Foreigners', *Contemporary Review* (June 1888), p. 861.

7 Fox, 'Pauper Foreigners', pp. 856, 866.

8 Booth, *Life and Labour*, vol. 3, p. 178.

9 Booth, *Life and Labour*, vol. 3, p. 186.

10 Potter, 'East End Labour', p. 177.

11 Mearns, *Bitter Cry*, p. 74.

12 Gareth Stedman Jones, *Outcast London* (Oxford: Clarendon Press, 1971), pp. 219–20, 325.

13 Arnold White, *Problems of a Great City* (London: Remington & Co., 1886), p. 131.

14 Anonymous, 'The Inhabitants of East London', *Quarterly Review* (July–October 1889), pp. 453–4.

15 *Lancet* (10 May 1890), p. 1036.

16 White, *Problems*, pp. 136–8.

17 W. J. Fishman, *East End 1888* (London: Duckworth, 1988), pp. 8, 18.

18 George Sims, *How the Poor Live and Horrible London* (London: Chatto and Windus, 1889; repr. New York: Garland, 1984), pp. 106–7.

19 Octavia Hill, *Homes for the London Poor* (London: Chatto and Windus, 1883), p. 88.

20 Parliamentary Papers, House of Commons, 22 Nov. 1888, 330, p. 1819.

21 Stuart-Wortley, 'East End', p. 375.

22 See Douglas Browne, *The Rise of Scotland Yard* (New York: Harrap, 1956), p. 207; Fraser Harrison, *The Dark Angel: Aspects of Victorian Sexuality* (London: Sheldon Press, 1977), pp. 225, 232–3, 241; and E. M. Sigsworth and T. J. Wyke, 'A Study of Victorian Prostitution and Venereal Disease', in Martha Vicinus (ed.), *Suffer and Be Still: Women in the Victorian Age* (Bloomington, IN: Indiana University Press, 1972), p. 81.

23 Robert Storch, 'Police Control of Street Prostitution in Victorian London', in David H. Bayley (ed.), *Police and Society* (Beverly Hills, CA: Sage, 1977), p. 51.

24 See Eric Trudgill, 'Prostitution and Paterfamilias', in Dyos and Wolff, *The Victorian City*, vol. 2, p. 701.

25 See Judith Walkowitz, *Prostitution and Victorian Society* (Cambridge: Cambridge University Press, 1980), pp. 13–15, 29–31, and Paul McHugh, *Prostitution and Victorian Social Reform* (London: Croom Helm, 1980), pp. 17–18, 262–4.

26 Harrison, *Dark Angel*, p. 241.

27 Walkowitz, *Prostitution*, p. 251.

28 Brian Harrison, 'State Intervention and Moral Reform', in Patricia Hollis (ed.), *Pressure from Without in Early Victorian England* (London: Edward Arnold, 1974), pp. 306–7.

29 Judith Walkowitz, 'Jack the Ripper and the Myth of Male Violence', *Feminist Studies* (Fall 1982), p. 558; Walkowitz, *Prostitution*, p. 252; and Storch, 'Police Control of Prostitution', p. 56.

30 Fishman, *East End 1888*, pp. 6, 202–3.

31 Sims, *How the Poor Live*, p. 11.

32 Sims, *How the Poor Live*, pp. 11–12, 70.

33 Sims, *How the Poor Live*, p. 137; see also Fishman, *East End 1888*, p. 208.

34 Philip Smith, *Policing Victorian London* (Westport, CN: Greenwood Press, 1985), p. 12; see also V. A. C. Gatrell, 'The Decline of Theft and Violence in Victorian and Edwardian England', in V. A. C. Gatrell, Bruce Lenman and Geoffrey Parker (eds), *Crime and the Law* (London: Europa, 1980), pp. 282, 286.
35 Sims, *How the Poor Live*, p. 119.
36 Anonymous, 'Inhabitants of East London', p. 441.
37 Jones, *Outcast London*, pp. 284–5.
38 Smith, *Policing Victorian London*, p. 28; see also Jones, *Outcast London*, p. 11.
39 Jones, *Outcast London*, p. 292; see also Samuel Barnett, 'Distress in East London', *Nineteenth Century* (November 1886), p. 679, and Basil Thomson, *The Story of Scotland Yard* (Garden City, NY: Doubleday, Doran, 1936), p. 187.
40 See Victor Bailey, 'The Metropolitan Police, the Home Office and the Threat of Outcast London', in Victor Bailey (ed.), *Policing and Punishment in Nineteenth Century Britain* (London: Croom Helm, 1981), p. 108.
41 See Jones, *Outcast London*, p. 291; Thomson, *The Story of Scotland Yard*, pp. 186–7; and David Ascoli, *The Queen's Peace* (London: Henry Hamilton, 1979), pp. 160–1.
42 *The Times*, 14 November 1887.
43 James Stuart, 'The Metropolitan Police', *Contemporary Review* (April 1889), p 628
44 Walkowitz, 'Myth of Male Violence', pp. 544–5.
45 Basil Thomson, *My Experiences at Scotland Yard* (Garden City, NY: Doubleday, Page & Co., 1923), p. 2.
46 L. S. F. Winslow, *Recollections of Forty Years* (London: John Ouseley, 1910), p. 261.
47 Paul Begg, *Jack the Ripper: The Uncensored Facts* (London: Robson, 1988), p. 137.
48 Frederick Wensley, *Forty Years of Scotland Yard* (Garden City, NY: Doubleday, Doran & Co., 1931), pp. 7–8.
49 Cited in Leonard Matters, *The Mystery of Jack the Ripper* (London: Hutchinson & Co., 1929), p. 33.
50 Cited in George MacCormick, *The Identity of Jack the Ripper* (London: Jarrolds, 1959), p. 26.
51 Begg, *Jack the Ripper*, p. 79.
52 McCormick, *Identity of the Ripper*, p. 45.
53 *The Times*, 2 October 1888; see also Matters, *Mystery of the Ripper*, pp. 92–3.
54 The killing itself had taken place outside of a club for Russian, Polish and Jewish socialists.
55 Begg, *Jack the Ripper*, p. 126; see also *The Times*, 12 October 1888.
56 *The Times*, 16 October 1888; see also McCormick, *Identity of the Ripper*, p. 99.
57 *The Times*, 19 September 1888.

58 Cited in McCormick, *Identity of the Ripper*, p. 95.
59 *The Times*, 4 October 1888.
60 *The Times*, 6 October 1888.
61 *The Times*, 4 October 1888.
62 *The Times*, 8 September 1888. It is interesting to note that a play based on Robert Louis Stevenson's novel, *The Strange Case of Dr Jekyll and Mr Hyde* (1886), was a big hit in London at this time.
63 See the *The Times*, 13, 28 September, 19 October and 12 November.
64 Winslow, *Recollections*, p. 255.
65 *The Times*, 12 September 1888.
66 *The Times*, 1 October 1888.
67 Winslow, *Recollections*, p. 262.
68 Cited in Begg, *Jack the Ripper*, p. 89.
69 *The Lancet*, 29 September 1888, p. 637.
70 *The Times*, 15 November 1888; see also 14 September 1888.
71 See *The Times*, 28 September 1888, and David Rumbelow, *The Complete Jack the Ripper* (London: W. H. Allen, 1975), pp. 73–4.
72 Cited in Begg, *Jack the Ripper*, p. 124; see also Matters, *Mystery of the Ripper*, pp. 54–5.
73 Rumbelow, *Complete Jack the Ripper*, p. 222.
74 See *The Times*, 10 November 1888.
75 *The Lancet*, 6 October 1888, p. 683; see also *The Times*, 29 September 1888.
76 *The Times*, 6 October 1888.
77 *The Times*, 18 September 1888.
78 See *The Times*, 26 and 29 October 1888. For an overview of the various responses see Walkowitz, 'Myth of Male Violence', p. 568.
79 Fishman, *East End 1888*, p. 213; see also *The Times*, 17 September 1888.
80 *The Times*, 8 October 1888.
81 Parliamentary Papers, House of Commons, 12 November 1888, 330, p. 904.
82 *The Times*, 15 November 1888. Other examples of like behaviour can be found on 10 and 12 November.
83 Rumbelow, *Complete Jack the Ripper*, pp. 86–7.
84 Mr Haggard wishes to thank Mr Lenard Berlanstein, Mr Nicholas Edsall and Ms Susan Eisley for advice on both the style and content of this essay.

13

'Who kills whores?' 'I do,' says Jack: race and gender in Victorian London

Sander L. Gilman

'I am down on whores and I shan't quit ripping them till I do get buckled', wrote Jack the Ripper to the Central News Agency on 18 September 1888.[1] The question I raise in this essay reflects not on the reality of Jack the Ripper – real he was, and he never did get buckled – but on the contemporary fantasy of what a Jack the Ripper could have been. To understand the image of Jack, however, it is necessary to understand the image of the prostitute in Victoria's London. It is also necessary to comprehend the anxiety that attended her image in 1888, an anxiety that, like our anxieties a hundred years later, focused on diseases labelled sexual and attempted to locate their boundaries within the body of the Other.[2] Who could truly kill the prostitute but the prostitute herself? Who else could expiate her sins against the male? For the prostitute's life must end in suicide.

[...]

The physician's eye is always cast to examine and find the source of pathology, in the role assigned by society. Here again it is the male physician opening the body of the woman to discover the source of disease, hidden within the woman's body.

But in the fantasy of the nineteenth century the physician could not remove the prostitute from the street. Only the whore could kill the whore. Only the whore, and Jack. Killing and dismembering, searching after the cause of corruption and disease, Jack could kill the source of infection because he too was diseased. The paradigm for the relationship between Jack and the prostitutes can be taken from the popular medical discourse of the period: *Similia similibus curantur*, 'like cures like', the motto of C. F. S. Hahnemann, the founder of homeopathic medicine. The scourge of the streets, the carrier of disease, can be eliminated only by one who is equally corrupt and diseased. And that was Jack.

Jack, as he called himself, was evidently responsible for a series of murders that raised the anxiety level throughout London to fever pitch in the cold, damp fall of 1888. The images of the murders in the London

Illustrated Police News provide an insight into how the murderer was seen and also how the 'real' prostitute, not the icon of prostitution or of seduction, was portrayed in mass art. The murders ascribed to Jack the Ripper all took place in the East End of London, an area that had been the scene of heavy Eastern European Jewish immigration. Who, within the fantasy of the thought collective, can open the body? Who besides the physician? No one but Jack, the emblem of human sexual perversion out of all control, out of all bounds. Jack becomes the sign of deviant human sexuality destroying life, the male parallel to the destructive prostitute. He is the representative of that inner force, hardly held under control, that has taken form - the form of Mr Hyde. Indeed, an extraordinarily popular dramatic version of Robert Louis Stevenson's *Dr Jekyll and Mr Hyde* was playing in the West End while Jack (that not-so-hidden Mr Hyde) terrorized the East End.

The images of the victims of 'Jack' – ranging in number from four to twenty depending on which tabulation one follows – were portrayed as young women who had been slashed and mutilated. But because of the sensibilities of even the readers of the *Illustrated Police News*, the mutilation presented is the mutilation of the face (as in the image of Catherine Eddowes). The reality, at least the reality that terrified the London of 1888, was that the victims were butchered. Dr Bagster Philips, who undertook the postmortem description of Mary Kelly, described the process:

> The body had been completely disembowelled and the entrails flung carelessly in a heap on the table. The breasts had been cut off, hacked for no apparent purpose, and then hung on nails affixed to the walls of the room. Lumps of flesh, cut from the thighs and elsewhere, lay strewn about the room, so that the bones were exposed. As in some of the other cases, certain organs had been extracted, and, as they were missing, had doubtless been carried away.[3]

The police photographs of the eviscerated prostitute appeared at the time only within 'scientific' sources such as Alexandre Lacassagne's 1889 study of sadism. In the public eye the prostitutes were their faces, the face of the prostitute in death. But the true fascination was with those 'certain organs [that] had been extracted' and had 'been carried away'. The whore's body had not merely been opened; her essence, her sexuality, had been removed. These images are quite in contrast to those of the contemporary 'Whitehall' murder, where a decapitated torso was discovered and the body reconstructed with limbs found throughout the city. The mutilated body was understood over the course of further killings to be one of Jack's victims, even though it contrasted with the bodies of the prostitutes he killed. The bodies of Jack's victims were opened and their viscera removed. Such sexual disfigurement, along with the amputation of the breasts of some of the victims, made it clear to both the police and the general public that his actions were sexually motivated. And indeed, most of the theories concerning Jack's identity assumed that he (or a close family member) had been infected with syphilis by a prostitute and was simply (if insanely) taking his revenge. But the vague contours of Jack the 'victim' soon gave way to a very specific visual image of Jack.

'Jack' is the caricature of the Eastern Jew. Indeed, the official description was of a man 'age 37, rather dark beard and moustache, dark jacket and trousers, black felt hat, spoke with a foreign accent'.[4] There appeared scrawled on the wall in Goulston Street, near the place where a blood-covered apron was discovered, the cryptic message: 'The Juwes are the men that will not be blamed for nothing'.[5] The image of the Jews as sexually different, the Other even in the killing of the Other, led to the arrest of John Pizer, 'Leather Apron', a Polish-Jewish shoemaker. Pizer was eventually cleared and released, but a high proportion of the 130 men questioned in the Ripper case were Jews.

Sir Robert Anderson, the police official in charge of the case, noted in his memoir:

> One did not need to be a Sherlock Holmes to discover that the criminal was a sexual maniac of a virulent type; that he was living in the immediate vicinity of the scenes of the murders; and that, if he was not living absolutely alone, his people knew of his guilt, and refused to give him up to justice. During my absence abroad the Police had made a house-to-house search for him, investigating the case of every man in the district whose circumstances were such that he could go and come and get rid of his blood-stains in secret. And the conclusion we came to was that he and his people were low-class Jews, for it is a remarkable fact that people of that class in the East End will not give up one of their number to Gentile justice. ... I will only add that when the individual whom we suspected was caged in an asylum, the only person who had ever had a good view of the murderer at once identified him, but when he learned the suspect was a fellow-Jew he declined to swear to him.[6]

The claim that Jack the Ripper was a 'sexual maniac' and a Jew led to repercussions with the East End community. When the body of Elizabeth Stride was found on 30 September outside the International Working Men's Educational Club by a Jew, a pogrom almost occurred in the East End, at least according to the *East London Observer* (15 October 1888): 'On Saturday the crowds who assembled in the streets began to assume a very threatening attitude towards the Hebrew population of the District. It was repeatedly as serted that no Englishman could have perpetrated such a horrible crime as that of Hanbury Street, and that it must have been done by a Jew - and forthwith the crowds began to threaten and abuse such of the unfortunate Hebrews as they found in the streets.'[7] The powerful association between the working class, revolutionaries and the Jews combines to create the visualization of Jack the Ripper as a Jewish worker, marked by his stigmata of degeneration as a killer of prostitutes. Here Jack had to intervene. In one of his rhyming missives sent in 1889 to Sir Melville MacNaghten, chief of the Criminal Investigation Division at Scotland Yard, he wrote:

> I'm not a butcher, I'm not a Yid
> Nor yet a foreign skipper,
> But I'm your *own* light-hearted friend,
> Yours truly, Jack the Ripper.[8]

When during the 1890s the German playwright Frank Wedekind visualized his Jack the Ripper killing the archwhore Lulu, he represented him as a degenerate working-class figure: 'He is a square-built man, elastic in his movements, with a pale face, inflamed eyes, thick arched eyebrows, drooping moustache, sparse beard, matted sidewhiskers and fiery red hands with gnawed finger nails. His eyes are fixed on the ground. He is wearing a dark overcoat and a small round hat.'[9] This primitive figure was quite in line with the views shared by the Italian forensic psychiatrist Cesare Lombroso and his French rival, Alexandre Lacassagne, as to the representative image (if not origin) of the criminal, but specifically the sadist. For the Germans, at least for liberals such as Wedekind, Jack was also seen as a member of the lumpenproletariat in reaction to the charge, made in 1894 in the anti-Semitic newspapers in Germany, that Jack was an Eastern European Jew functioning as part of the 'international Jewish conspiracy'.[10] But in Britain this image evoked a very specific aspect of the proletariat, that of London's East End, the Eastern Jew.

But why Eastern European Jews? The charge of ritual murder, the murder of Christian women by Polish Jews, appeared in *The Times* during this period, but this was only a subissue or perhaps a more limited analogy to the events in Whitechapel. Nor can we simply recall the history of British anti-Semitism, from the Norwich pogrom of 1144, caused by the charge of the ritual murder of a child, to the King's Road murders of 1771, which were laid at the feet of the Jews. The 'real' parallel to the fantasy about the Jewish Jack the Ripper as a sexual monster was played out in the courts of London in the accusation of murder lodged against the Eastern European Jew Israel Lipski in 1887, the year before the Ripper murders. Lipski was accused of having murdered a pregnant Jewish woman by pouring nitric acid down her throat. Her exposed body was discovered with Lipski hiding under the bed. This case was widely publicized and found detailed coverage in the press of the day. Lipski's conviction was understood (at least by his supporters) as a sign of the prejudice against 'foreign' Jews in London. Lipski was hanged in 1887. His case was widely debated; it was charged that he had been accused because he was an Eastern European Jew. Indeed, the most recent commentator on the case agrees that Lipski was most probably not given a truly fair trial because of his identity as a Jew.[11]

The search for Jack the Ripper was the search for an appropriate murderer for the Whitechapel prostitutes. The murderer had to be representative of an image of sexuality that was equally distanced and frightening. Thus the image of Jack the Ripper as the shochet, the ritual butcher, arose at a moment when there was a public campaign by the anti-vivisectionists in England and Germany against the 'brutality' of the ritual slaughter of kosher meat. This image of the Jewish Jack rested on a long association of the Jew in the West with the image of the mutilated, diseased, different appearance of the genitalia. This mark of sexual difference was closely associated with the initial image of the syphilitic Jack. The Jew remains the representation of the male as outsider, the act of circumcision marking the Jewish male as sexually apart, as anatomically different. (It is important to remember that there is a constant and purposeful confusion throughout the late nineteenth and early twentieth centuries of circumcision with castration.) The prostitute is the embodiment of the degenerate and diseased female genitalia in the nineteenth century. From the normative perspective of the European middle class, it is natural that the Jew and the prostitute must be in conflict and that the one 'opens up' the other, since both are seen as 'dangers' to the economy of the state, both fiscal and sexual. This notion of the association of the Jew and the prostitute is also present in the image of 'spending' semen (in an illicit manner) that dominates the literature on masturbation in the eighteenth and early nineteenth centuries. For the Jew and the prostitute are seen as negating factors, outsiders whose sexual images represent all the dangers felt to be inherent in human sexuality. And to constantly destroy, indeed touch, the polluting force of the Other, one must oneself be beyond the boundaries of acceptability.

The linkage between Jew and prostitute is much older than the 1880s. This association is related to the image of the black and the monkey (two icons of 'deviant' sexuality) in the second plate of Hogarth's *A Harlot's Progress*. Here Moll Hackabout, the harlot, has become the mistress of a wealthy London Jew. The Jew has been cheated by the harlot; her lover is about to leave the scene. But her punishment is forthcoming. She will be dismissed by him and begin her slow slide downward. Tom Brown,

Hogarth's contemporary and the author of 'A Letter to Madam ——, Kept by a Jew in Covent Garden', which may well have inspired the plate, concludes his letter on the sexuality of the Jew by asking the young woman 'to be informed whether Aaron's bells make better music than ours'.[12] It is this fascination with the sexual difference of the Jew, parallel to the sexual difference of the prostitute, that relates them even in death. Each possesses a sexuality different from the norm, a sexuality that is represented in the unique form of their genitalia.

The relationship between the Jew and the prostitute also has a social dimension. For both Jew and prostitute have but one interest, converting sex into money or money into sex. 'So then', Brown writes to the lady, ' 'tis neither circumcision nor uncircumcision that avails any thing with you, but money, which belongs to all religions'.[13] The major relationship, as Tom Brown and Hogarth outline, is a financial one; Jews buy specific types of Christian women, using their financial ability as a means of sexual control. 'I would never have imagined you ... would have ever chosen a gallant out of that religion which clips and diminishes the current coin of love, or could ever be brought to like those people that lived two thousand years on types and figures'.[14]

By the end of the nineteenth century this linkage had become a common place in all of Christian Europe. In 1892 there reappeared in London an early nineteenth-century (1830s) pornographic 'dialogue between a Jew and a Christian, a Whimsical Entertainment, lately performed in Duke's Palace', the *Adventures of Miss Lais Lovecock*.[15] This dialogue represents the Jew, and it represents him in a very specific manner. First, the Jew speaks in dialect. By 1888 the British Jewish community had become completely acculturated. With Disraeli's terms as prime minister, as well as with the Prince of Wales (later King Edward VII) attending the wedding of Leopold de Rothschild on 14 January 1881 at a London synagogue, the boundary between the 'native' Jews and the 'foreign' Jews had to be drawn. This explains the use of dialect, which in 1892 would point toward the Eastern Jew, toward Jack the Ripper, who could not command written English, at least about the 'Juwes'.

The text may well have reflected the image of the Jew in the 1830s, but it clearly had a very different set of associations after Jack the Ripper's appearance. The Jew, Isaac, describes his seduction of his father's Jewish (and therefore, since all Jews are deviants in one way or another, hermaphroditic) maid, who has a 'clitoris, which was hard and shaped like a penis', while he seduces the Christian prostitute Polly. She is described by him as having 'little feet and ankles, I think of your pretty legs, and den I think of your snowy thighs, and den my fancy glowing hot got to de fountain of bliss, and dere I vill go immediately'.[16] She is the object of

13 A sketch of the Whitechapel murderer shows a particular Jewish bias.

the Jew's desire, for his women (servant girls or whores) are as sexually marginal as he is himself. But it is only for money that Polly is willing to ring 'Aaron's bells', for 'nothing under three hundred a year'.[17] The prostitute is little more than a Jew herself. Both are on the margins of 'polite' society. And as we know from the degeneration of Hogarth's Moll Hackabout following her relationship with the Jewish merchant, such sexuality in women leads to corruption and physical decay. The Jew, with all of his associations with disease, becomes the surrogate for all marginal males, males across the boundary from the (male) observer, males who, like women, can be the source of corruption, if not for the individual, then for the collective.

The association of the venality of the Jew with capital is retained even into the latter half of the twentieth century. In a series of British comic books from the 1980s in which an anthropomorphized phallus plays the central role, the Jew is depicted as masturbating, committing an 'unnatural' act (whereas the other phalluses are depicted as having a potential female partner) while reading a financial journal. What is striking in these comics is that all the phalluses are circumcised.[18] This is a problem of contemporary culture. In the post-second World War decades circumcision became a commonplace – even among non-Jews – in the United States and (less so, but more prominently than before World War II) Great Britain. How then to differentiate between the Jew and the non-Jew, between the 'deviant' and the 'normal'? We are faced with a problem analogous to why George Eliot's eponymous character Daniel Deronda did not know he was a Jew. Did he ever look at his penis? Here the hidden is not marked upon the skin, for the skin hides rather than reveals. It is the Jew within that surfaces. Here, in seeing a financial journal as the source of power and therefore of sexual stimulation; in Eliot's novel, with the 'natural' sexual attraction between the crypto-Jew Deronda and the beautiful Jewess Mirah Cohen. (Deronda never defines himself as sexually different, for his own body is the baseline that defines for him the sexually 'normal'. His circumcised penis is not a sign of difference until he understands himself to be a Jew.)

The image of the Jew revealed in his sexuality seems to be an accepted manner of labelling the image of the deviant. Even his phallus does not know for sure until he performs a 'perverse' act. Here the icon is a reversal of the traditional image of the phallus as the beast out of control. In this image it is the man, not his phallus, who is bestial (read Jewish). The perversion of the Jew (and thus the 'humour' of this depiction of the phallus) lies in his sexualized relationship with capital. This of course echoes the oldest and most basic calumny against the Jew, his avarice, an avarice for the possession of 'things', of 'money', which signals his inability to understand (and produce) anything of transcendent aesthetic value. The historical background to this is clear. Canon law forbade charging interest, which according to Thomas Aquinas was impossible, since money, not being alive, could not reproduce. Jews, in charging interest, treated money as a sexualized object. The Jew takes money, as does the prostitute, as a substitute for higher values, for love and beauty. And thus the Jew becomes the representative of the deviant genitalia, the genitalia not under the control of the moral, rational conscience.

But the image of the Jew as prostitute is not merely a reflection of the economic parallel between the sexuality of the Jew and that of the prostitute. That relationship also reveals the nature of the sexuality of both Jew and prostitute as diseased, as polluting. Just as the first image of Jack the Ripper was that of the victim of the prostitute, the syphilitic male, so too were the Jews closely identified with sexually transmitted diseases. For the Jew was also closely related to the spread and incidence of syphilis. This charge appeared in various forms, as in the anti-Semitic tractate *England under the Jews* (1901) by Joseph Banister, in which there is a fixation on the spread of 'blood and skin diseases'.[19] Such views had two readings. Banister's was the more typical. The Jews were the carriers of sexually transmitted diseases and spread them to the rest of the world. This view is to be found in Hitler's discussion of syphilis in *Mein Kampf*, and there he links it to the Jew, the prostitute and the power of money:

Particularly with regard to syphilis, the attitude of the nation and the state can only be designated as total capitulation ... The cause lies, primarily, in our prostitution of love ... The Jewification of our spiritual life and mammonization of our mating instinct will sooner or later destroy our entire offspring.[20]

Hitler's views, like those of Banister and the earlier British anti-Semites also linked Jews with prostitutes. Jews were the archpimps; Jews ran the brothels; Jews infected their prostitutes and caused the weakening of the national fibre. Indeed, according to Hitler, it was the realization of this 'fact' during the first few days of his stay in Vienna in 1907 that converted him to anti-Semitism. The hidden source of the disease of the body politic is the Jew, and his tool is the whore: 'If you cut even cautiously into such a tumour, you found, like a maggot in a rotting body, often dazzled by the sudden light – a kike!'[21]

Such a view of the Jew as the syphilitic was not limited to the anti-Semitic fringe of the turn of the century. It was a view that possessed such power that even 'Jewish' writers (writers who felt themselves stigmatized by the label of being 'Jewish') subscribed to it. One such was Marcel Proust, whose uncomfortable relationship with his mother's Jewish identity haunted his life almost as much as did his gay identity. In Proust's *Remembrance of Things Past*, the series of novels written to recapture the world of the 1880s and 1890s, one of the central characters, Charles Swann, is a Jew who marries a courtesan. This link between Jew and prostitute is mirrored in Proust's manner of representing the sexuality of the Jew. For Proust, being Jewish is analogous to being gay: it is 'an incurable disease'.[22] But what marks this disease for all to see? For in the *mentalité* of the turn of the century, syphilis in the male must be written on the skin, just as it is hidden within the sexuality of the female. Proust, who in the same volume discusses the signs and symptoms of syphilis with a detailed clinical knowledge, knows precisely what marks the sexuality of the Jew upon his physiognomy.[23] It is seen upon his face as 'ethnic eczema'.[24] It is a sign of sexual and racial corruption as surely as the composite photographs of the Jew that Francis Galton made at the time reveal the true face of the Jew.[25]

This mark upon the face is Hitler's and Banister's sign of the Jew's sexual perversion. It is the infectious nature of that 'incurable disease', the sexuality of the Jew, Proust's Jew fixated upon his courtesan. (This is an interesting reversal of one of the subthemes of Zola's *Nana*. There Nana, like Moll Hackabout, is first the mistress of a Jew whom she, quite easily reversing the role of Jack the Ripper, bankrupts and drives to suicide.) The Jew's sexuality, the sexuality of the polluter, is written on his face in the skin disease that announces the difference of the Jew. For

Proust, all his Jewish figures (including Swann and Bloch) are in some
way diseased, and in every case this image of disease links the racial with
the sexual, much as Proust's image of the homosexual links class (or at
least the nobility) with homosexuality. ('Homosexuality' is a 'scientific'
label for a new 'disease' coined by Karoly Benkert in 1869 at the very
same moment in history when the new 'scientific' term for Jew hating,
'anti-Semitism', was created by Wilhelm Marr.) The image of the infected
and infecting Jew also had a strong political as well as personal dimension for Proust. For the ability to 'see' the Jew who was trying to pass as
a non-Jew within French society is one of the themes of the novels, a
theme that, after the Dreyfus affair, had overt political implications.
Seeing the Jew was seeing the enemy within the body politic, seeing the
force for destruction. And Proust's 'racial' as well as sexual identity was
tied to his sense of the importance of class and society in defining the individual. Thus Proust's arch-Jew Swann was visibly marked by him as the
heterosexual syphilitic, as what he was not (at least in his fantasy about
his own sexual identity).

The second model existing at the close of the nineteenth century that
represented the relation between Jews and sexually transmitted disease
postulated exactly the opposite – that Jews had a statistically lower rate
of syphilitic infection – because they had become immune to it through
centuries of exposure. Syphilis was understood at the close of the nineteenth century as an African disease predating Columbus. In the medical
literature of the period, reaching across all of European medicine, it was
assumed that Jews had a notably lower rate of infection. In a study of
the incidence of tertiary lues (the final stage of the syphilitic infection)
undertaken in the Crimea between 1904 and 1929, the Jews had the
lowest consistent rate of infection.[26] In an eighteen-year longitudinal
study H. Budel demonstrated the extraordinarily low rate of tertiary lues
in Estonia during the prewar period.[27] All these studies assumed that bio-
logical difference as well as the social difference of the Jews was at the
root of their seeming 'immunity'.

Jewish scientists also had to explain the 'statistical' fact of their immunity to syphilis. Studying the rate of tertiary lues during the First World
War, the Jewish physician Max Sichel addressed the general view that the
relative lower incidence of infection among Jews resulted from their
sexual difference.[28] He responded – out of necessity – with a social argument. The Jews, according to Sichel, evidenced lower incidence because
of their early marriage and the patriarchal structure of the Jewish family,
but also because of their much lower rate of alcoholism. They were therefore, according to the implicit argument, more rarely exposed to the
infection of prostitutes, whose attractiveness was always associated with

the greater loss of sexual control in the inebriated male. He made the relation between these two 'social' diseases into a cause for the higher incidence among other Europeans. The Jews, because they were less likely to drink heavily, were less likely to be exposed to both the debilitating effects of alcohol (which increase the risk for tertiary lues) and the occasion for infection.

There is a hidden agenda in these comments. According to Sichel, the prostitute is the source of infection. And the prostitute is the offspring of alcoholic parents, according to one common theory of nineteenth-century psychopathology. If you have no Jewish alcoholics then you have no Jewish prostitutes, and thus the Jews are isolated from any charge of being the 'source of pollution', one of the common calumnies lodged against them from the Middle Ages through the nineteenth century.

In 1927 H. Strauss looked at the incidence of syphilitic infection in his hospital in Berlin in order to demonstrate whether the Jews had a lower rate, but also to see (as in the infamous Tuskegee experiments among blacks in the United States[29]) whether they had 'milder' forms of the disease because of their lifestyle or background. He found that Jews indeed had a much lower incidence of syphilis (while having an extraordinarily higher rate of hysteria) than the non-Jewish control group. He proposed that the disease might well have a different course in Jews than in non-Jews. The reason given by non-Jewish scientists was the inherited tendency of male Jews to be more 'immune'. Just as 'Jewishness' was an inherited tendency, so too was the nature of a 'Jewish sexuality', a sexuality so markedly different that some Jewish male infants were even born circumcised.[30]

Both of these arguments saw the Jew as having a 'special' relation to syphilis (through the agency of the prostitute) and carried on the association between the Jew and the prostitute. But this special relation could literally be seen on the Jew. Joseph Banister saw the Jews as bearing the stigmata of skin disease (as a model for discussing sexually transmitted disease):

> If the gentle reader desires to know what kind of blood it is that flows in the Chosen People's veins, he cannot do better than take a gentle stroll through Hatton Garden, Maida Vale, Petticoat Lane, or any other London 'nosery'. I do not hesitate to say that in the course of an hour's peregrinations he will see more cases of lupus, trachoma, favus, eczema, and scurvy that he would come across in a week's wanderings in any quarter of the Metropolis.[31]

Banister is fixated on the nose of the Jew, a not so subtle anti-Semitic reference to the circumcised and, thus, diseased, phallus. For the 'nose' is the iconic representation of the Jew's phallus throughout the nineteenth century. Indeed, Jewish social scientists, such as the British savant Joseph Jacobs, spend a good deal of their time denying the salience of 'nostrility' as a sign of the racial cohesion of the Jews.[32] It is clear that for Jacobs (as for Wilhelm Fliess in Germany) the nose is the displaced locus of anxiety associated with the marking of the male Jew's body through circumcision, given the debate about the 'primitive' nature of circumcision and its reflection on the acculturation of the Western Jew during the late nineteenth century.[33]

Jews bear their diseased sexuality on their skin. Indeed, they bear the salient stigma of the black skin of the syphilitic. For at least in the Latin tradition, syphilis (like leprosy, another disease understood to be sexually transmitted) was understood to turn one black, the syphilitic rupia. Francisco Lopez de Villalobos, court physician to Charles V, in his long poem on syphilis of 1498, observes that the 'colour of the skin becomes black' when one has the 'Egyptian disease', the plague of boils recounted in the account of the Jews' escape from slavery.[34] Blackness marks the sufferer from disease, sets him outside the world of purity and cleanliness.

The Jews are black, according to nineteenth-century racial science, because they are 'a mongrel race which always retains this mongrel character'. So says Houston Stewart Chamberlain, arguing against the 'pure' nature of the Jewish race.[35] Jews had 'hybridized' with blacks in Alexandrian exile, and they were exposed to the syphilis that becomes part of their nature. They are, in an ironic review of Chamberlain's work by the father of modern Yiddish scholarship, Nathan Bimbaum, a 'bastard' race whose origin was caused by their incestuousness. But the Jews were also seen as black.[36] Adam Gurowski, a Polish noble, 'took every light-coloured mulatoo for a Jew' when he first arrived in the United States in the 1850s.[37] Jews are black because they are different, because their sexuality is different, because their sexual pathology is written upon their skin.

Gurowski's contemporary Karl Marx associates leprosy, Jews and syphilis in his description of his archrival Ferdinand Lassalle (in 1861): 'Lazarus the leper, is the prototype of the Jews and of Lazarus-Lassalle. But in our Lazarus, the leprosy lies in the brain. His illness was originally a badly cured case of syphilis'.[38] Jews = lepers = syphilitics = prostitutes = blacks. This chain of association presents the ultimate rationale for the Jewish Jack the Ripper, for the diseased destroy the diseased, the corrupt the corrupt. They corrupt in their act of touching, of seducing the pure and innocent, creating new polluters. But they are also able in their sexual frenzy to touch and kill the sexual pariahs, the prostitutes, who like Lulu at the close of Frank Wedekind's play (and Alban Berg's opera) go out to meet them, seeking their own death. Being unclean, being a version of the female genitalia (with his amputated genitalia), the male Jew is read (as Jack's Viennese contemporary Otto Weininger had read him) as really nothing but a type of female. The pariah can thus touch and kill the pariah, the same destroy the same. Wedekind's Lulu dies not as a suicide but as the victim of the confrontation between two libidinal forces – the unbridled, degenerate sexuality of the male and the sexual chaos of the sexually emancipated female. But die she does, and Jack leaves the stage, having washed his hands like Pontius Pilate, ready to kill again.

Notes

1 Michael Parry (ed.), *Jack the Knife: Tales of Jack the Ripper* (London: Mayflower, 1975), p. 12.
2 Dorothy Nelkin and Sander L. Gilman, 'Placing the Blame for Devastating Disease', *Social Research* 55 (1988), pp. 361–78.
3 Parry, *Jack the Knife*, p. 14.
4 Christopher Frayling, 'The House That Jack Built: Some Stereotypes of the Rapist in Popular Culture', in Sylvana Tomaselli and Roy Porter (eds), *Rape* (Oxford: Blackwell, 1986), p. 183.
5 Frayling, 'The House that Jack Built', p. 187.
6 Robert Anderson, 'The Lighter Side of My Official Life', *Blackwood's Magazine*, 187 (1910), pp. 356–7.
7 Frayling, 'The House That Jack Built', p. 189.
8 Alexander Kelley and Colin Wilson, *Jack the Ripper: A Bibliography and Review of the Literature* (London: Association of Assistant Librarians, 1973), p. 14.
9 Frank Wedekind, *Five Tragedies of Sex*, trans. Frances Fawcett and Stephen Spender (New York: Theatre Arts Books, n.d.), p. 29.
10 Peter Pulzer, *The Rise of Political Anti-Semitism in Germany and Austria* (London: Halban, 1988), p. 6.
11 Martin L. Friedland, *The Trials of Israel Lipski: A True Story of a Victorian Murder in the East End of London* (New York: Beaufort, 1984).
12 Tom Brown, *Amusements Serious and Comical and Other Works*, ed. Arthur L. Hayward (London: Routledge, 1927), p. 200.
13 Brown, *Amusements*, p. 199.
14 Brown, *Amusements*, p. 199.
15 *Bagnio Miscellany Containing the Adventures of Miss Lais Lovecock* (London: Printed for the Bibliophilists, 1892), pp. 54–5.
16 *Bagnio Miscellany*, p. 66.
17 *Bagnio Miscellany*, p. 62.
18 Gray Joliffe and Peter Mayle, *Man's Best Friend* (London: Pan, 1984).
19 Joseph Banister, *England Under the Jews* ([1901] London: J. Banister, 1907), p. 61.

20 Adolf Hitler, *Mein Kampf*, trans. Ralph Manheim (Boston: Houghton Mifflin, 1943), p. 247.

21 Hitler, *Mein Kampf*, p. 57.

22 Marcel Proust, *Remembrance of Things Past*, trans. C. K. Scott Moncrieff and Terence Kilmartin, 3 vols (Harmondsworth: Penguin, 1986), vol. 2, p. 639.

23 Proust, *Remembrance*, vol. 2, p. 186.

24 Proust, *Remembrance*, vol. 1, p. 326.

25 Joseph Jacobs, *Studies in Jewish Statistics, Social, Vital and Anthropometric* (London: Nutt, 1891), p. xl.

26 N. Balban and A. Molotschek, 'Progressive Paralyse beiden Bevölkerungen der Krim', *Allegmeine Zeitschrift für Psychiatrie* 94 (1931), pp. 373–83.

27 H. Budel, 'Beitrag zur Vergleichenden Rassenpsychiatrie', *Monatsschrift für Psychiatrie und Neurologie* 37 (1915), pp. 199–204.

28 Max Sichel, 'Die Paralyse der Juden in Sexuologischer Beleuchtung', *Zeitschrift für Sexualwissenschaft* 7 (1919–20), pp. 986–1004.

29 James H. Jones, *Bad Blood: The Tuskegee Syphilis Experiment* (New York: Free Press, 1981).

30 Sander L. Gilman, 'The Indelibility of Circumcision', *Koroth* 9 (1991), pp. 806–17.

31 Banister, *England Under the Jews*, p. 61.

32 Jacobs, *Jewish Statistics*, pp. xxxii–xxxiii.

33 Frank J. Sulloway, *Freud: Biologist of the Mind* (New York: Basic, 1979), pp. 147–58.

34 Francisco Lopez de Villalobos, *El Somario de la medicina con un tratado sobre las pestiferas bubas*, ed. María Teresa Herrera (Salamanca: Instituto de Historia de la Medicina Española, 1973), pp. 159–61.

35 Proust, *Remembrance*, vol. 1, pp. 388–9.

36 Nathan Birnbaum, 'Über Houston Stewart Chamberlain', *Ausgewählte Schriften zur jüdischen Frage*, 2 vols (Czernowitz: Birnbaum und Kohut, 1910), vol. 2, p. 201.

37 Adam G. de Gurowski, *America and Europe* (New York: Appleton, 1857), p. 177.

38 Karl Marx, *The Letters of Karl Marx*, ed. and trans. Saul K. Padover (Englewood Cliffs, NJ: Prentice Hall, 1979), p. 459.

14

Crime and punishment

William J. Fishman

It was in accord with current belief in British pride and moral superiority, that no Christian Englishman could have perpetrated such abominations as the Whitechapel murders; therefore it *must* have been a foreigner. Easiest to pinpoint were the Russians, settled locally, and one commentator referred to an article in a Russian paper naming a Russian anarchist, Nicolai Vassilyev, who in the 1870s emigrated to Paris, where he shortly went insane and, after murdering several prostitutes, was incarcerated in a lunatic asylum. His mania was driven by the conviction that fallen women could only atone for their sins and obtain redemption by being killed. Shortly before the first Whitechapel outrage he was discharged as cured and crossed over to East London. After the Turner murder he went underground.[1]

It was inevitable that suspicion would fall on the old scapegoat, the foreign Jew. After the Hanbury Street crime, a poor Polish boot-finisher, Jacob Pizer, nicknamed 'Leather Apron' and associated with 'a man of sinister appearance, wearing a leather apron, who terrorised women of the streets', was arrested. A collection of long-bladed knives found in his house were ostensibly tools of his trade, but a series of impeccable alibis proved his innocence. This did not prevent a minor outbreak of Judeophobia which a local editor observed under the heading 'A Riot against the Jews':

> On Saturday in several quarters of East London the crowds who assembled in the streets began to assume a very threatening attitude towards the Hebrew population of the District. It was repeatedly asserted that no Englishman could have perpetrated such a horrible crime as that of Hanbury Street, and that it must have been done by a Jew – and forthwith the crowds began to threaten and abuse such of the unfortunate Hebrews as they found in the streets. Happily the presence of a large number of police ... prevented a riot actually taking place.[2]

Anti-Semitism was prevalent in the hierarchy of the Metropolitan Police. Sir Robert Anderson, appointed Assistant Commissioner and head of the

CID in September, was convinced that the Ripper was a Jew. (His chief, Sir Charles Warren, who disliked him, took the opposite view and was determined to refute anti-Jewish accusations.)

After the Hanbury Street affair the ill-timed publication of an article in *The Times* by its Vienna correspondent heightened such suspicions. It referred to a Galician *cause célèbre* concerning one Moses Ritter, who had only just been acquitted of raping a Christian girl 'and in order to destroy all evidence of the fact had caused his victim to be murdered'. The real criminal was proved to have been a Christian peasant only after Ritter, his wife and a Polish Christian stockbroker had been in prison for more than two years pending trial. Nevertheless the correspondent added that 'there was no doubt that Ritter was innocent, but that the evidence to this superstition was never wholly disproved', implying the possibility of the age-old anti-Jewish libel of ritual murder. The Chief Rabbi promptly protested:

> The impropriety and injustice of the libel is only equalled by the danger involved in telegraphing it ... no one knows what an excited mob is capable of believing against any class which differs from the mob majority by well-marked characteristics. Many English and Irish workpeople in the East End are inflamed against the immigrant Jews by the competition for work and houses, by the stories of the sweaters and the sweated. If these illogical and ignorant minds should come to believe in the report heedlessly spread by a writer who is not quite just nor well informed himself, the results might be terrible.

Letters to *The Times* from both the Chief Rabbi and the equally respected Revd M. Gaster rejected, with the full force of Talmudic erudition, the myth that a Jew could attain spiritual absolution by murdering the Christian woman with whom he had fornicated.[3] Rabbinical fears were subsequently borne out by events. On 6 October *Commonweal* reported that 'the excitement caused by the murder outside the Berners Street club prevented the usual meeting here on Sunday [30 September]'. Whoever the Ripper was, it certainly suited him to cast suspicion on the Jews. The fourth murder[4] was committed within the precincts of a predominantly Jewish club; and, after the fifth, it was he who wrote on the walls of the model dwellings in Goulston Street inhabited mainly by Jews, a message in large chalk letters: 'The Jewes are the men who will not be blamed for nothing'. Thanks to the initiative of the Metropolitan policeman who first discovered it, another violent outbreak against Jews was scotched. He consulted his superiors, who agreed to order its immediate removal.[5]

There was no shred of evidence that the killer was a Jew. On the contrary, Margaret Harkness, declaring her own views in the contemporary novel *In Darkest London*, completely exonerates the Jews. A dying slaughterer confesses to the Salvation Army officer that he is the Ripper, and explains the evil dynamic that drove him to commit murder: 'people must eat and someone must kill beasts; but to kill makes a man like a cannibal, it gives him a thirst for blood, and I got to feel at last that nothing would quench my thirst but human blood, human flesh'. His blood lust reached saturation point when he 'could not go on butchering' and sought some kind of sanctuary in the ghetto: 'I hid myself here among the Jews who hate blood and never spill it. I'm not a Jew. I'm a gentile'.[6] This accords with the peculiar horror entertained by Jews of any mutilation of the human body before or after death, an act strictly forbidden by Talmudic Law.

Speculation on identity persisted and rumour was rife. Some even deduced that it could be a woman, perhaps a midwife who had knowledge of anatomy and could have explained away her presence in the streets at night in bloodstained clothing. Suspicion of evil in high places was fed by the nocturnal activities of the young Duke of Clarence; and later, in retrospect, a theory was put forward which detected the Masonic hand behind the murders, perpetrated according to ritual to protect the Duke, and through him the integrity of the monarchy.[7]

Whoever the Ripper was, his deeds had ramifications both locally and beyond their time or place. One casualty along the way was public respect for the police, which deteriorated as the killings went on. Well before the first outrage the *East London Observer* was questioning the efficiency of Old Bill on the beat.[8] Such doubts were strongly voiced after the third murder. A powerful attack on the Police Commissioner, Sir Charles Warren, was mounted by the *East London Advertiser* on 15 September. It described him as 'a martinet of apparently a somewhat inefficient type' who was guilty of:

> The double folly of weakening his detective force and strengthening his ordinary police force from the ranks of reservemen and others of a military or semi-military type that destroys two safeguards of a community ... It deprives it of a specially trained force, consisting of men of superior intellect and specially adapted powers for detective purposes ... It substitutes for the old parish constable the man with the few years military service but with no other qualification for serving the public ... Nothing, indeed has been more characteristic of the hunt after the Whitechapel murderer than the want of local knowledge displayed by the police. They seem to know little of bad haunts of the neighbourhood and still less of the bad characters who infest them.

By the third murder there was, according to the *Advertiser*, already 'no confidence in the police'. On 17 September a Mile End Vigilantes

Committee was formed at the Crown, 74 Mile End Road, under the auspices of a Mr Baron. A letter to the Home Secretary was drafted demanding the offer of a reward, which was rejected on the basis that 'the
practice was discontinued ... because experience showed that such offers
tended to produce more harm than good'. This prompted the *Advertiser*
('Economist', 29 September) to follow up its attack with the accusation
that 'the police force of 13,000 men in the Metropolis was inadequate
and disproportionally distributed – the most patrolling the richer districts, a consequence of which was that the low, crowded and vicious
districts within it are insufficiently guarded'. The age-old complaint
was repeated that 'when a crime has been committed the police come so
late that criminals have had every advantage in their efforts to get away'.
After the fifth murder the *East End News* (5 October) added insult
to injury:

> The marvellous inefficiency of the police in the detection was forcibly
> shown in the fact that in the very same block as that containing Mitre
> Square, in the great leading thoroughfare, and at a moment when the whole
> area was full of police just after the murder, the Aldgate Post Office was
> entered and ransacked, and property to the value of hundreds of pounds
> taken clean away under the very noses of the 'guardians of peace and
> order'!

Such was considered to be the state of lawlessness and terror that on
2 October the Whitechapel Board of Works was bemoaning the injurious effects on trade. One coffee-house keeper informed a member that
'emigrants were refusing to be located in Whitechapel en route for the
West', while the Revd Dan Greatorex went further, declaring that
'Whitechapel was becoming notorious all over the world as a place to be
shunned and feared'. The *Advertiser* added the suggestion that, given
police attitudes towards prostitutes, their very presence inadvertently
helped the killer. 'Constables are carefully watched off their beats by
these poor wretches, and so the victim and the murderer are in a kind of
conspiracy to accomplish a murder.'[9] At the meeting of the Whitechapel
Vestry on 3 October such criticisms of police ineptitude reached a peak.
Attacks centred on the person of Sir Charles Warren, who was censored
for not agreeing to offer a reward, with the Rector of Whitechapel
demanding that 'bloodhounds should be employed with the object of
tracking the murderer'. (Warren subsequently carried out an exercise on
Tooting common involving two bloodhounds, which proved a fiasco and
rendered him the laughing stock of London.)

The radical press joined the fray. For the 'real' causes of the Ripper
phenomenon their diatribes centred on the evils of society and the antics

of its current 'protector', the Police Commissioner. *Justice* (6 October) was quick off the mark. In a humorous article, meant for serious application, H. M. Hyndman, leader of the Social Democratic Federation, slated the 'cant' exuded by 'bourgeois' attitudes towards the murders, and wrote scathing denunciation of poor Warren:

> The very people who are now the most vehement in their denunciation of this almost certainly demented murderer don't turn a hair when hundreds or even thousands of women of the same class as his victims rot to death with syphilis in a Lock Hospital . . . Who cares, too, how many young girls have their jaws eaten out of their heads by phosphorous in order that matches should be sold cheaper and shareholders should get a higher percentage for their investment? Not even a fraction of those of the non-producing classes who are harrowing up their feelings so pleasantly with the details of the unlicensed dissections in the East End of London.
>
> All this hysterical cant will die down, as it has died down time after time before, and men, women and children will be left in precisely the same conditions of life as those which render these murders possible. None the less, however, these murders and the impunity of the murderer teach a plain lesson to the police. They are paid to protect the public ... instead of this they batter in the heads of their real paymasters, the working people, with truncheons, let murder after murder pass undetected in our midst ... If the assassin of Whitechapel is cranky on the uterus or has gone daft on the purity question, the South African filibuster is certainly clean 'off his head' at the prospect of the anniversary of the French Revolution.

In the next issue (13 October) he contemptuously dismissed Warren's letter urging the Whitechapel Board of Works to 'dissuade the unfortunate women about Whitechapel from going into lonely places in the dark with any persons, whether acquaintances or strangers'.

> A more lamentable ignorance of the true position of these women could scarcely have been made public. Everyone, we should think, save Sir Charles Warren, must know perfectly well that the vast majority of East End prostitutes are compelled to earn the 3d or 4d for their bed before they can obtain a night's lodging. There are no comfortable brothels for them like those at the West End. Thus, if these poor unfortunate creatures are not to run the risk of murder and mutilation by 'going into lonely places in the dark' they must walk the streets all night, and it is questionable whether, even then, the danger will be in any way avoided ... And, be it remembered, one at least, of the women who had fallen a victim to the maniac's knife went on the streets only when driven to do so by sheer dread of starvation.

Williams Morris's *Commonweal* was also in bantering mood before putting in the knife. Its 'Notes and News' referred to the latest theory accusing Warren of arranging the murders to back up his demands for more police. Conceding that this was not credible, the writer went on, 'but if he is not a scoundrel he is at least a fool', whose folly was now revealed to all. Thus:

> The gentleman who occupies his spare time in mutilating and murdering in the neighbourhood of Whitechapel, has quite intentionally done Society a service. By his latest masterpiece he has made Sir Charles Warren's position almost untenable, and it will probably not be long before the London Socialists will bid adieu to their best friend.

Warren's departure might be to the detriment of the Revolution for which all 'true' radicals were striving. The *Commonweal* therefore bemoans, albeit sarcastically (and prophetically), his imminent dismissal:

> His loss will leave us inconsolable. Oh, if he could stay another year and give us another Trafalgar Square performance! The small Radical remnant who have not yet accepted the Gospel of Revolution at his hands might then be driven, by dint of hard knocks and furious charges of mounted men into our ranks ... to the only religion which any sane person professes.[10]

There was also severe criticism from the highest in the land. Queen Victoria personally intervened to offer royal advice. On 10 November, she wired the Marquis of Salisbury from Balmoral. 'All these courts must be lit, and our detectives improved. They are not what they should be.' In the follow-up correspondence she repeated that 'the detective department is not so efficient as it might be' and outlined practical suggestions on how to improve methods of investigation.[11] Her last words on the matter spelt *finis* to Warren's career. On 17 November the editor of *Justice* joyfully announced that on Tuesday 13th the Police Commissioner had 'been ignominiously kicked out of office by the same Tory Home Secretary amid the jeers and execrations of the whole community'. The nature of his dismissal brought into the public eye the internal wranglings and rivalries within the hierarchy: that is, the antagonisms between Warren and Home Secretary Matthews and between the Metropolitan and City forces. It meant a loss of confidence in the police which precipitated an overall scrutiny of their operations culminating in the major reforms of 1894.

The social implications of the murders endured well after the hue and cry had died down. Discussions of the Ripper phenomenon persisted as a national disease. Locally there were immediate repercussions. Hooliganism increased as youths, pretending they were the killer, went on the rampage frightening old women and girls. Drunken attacks on women were stepped up, notably violence against prostitutes. While police efforts were concentrated on catching their prime target, the burglars successfully increased their operations on the periphery of the Ripper's killing ground. This was all good copy for the press and high

14 Jack the Ripper begins to evolve into myth.

drama for the popular theatre. *Punch* pointed an accusing finger at the latter for helping to exacerbate the incidence of crime:

> Is it not within the bounds of probability that to the highly coloured pictorial advertisements to be seen on almost all the hoardings in London, vividly representing sensational scenes of murder, exhibited as the great attraction of certain dramas, the public may be to a certain extent indebted for the horrible crime in Whitechapel? We say it most seriously; imagine the effect of these gigantic pictures of violence and assassination by knife and pistol on the morbid imagination of unbalanced minds. These hideous picture-posters are a blot on our civilization and a disgrace to the drama.
> 'On Horror's Head Horrors Accumulate!'
> Here are a few clippings from one day's papers:
> 'Shocking murder of a servant'
> 'The Italian stabbing case'
> 'Cruelty to a child'
> 'Knocking a man's eye out'
> 'Revolutionary murder in Whitechapel'[12]

On the positive side, the Whitechapel incidents certainly led to greater emphasis on socio-economic and environmental causes rather than character defects in considering the poverty of human and moral propensities supposedly inherent in East End life. They helped register a more favourable climate for the reception of Charles Booth's findings and provided a catalyst to unify all reform interests with others hitherto unconcerned with the problems of deprived areas. The *Daily Telegraph* (6 October), commenting on the murder of Annie Chapman, focused the issue:

> She has forced innumerable people who never gave a serious thought before to the subject to realise how it is and where it is that our vast floating population, the waifs and strays of our thoroughfares, live and sleep at night and what sort of accommodation our rich and enlightened capital provides for them.

It was the Ripper terror which persuaded authorities to embark on improvements in both health and housing for the 'lower classes'. The *Lancet* (6 October) conceded that 'modern society is more promptly awakened to a sense of duty by the knife of a murderer than by the pens of many earnest writers'. The Revd Samuel Barnett's letter to *The Times* on 19 September forcefully projected the desperate social problems of East London on to the national stage. He posited four practical suggestions: efficient police supervision; adequate lighting and cleaning, and the control of tenement houses by responsible landlords. ('At present there is lease under lease, and the acting landlord is probably one who encourages vice to pay his rent' for 'vice can afford to pay more than honesty!'[13]) Henrietta Barnett's petition to the Queen, signed by over 4,000 'women for the labouring classes of East London', pleading that she call on her 'servants in authority to close bad houses', brought a favourable response and, no doubt, reinforced Barnett's urgent demands for local improvements.[14]

The first priority was to light up the dark alleyways and courtyards. As early as February the Commercial Gas Company was informing both the Whitechapel and St George's Board of Works that the price of gas for public lamps was being reduced to £3 9s per annum.[15] The offer had little effect until the killer struck. On 18 August the *East London Advertiser* noted that the Whitechapel Board voted 'that lamps with double the illuminating power be fixed at the corner of the following streets, viz. Wentworth Street West Corner, Thrawl Street, Flower and Dean Street, Vine Court, Quaker Street, Worship Square, White Lion Street and Spital Square'. By November the same board had appointed a standing Lighting Committee with powers of spending up to £2,200 (until March 1889), the third largest expenditure allowance for the district. But the prospect of electric lighting for Whitechapel was already in the offing. On 10 December, the Works Committee 'reported that they had under consideration the bill introduced into Parliament by the London Electrical Supply Corporation for the supply and sale of electric light in various parishes of the metropolis under the Electric Lighting Acts of 1882 and 1888, the area of Whitechapel being included'. By the last month of the year street lighting had been extended in both the Mile End and Limehouse districts.[16]

The murders led to the escalation of new housing policies. The *Lancet* (6 October) was in the forefront, urging for new public health legislation relevant to improved housing. In a milder reiteration of Shaw's terse polemic it conceded that 'modern society is more promptly awakened to a sense of duty by the knife of a murderer than by the pens of many earnest writers'. Gauldie confirms that the crimes engendered two important Acts:

i.   The Housing of the Working Classes Act 1890 was a comprehensive act consolidating all previous Housing Acts. It opened the way for progressive local authorities to begin the development schemes ... Its most useful provision was to allow authorities in the Metropolitan Area to purchase as much land as might prove necessary for the long-term planning of an effective improvement scheme.

ii. The Public Health Amendment Act 1890 extended the provisions of the 1875 Act to empower every urban authority to make by-laws about the keeping of WCs supplied with flushing water, the structure of flows, hearths and staircases and the height of rooms, the paving of yards, the provision of means of access for refuse removal and to forbid the use as human habitations of rooms over privies, middens, cesspools and ash pits.[17]

Their implementation was made possible by the terms of the Local Government Act of 1888, which created both the structure and the permanent officials to design and construct mass low-cost housing within the auspices of the new London County Council.

At the local level there was an immediate response, especially by the increased activity of the Warden of Toynbee Hall. Practically all the remainder of the foulest enclaves within the Flower and Dean Street complex were demolished. The 4 per cent Dwelling Company purchased the north-east side and erected Nathaniel Dwellings, completed by 1892, with 170 apartments accommodating 800 people. From the rubble of the rookeries rose Stafford House on the north side of Wentworth Street, thanks to the eagerness of the land-owning Henderson family to dispose of property tainted by association with the recent horrors. In the 1890s demolitions continued between Flower and Dean and Thrawl Streets where Abraham Davis, a speculative builder, added a further six tenements, each four storeys high, with ground-floor shop fronts. Thus within the parameters of Flower and Dean, Lolesworth and Thrawl Streets a further 163 flats were constructed. The historian Jerry White concurs that 'within six years Jack the Ripper had done more to destroy the Flower and Dean Street rookery than fifty years of road building, slum clearance and unabated pressure from the police, Poor Law Guardians, Vestries and sanitary officers ... by 1897 the area was entirely dominated by the tenement blocks'.[18]

Another positive outcome was the refocusing of national attention on the plight of children in the common lodging houses. The social backcloth revealed by the murders stimulated renewed concentration of effort to alleviate the terrible incidence of homeless and abandoned children – a running sore of the metropolis. Their role as perpetual recruits to criminal gangs had been underlined by Dickens, and Barnardo had helped pioneer the movement to rescue them from the streets. He was quick to seize this opportunity. In a letter to *The Times* (6 October) he emphasized the dangers threatening young children forced to live in lodging houses. He demanded government intervention to rescue 'boys and girls from the foul contamination of these human sewers' and to 'make it illegal for the keepers of licensed lodging houses to which adults resort to admit young children upon any pretext whatever'. He stressed that 'provision is urgently required for the shelter of young children of the casual or tramp class, something between the casual wards of the workhouse and the lodging house itself, places where only young people under

16 would be admitted'; and ended with the forceful plea that 'surely the awful revelations consequent upon the recent tragedies should stir the whole community up to action and to resolve to deliver the children of today, who will be the men and women of tomorrow, from so evil an environment'.

In fact Barnardo had caught the current mood. His exhortations certainly provided ammunition for those involved with him in child aid, and had both the immediate and long-term effect of mobilizing public concern for the welfare of deprived children: 'A great empire could not develop its potential strength while its own heart was weakened by disease. This disease was the poverty to which the crude existing social system condemned so many.' This was brought home vividly to the young Lloyd George, who had caught a glimpse of it when, with a fellow Welshman, Sir Alfred Danes, the Caernarvon-born Superintendent of the Metropolitan Police, he made an expedition to the scenes of 'Jack's' recent operations. He was apparently fascinated by 'this Hogarthian Picture ... and appalled by its degradation'.[19] There is no doubt that this experience helped to foster a passionate concern for the poor which he later transformed into practical welfare legislation to address the fundamental causes of the horrific crimes.

To some extent, analysis of the causes depended on the religion, class or politics of the analyst. Radical opinion played on the socio-economic implications behind the murders. Hyndman's *Justice* had a field day: 'Whoever may be the wretch who committed these sanguinary outrages, the real criminal is the vicious bourgeois system which, based on class injustice, condemns thousands to poverty, vice and crime, manufactures criminals, and then punishes them!' After the Hanbury Street affair, it poured scorn on the fears of local middle-class sermonizers, as reflected in the warning expressed by the Revd S. Barnett that 'if they don't look out – that's the moral of it – the rich will get their throats cut and their carcasses mangled like the poor wretched women of the slums'; rejecting such 'mawkish twaddle' with the argument that nothing will be done by 'individual effort' save by an 'organised and vigorous Social Democracy'. In the SDF's reckoning the current 'unemployment meetings in Hyde Park which have received so much of police attention, and the Whitechapel murders which have received so little, are both effects of the same cause'.[20] William Morris, in his *Commonweal*, was even more explicit in his condemnation of the bourgeois mores that perpetuated such infamies: that is 'the *exclusive* culture of those whose sensibilities are so shocked by the brutality, the responsibility for which their greed and cowardice evades ... and when the dark side of this inglorious inequality is thrust on their notice, they are shocked and read moving articles in the newspapers – and go on eating, drinking and making merry, and hoping it will last for ever – Whitechapel murders and all'. Yet a month later a contributor, H. Davis, concedes that 'at length our masters are aroused, and behold! a Royal Commission is enquiring into the particulars of the housing of the poor', and that 'in our age of contradictions and absurdities, a fiend murderer may become a more effective reformer than all the honest propagandists in the world'.[21] Certainly one outcome of the murders was the focusing of national attention on East London, which, together with other political 'happenings' there, would give rise to a wider sympathetic appreciation of the dockers' case in their strike the following year, another important factor in the making of the New Unionism.

Diagnosticians from the respectable middle classes reckoned the Ripper phenomenon a symptom of other social diseases. Theologians posed such simple arguments as the reading of sensational French novels and detective thrillers, habits that activated hitherto suppressed murderous instincts in a criminal. Would-be social psychologists, quoting the current popularity of *Dr Jekyll and Mr Hyde* at the Lyceum Theatre, were wont to concur with the clerics, yet were curiously suspicious of the Salvation Army 'blood and thunder' dramatics as a possible stimulant for bloody deeds by a religious maniac. Social workers in the field put forward a confused mixture of causes: the lack of good housing; educational facilities which excluded any appreciation of aesthetics as well as the need for improvement of normal schooling; and, of course, drink and the lack of thrift which must ultimately result in a state of dehumanization that could produce such a monster.

In a letter to *The Times* the aristocratic polemicist Lord Sydney Godolphin Osborne blamed the Society for the Propagation of the Christian Gospel for dereliction of duty among those on its own doorstep:

> I believe nearly half a million of pounds is yearly raised in this country by societies having their headquarters in London to propagate the Gospel in foreign parts, to support the Established Church system, to send missions to convert the heathen in other lands ... all this within cheap cab hire of that portion of Eastern London, which for many years has been known to have been in a social condition utterly devoid of the commonest attributes of civilisation, so saturated with all that can contribute to heathenise as to be a standing shame to the nation.

After the third murder he warned: 'Wealth and station in its embodiment may at one moment be inclined to cry, "Ah, ha, I am warm" ... In my poor opinion these are just the days when apathy to the condition of the lowest classes is most fraught with danger to all other classes'. Such sentiments expressed by outsiders on the East End did not go unopposed by local worthies. The *East London Advertiser* had quickly responded to the hiatus following the first murder. The editor referred to the Mrs Grundy ('who has every sympathy for those "rich in the world's goods" ') attitude towards 'the poor savages in the howling wild corners of the East End' where 'the inhabitants of particular parts are all ruffians and viragos who acquired a taste for thieving and violence in their mothers' arms'. He counter-claimed that statistics of criminal offences were no greater or less than for any other part of the metropolis or Great Britain. On the contrary, East London was 'not in a moral and social downgrade ... but surely being reached by the influence of a better age and truer charity'.[22]

Such definitive postures proved inconsequential as the Ripper got into his stride. Other acts of extreme violence and homicide continued unabated, reinforcing the insalubrious image of the East End. A case of fratricide in Watney Street in July, and an attempted murder of a chemist in Berners Street in early September, made the national headlines. On 12 August a brutal murder took place on the Isle of Dogs, where an old eccentric, 'Mad Dick' Bartlett, battered his wife to death with a hammer.[23] There was no let-up in criminal high jinks during the Christmas festivities. The *Advertiser* summed up the score:

Holiday Charges
Of course there is always the swing of the pendulum, and at the Thames Police Court on Wednesday there were 38 charges arising out of Christmas Day, and four remands down for hearing, which is about the average number on Monday mornings. The former consisted of 14 on account of drunkenness etc, 3 for wilful damage, 6 on account of assault, 1 for being drunk in charge of a pony and barrow and furious driving, 1 for drunkenness and violent assault, 1 for drunkenness and arson, 1 for unlawful possession, and the remainder were felonies.

Two days later the body of a strangled woman, a known prostitute, was found in the early hours of the morning by a patrolling Police Sergeant in Charles Yard, a grim rookery off the Poplar High Street. Such news aroused fear and trembling locally. It would appear that Old Jack was back in business, and it boded ill for the coming New Year.[24]

Notes

1 'Jack the Ripper – in Russia', *East London Advertiser*, 1 December.
2 *East London Observer*, 15 December.
3 See *Jewish Chronicle*, 5 October for comments of Chief Rabbi on the Ritter case, and notes on the two rabbinical letters to *The Times*.

4 Fishman is attributing six murders to Jack the Ripper, starting with Martha Tabram. By fourth and fifth victims he means Elizabeth Stride and Catherine Eddowes. [ed.]

5 For details of the murders see accounts given in Leonard W. Matters, *The Mystery of Jack the Ripper* (London: W. H. Allen, 1948). On the Jewish association see pp. 48, 82 and 93. For contemporary information on the Jewish factor see also *Jewish Chronicle*, 12 October, *East London Advertiser*, 13 October and *Commonweal*, 20 October.

6 John Law (Margaret Harkness), *In Darkest London* (London: W. Reeves, 1893), p. 208.

7 Stephen Knight, *Jack the Ripper: The Final Solution* (London: Harrap, 1976).

8 'One of the East End representatives might do service by looking into the police arrangements in the East End of London, for there is room for grave doubt whether our end of town has its fair return for money in the matter of police protection.' It went on to evidence assaults by night in localities where 'the guardian of the night' was notably absent. 'Where was the police?' it demanded.

9 'The Mysterious Atrocities', 'Here and There – Rambler', *East London Advertiser*, 6 October.

10 *Commonweal*, 13 October.

11 *The Letters of Queen Victoria, vol. 1, 1886–1890* (London: Murray, 1930).

12 *East End News*, 14 September. Reporting on the *Punch* article of 11 September.

13 The full text of his letter to *The Times* on 13 September is well worth scrutiny. His major object was to press for an immediate rehousing programme. Barnett was resolved to rebuild the 'whole bad quarter'.

14 *East London Advertiser*, 27 October reproduced a copy of the letter.

15 See *East London Observer*, 11 February.

16 Note Local Government reports in *East London Advertiser*, 8, 15 and 22 December.

17 Enid Gauldie, *Cruel Habitations* (London: Allen and Unwin, 1974), p. 293. In effect the murders helped to create a climate ready to reassess means of ending overcrowding in the slums and generated a thrust towards more municipal housing rather than philanthropic projects as proposed by Octavia Hill and others.

18 Jerry White, *The Rothschild Buildings: Life in a Tenement Block, 1887–1920* (London: Routledge & Kegan Paul, 1980), pp. 29–30.

19 Frank Owen, *Tempestuous Journey: Lloyd George and His Times* (London: Hutchinson, 1954), pp. 63–4.

20 See *Justice* 15 and 22 September, 13 October for its observations on the Ripper murders.

21 *Commonweal*, 6 October and 3 November. In the twenty-ninth issue, anarchist David Nicoll rejects the charge by the 'renegade' radical paper the *Echo*, that the murders 'have their origin in the incendiary speeches of Trafalgar Square agitators'.

22 'Crime in East London', *East London Advertiser*, 25 August.
23 For the case of fratricide see *East London Advertiser*, 21 July; for the attempted murder see *East London Advertiser*, 6 October. Bartlett's crime is reported in full in the *East London Advertiser*, 25 August, and his subsequent trial and sentencing to death on 27 October.
24 See *East London Advertiser*, 29 December for the reports on Christmas charges and the murder in Charles Yard.

Select bibliography and filmography

Ackroyd, Peter, *London: A Biography* (London: Chatto and Windus, 2000).

Begg, Paul, *Jack the Ripper: The Definitive History* (London: Pearson, 2003).

Begg, Paul, Martin Fido and Keith Skinner, *Jack the Ripper: A–Z* (London: Headline, 1991).

Belloc Lowndes, Marie, *The Lodger* (Chicago: Academy Chicago, 1988).

Bland, Lucy, *Banishing the Beast: English Feminism and Sexual Morality 1885–1914* (Harmondsworth: Penguin, 1995).

Booth, Charles, *Life and Labour of the People of London* (London: Macmillan, [1889] 1892).

Box, Steven, *Power, Crime and Mystification* (London: Routledge, 1990).

Bronfen, Elisabeth, *Over Her Dead Body: Death, Femininity and the Aesthetic* (Manchester: Manchester University Press, 1992).

Browne, Douglas, *The Rise of Scotland Yard: A History of the Metropolitan Police* (London: George G. Harrap and Co., 1956).

Cameron, Deborah and Elizabeth Frazer, *The Lust to Kill: A Feminist Investigation of Sexual Murder* (Cambridge: Polity, 1987).

Canter, David, *Mapping Murder* (London: Virgin, 2003).

Caputi, Jane, *The Age of Sex Crime* (London: The Women's Press, 1988).

Cawelti, John G., *Adventure, Mystery and Romance: Formula Stories as Art and Popular Culture* (Chicago: University of Chicago Press, 1976).

Chesney, Kellow, *The Victorian Underworld* (London: Penguin, 1974).

Chisholm, Alex, Christopher Michael DiGrazia and Dane Yost, *The News from Whitechapel: The Whitechapel Murders in the Daily Telegraph* (Jefferson NC: McFarland and Company, 2002).

Cullen, Tom, *Autumn of Terror: Jack the Ripper, His Crimes and Times* (London: Bodley Head, 1965).

Douglas, John and Mark Olshaker, *Mindhunter: Inside the FBI's Elite Serial Crime Unit* (London: Arrow Books, 1995).

Dyos, H. J. and Michael Wolff (eds), *The Victorian City: Images and Realities* (London and Boston: Routledge & Kegan Paul, 1973).

Evans, Stewart and Keith Skinner (eds), *Jack the Ripper and the Whitechapel Murders: Contemporary Documents* (Surrey: Public Record Office, 2002).

Friedland, Martin L., *The Trials of Israel Lipski: A True Story of a Victorian Murder in the East End of London* (London: Macmillan, 1984).

From Hell (Dir. Albert and Allen Hughes, 2001).

Gauldie, Enid, *Cruel Habitations* (London: Allen and Unwin, 1974).

Glinert, Ed, *East End Chronicles* (London: Penguin, 2005).

Gotham by Gaslight (New York: DC Comics, 1989).

Halstead, D. G., *Doctor in the Nineties* (London: Christopher Johnson, 1959).

Harrison, Shirley, *The Diary of Jack the Ripper* (London: Smith Gryphon, 1993).

Hill, Octavia, *Homes for the London Poor* (London: Longman, [1883] 1970).

Jack the Ripper (Dir. David Wickes, 1988).

Jenkins, Philip, *Using Murder: The Social Construction of Serial Homicide* (New York: Aldine de Gruyter, 1994).

Keating, Peter, *The Working Classes in Victorian Fiction* (London: Routledge & Kegan Paul, 1979).

Knight, Stephen, *Form and Ideology in Crime Fiction* (Bloomington: Indiana University Press, 1980).

Knight, Stephen, *Jack the Ripper: The Final Solution* (London: Harrap, 1976).

Krafft-Ebing, Richard von, *Psychopathia Sexualis – With Especial Reference to Contrary Sexual Instinct: A Medico-Legal Study*, trans. Charles G. Chaddock (London and Philadelphia: F. A. Davis, 1892).

Law, John (Margaret Harkness), *In Darkest London* (London: W. Reeves, 1893).

Ledger, Sally and Roger Luckhurst (eds), *The Fin de Siècle: A Reader in Cultural History c.1800–1900* (Oxford: Oxford University Press, 2000).

Marcus, Steven, *The Other Victorians: A Study of Sexuality and Pornography in Mid-nineteenth Century England* (London: Weidenfeld and Nicolson, 1966).

Matters, Leonard W., *The Mystery of Jack the Ripper* (London: W. H. Allen, 1948).

Mayhew, Henry, *London Labour and the London Poor* (Harmondsworth: Penguin, [1861] 1985).

McHugh, Paul, *Prostitution and Victorian Social Reform* (London: Croom Helm, 1980).

Mighall, Robert, *A Geography of Victorian Gothic Fiction: Mapping History's Nightmares* (Oxford: Oxford University Press, 1999).

Moore, Alan and Eddie Campbell, *From Hell* (London: Knockabout, 2000).

Murder by Decree (Dir. Bob Clark, 1979).

Moretti, Franco, *Atlas of the European Novel 1800–1900* (London and New York: Verso, 1998).

Nordau, Max, *Degeneration* (Lincoln, NE and London: University of Nebraska Press, 1993).

Parry, Michael (ed.), *Jack the Knife: Tales of Jack the Ripper* (London: Mayflower, 1975).

Priestman, Martin, *Crime Fiction from Poe to the Present* (Plymouth: Northcote House, 1998).

Pykett, Lynn (ed.), *Reading Fin de Siècle Fictions* (London: Longman, 1996).

Queen, Ellery, *Sherlock Holmes Versus Jack the Ripper* (London: Gollancz, 1967).

Rumbelow, Donald, *The Complete Jack the Ripper*, rev. edn (London: Penguin, 2004).

Seltzer, Mark, *Serial Killers: Life and Death in America's Wound Culture* (London: Routledge, 1998).

Sims, George, *How the Poor Live and Horrible London* (New York: Dover, [1889] 1984).

Sinclair, Iain, *White Chappell, Scarlet Tracings* (London: Granta, [1987] 1998).

Smith, Anthony, *The Newspaper: An International History* (London: Thames and Hudson, 1979).

Smith, Joan, *Misogynies* (London: Faber & Faber, 1989).

Stedman Jones, Gareth, *Languages of Class: Studies in Working Class History 1832–1982* (Cambridge: Cambridge University Press, 1983).

Stewart, William, *Jack the Ripper: A New Theory* (London: Quality Press, 1939).

Sugden, Philip, *The Complete History of Jack the Ripper*, rev. edn (London: Robinson, 2002).

The Lodger (Dir. John Brahm, 1944).

The Lodger: A Story of the London Fog (Dir. Alfred Hitchcock, 1926).

The Man in the Attic (Dir. Hugo Fregonese, 1953).

'The Whitechapel Murders: A Tale of Sheerluck Holmes and Dr Witsend,' *Morecambe and Wise Special*, 1977.

Walkowitz, Judith R., 'Jack the Ripper and the Myth of Male Violence', *Feminist Studies* 8 (1982), pp. 543–74.

Walkowitz, Judith R., *Prostitution and Victorian Society* (Cambridge: Cambridge University Press, 1982).

White, Arnold, *Problems of a Great City* (New York: Dover, [1886] 1985).

White, Jerry, *The Rothschild Buildings: Life in a Tenement Block, 1887–1920* (London: Routledge & Kegan Paul, 1980).

Whittington-Egan, Richard, *A Casebook on Jack the Ripper* (London: Wildy and Sons, 1975).

Wilson, Colin and Alexander Kelley, *Jack the Ripper: A Bibliography and Review of the Literature* (London: Association of Assistant Librarians, 1973).

Wilson, Colin and Robin Odell, *Jack the Ripper: Summing Up and Verdict* (London: Bantam, 1987).

Wright, Patrick, *On Living in an Old Country* (London and New York: Verso, 1985).

Wright, Patrick, *Journey Through the Ruins* (London: Flamingo, 1993).

Index